THE CAMBRIDGE COMPANION TO WILLIAM CARLOS WILLIAMS

This *Companion* contains thirteen new essays from leading international experts on William Carlos Williams, covering his major poetry and prose works – including *Paterson, In the American Grain,* and the Stecher Trilogy. It addresses central issues of recent Williams scholarship and discusses a wide variety of topics: Williams and the visual arts, Williams and medicine, Williams's version of local modernism, Williams and gender, Williams and multiculturalism, and more. Authors examine Williams's relationships with figures such as Ezra Pound, Wallace Stevens, H. D., and Marianne Moore, and illustrate the importance of his legacy for Allen Ginsberg, Amiri Baraka, Robert Creeley, Robert Lowell, and numerous contemporary poets. Featuring a chronology and an up-to-date bibliography of the writer, *The Cambridge Companion to William Carlos Williams* is an invaluable guide for students of this influential literary figure.

Christopher MacGowan is Professor of English at the College of William & Mary. He is the author of *Twentieth-Century American Poetry* and *William Carlos Williams's Early Poetry: The Visual Arts Background* and editor of numerous books, including *The Letters of Denise Levertov and William Carlos Williams* and *The Collected Poems of William Carlos Williams, Volumes I* (with A. Walton Litz) and *II.*

A complete list of books in the series is at the back of this book

CAMBRIDGE
COMPANIONS TO
LITERATURE

THE CAMBRIDGE
COMPANION TO
WILLIAM CARLOS
WILLIAMS

EDITED BY
CHRISTOPHER MACGOWAN
College of William & Mary

CAMBRIDGE
UNIVERSITY PRESS

CAMBRIDGE
UNIVERSITY PRESS

University Printing House, Cambridge CB2 8BS, United Kingdom

One Liberty Plaza, 20th Floor, New York, NY 10006, USA

477 Williamstown Road, Port Melbourne, VIC 3207, Australia

4843/24, 2nd Floor, Ansari Road, Daryaganj, Delhi - 110002, India

79 Anson Road, #06-04/06, Singapore 079906

Cambridge University Press is part of the University of Cambridge.

It furthers the University's mission by disseminating knowledge in the pursuit of
education, learning and research at the highest international levels of excellence.

www.cambridge.org
Information on this title: www.cambridge.org/9781107095151

© Cambridge University Press 2016

First published 2016

A catalogue record for this publication is available from the British Library

Library of Congress Cataloging in Publication data
MacGowan, Christopher J. (Christopher John), editor.
The Cambridge companion to William Carlos Williams / edited by Christopher
MacGowan, College of William & Mary.
New York, NY : Cambridge University Press, 2016. | Series: Cambridge companions to
literature | Includes bibliographical references, chronology, and index.
LCCN 2016005108 | ISBN 9781107095151 (hardback)
LCSH: Williams, William Carlos, 1883–1963 – Criticism and interpretation. | BISAC:
LITERARY CRITICISM / American / General.
LCC PS3545.I544 Z58255 2016 | DDC 811/.52–dc23
LC record available at https://lccn.loc.gov/2016005108

ISBN 978-1-107-09515-1 Hardback
ISBN 978-1-107-47908-1 Paperback

CONTENTS

CONTRIBUTORS

MILTON A. COHEN is Professor of Literary Studies at the University of Texas, Dallas, and the author of *Poet and Painter: The Aesthetics of E. E. Cummings's Early Work* (1987), *Movement, Manifesto, Melee: The Modernist Group, 1910–1914* (2004), *Hemingway's Laboratory: The Paris "in our time"* (2005), and *Beleaguered Poets and Leftist Critics* (2010). His current project is on Steinbeck, Wright, and Hemingway and leftist politics in the 1930s.

IAN COPESTAKE is an independent scholar based in Frankfurt am Main. He is the current editor of the *William Carlos Williams Review* and President of the William Carlos Williams Society. He is the author of *The Ethics of William Carlos Williams's Poetry* (2010) and the editor of *The Legacy of William Carlos Williams: Points of Contact* (2007), *Rigor of Beauty: Essays in Commemoration of William Carlos Williams* (2004), and *American Postmodernity: Essays on the Recent Fiction of Thomas Pynchon* (2003).

T. HUGH CRAWFORD teaches at Georgia Tech where he is an associate professor in the School of Literature, Media, and Communication. A specialist in the cultural studies of science and technology, he has published on literature and medicine, cinema and science, medical imaging technologies, the novels of Herman Melville, and the poetry of Williams. He is a past president of the Society for Literature, Science and the Arts, and past editor of *Configurations: A Journal of Science, Technology and Culture*. He is the author of *Modernism, Medicine and William Carlos Williams* (1993).

KERRY DRISCOLL is Professor of English at the University of Saint Joseph in Connecticut. Her publications include work on Williams, Levertov, and Twain. She is the author of *William Carlos Williams and the Maternal Muse* (1987), a contributing editor to the *William Carlos Williams Review*, and a past president of the William Carlos Williams Society.

CRISTINA GIORCELLI is Professor Emerita of Anglo-American literature at the University of Rome Three. She is a former president of the Italian Association of American Studies and Vice President of the European Association of American Studies. Her publications include essays on Washington Irving, Henry James, Kate

Chopin, Edith Wharton, Willa Cather, Denise Levertov, and Louis Zukofsky, as well as Williams. She is the co-editor of and a contributor to *The Rhetoric of Love in the Collected Poems of William Carlos Williams* (1993).

PETER HALTER is Professor Emeritus of American Literature at the University of Lausanne. He is the author of *The Revolution in the Visual Arts and the Poetry of William Carlos Williams* (1994) as well as a study on Katherine Mansfield and the short story. He has also published numerous articles, mainly on various aspects of modernism, with a special focus on the interaction of literature and the visual arts, including photography.

JOHN LOWNEY is Professor of English at St. John's University, New York. He is the author of *The American Avant-Garde Tradition: William Carlos Williams, Postmodern Poetry, and the Politics of Cultural Memory* (1997) and *History, Memory, and the Literary Left: Modern American Poetry, 1935–1968* (2006). He is currently completing a book titled "Jazz Internationalism: Literary Afro-Modernism and the Cultural Politics of Jazz."

CHRISTOPHER MACGOWAN, a professor of English at the College of William & Mary, is the editor, with A. Walton Litz, of *The Collected Poems of William Carlos Williams, Volume I: 1909–1939* (1986), and the editor of *The Collected Poems, Volume II (1939–1962)* (1988), *Paterson* (1992), and *The Letters of Denise Levertov and William Carlos Williams* (1998). He is the author of *William Carlos Williams Early Poetry: The Visual Arts Background* (1984), *Twentieth-Century American Poetry* (2004), and *The Twentieth-Century American Fiction Handbook* (2011).

GLEN MACLEOD is the author of *Wallace Stevens and Company* (1983) and *Wallace Stevens and Modern Art* (1993). He has published essays on Williams, Stevens, E. E. Cummings, Henry James, and Hawthorne, among others, and has edited special issues of *The William Carlos Williams Review* on Williams and Stevens, and Williams and Surrealism. He is a professor of English at the University of Connecticut, Waterbury.

ALEC MARSH is Professor of English at Muhlenberg College. He is the author of the prize-winning *Money and Modernity: Pound, Williams, and the Spirit of Jefferson* (1998), a biography of Ezra Pound (2011), *John Kasper & Ezra Pound: Saving the Republic* (2015), and numerous essays on Pound, Williams, and other modernist poets. He has for some years been one of the author reviewers for the annual *American Literary Scholarship* volumes.

J. A. MARZÁN/JULIO MARZÁN, poet, novelist, and scholar, teaches at SUNY/Nassau Community College, New York. He is the author of the award-winning *The Spanish American Roots of William Carlos Williams* (1994), and wrote the introduction to *By Word of Mouth: Poetry from the Spanish by William Carlos Williams*, ed. Jonathan Cohen (2011). In 2006 he was Visiting Professor of

Romance Languages at Harvard University, where he lectured on William Carlos Williams and Luis Palés Matos.

LISA M. STEINMAN is the Kenan Professor of English and Humanities at Reed College. A poet and teacher, her books include *Made in America: Science, Technology, and American Modernist Poets* (1987), *Invitation to Poetry: The Pleasures of Studying Poetry and Poetics* (2008), and *Absence and Presence* (2013), as well as a number of articles on Williams. Along with Jim Shugrue, she is co-editor of the poetry magazine *Hubbub*.

ERIN E. TEMPLETON is the Anne Morrison Chapman Distinguished Professor of International Study at Converse College. She has published essays on the gender dynamics of Williams's *Paterson* and Williams's relationship with Italian poet Emanuel Carnevali. She has also published essays and reviews on the work of Pound, Yeats, Eliot, and Moore, and she has been a contributing writer for the *Chronicle of Higher Education*'s blog "ProfHacker" since 2009.

ERIC B. WHITE is Senior Lecturer in American Literature at Oxford Brookes University. He is the author of *Transatlantic Avant-Gardes: Little Magazines and Localist Modernism* (2013) and has published a number of articles on Williams and his contemporaries. In 2013 he guest-edited the Thirtieth Anniversary number of the *William Carlos Williams Review*.

ACKNOWLEDGMENTS

Grateful acknowledgment is given to New Directions Publishing Corporation and Carcanet Press Ltd. for permission to quote from the following copyrighted works of William Carlos Williams.

The Autobiography of William Carlos Williams. Copyright 1984, 1951 by William Carlos Williams.

The Build-Up. Copyright 1946, 1952 by William Carlos Williams.

Collected Poems: Volume I, 1909–1939. Copyright 1938 by New Directions Publishing Corporation. Copyright © 1982, 1986 by William Eric Williams and Paul H. Williams.

Collected Poems: Volume II, 1939–1962. Copyright 1944, 1953, Copyright © 1962 by William Carlos Williams. Copyright © 1988 by William Eric Williams and Paul H. Williams.

The Doctor Stories. Copyright 1934, 1962 by William Carlos Williams.

The Embodiment of Knowledge. Copyright © 1974 by Florence H. Williams.

The Farmers' Daughters. Copyright 1934, 1950 by William Carlos Williams.

I Wanted to Write a Poem. Copyright © 1958 by William Carlos Williams.

Imaginations. Copyright © 1970 by Florence H. Williams.

In the American Grain. Copyright 1925 by James Laughlin. Copyright 1933 by William Carlos Williams.

In the Money. Copyright 1940 by Florence H. Williams.

Many Loves and Other Plays. Copyright 1948 by William Carlos Williams.

Paterson. Copyright © 1946, 1948, 1948, 1949, 1958 by William Carlos Williams.

Pictures from Brueghel. Copyright 1954, 1955, 1962 by William Carlos Williams.

A Recognizable Image. William Carlos Williams on Art and Artists. Copyright © 1978 by the Estate of Florence H. Williams.

Selected Letters of William Carlos Williams. Copyright 1957 by William Carlos Williams.

Something to Say: William Carlos Williams on Younger Poets. Copyright © 1985 by William Eric Williams and Paul H. Williams.

A Voyage to Pagany. Copyright 1928 by the Macauley Co. Copyright 1938 by New Directions Publishing Corporation.

White Mule. Copyright 1937 by New Directions Publishing Corporation.

The William Carlos Williams Reader. Copyright © 1966 by New Directions Publishing Corporation.

Yes, Mrs. Williams. Copyright © 1959 by William Carlos Williams.

Interviews with William Carlos Williams: Speaking Straight Ahead. Copyright © 1976 by the Estate of William Carlos Williams.

All previously unpublished material by William Carlos Williams quoted by permission of the estates of Dr William Carlos Williams and Dr William Eric Williams on behalf of Daphne Williams Fox, the executrix of both estates.

1883	September 17. Born in Rutherford, New Jersey. Oldest son of William George and Raquel Hélène Rose Hoheb Williams.
1884	Birth of brother Edgar Irving Williams.
1889–1896	Attends local schools in Rutherford.
1897–1899	First trip to Europe. Both brothers attend a year at Château de Lancy near Geneva. They then spend some months in Paris.
1899–1902	Commutes to attend Horace Mann School in New York City.
1902–1906	Studies medicine at the University of Pennsylvania, Philadelphia. Meets Ezra Pound, Hilda Doolittle, and Charles Demuth. Develops an interest in drama. Imitates Keats in his poetry.
1906–1908	Interns at French Hospital, New York City.
1908–1909	Interns at Child's Hospital, resigns on principle.
1909	First book, *Poems*, self-published, title page designed by Edgar. Proposes to Florence Herman, "Flossie," in July.
1909–1910	Studies pediatrics in Leipzig from September to February. Travels include France, Italy, Spain, and England – where he meets up with Pound in March.
1910	Begins medical practice at 131 West Passaic Avenue, Rutherford, in September.
1912	First magazine publication, in *The Poetry Review*, London: "A Selection from *The Tempers* ... With Introductory Note by Ezra Pound." Marries Florence Herman, December 12.
1913	*The Tempers* published in London by Elkin Mathews. In August publishes only medical article, in *Archives of Pediatrics*: "The Normal and Adventitious Danger Periods for Pulmonary Disease in Children." In November Williams and Florence move to 9 Ridge Road, where Williams sets up

	home and medical practice. Begins publishing regularly in *Poetry* and *The Egoist*.
1914	Birth of first child, William Eric Williams.
1915–1916	Through Pound contacts Grantwood, New Jersey, artists' colony. There and in New York meets Alfred Kreymborg, Marianne Moore, Wallace Stevens, Marcel Duchamp, and Man Ray.
1916	Birth of second child, Paul Herman Williams.
1917	*Al Que Quiere!* published in Boston by The Four Seas Company.
1918	Christmas Day. Death of his father.
1919	July, edits last issue of *Others*.
1920	*Kora in Hell: Improvisations* published. With Robert McAlmon edits *Contact*. Death of grandmother, Emily Dickinson Wellcome.
1921	Publishes *Sour Grapes*.
1923	*Spring and All* and *The Great American Novel* published in Paris. Begins a sabbatical year in the summer. Begins writing *In the American Grain*.
1924	January–June, in Europe with Flossie, visits France, Italy, Austria, and Switzerland. In Paris meets McAlmon, Pound, Joyce, Ford Madox Ford.
1925	*In the American Grain* published by Albert and Charles Boni, first commercial publication.
1926	Wins the *Dial* award for "Paterson" a precursor of the longer poem to come.
1927	September, final trip to Europe, with family. Returns end of the month while Flossie stays with the boys for their school year in Geneva. While in Paris Williams meets Gertrude Stein. *Voyage to Pagany* published.
1928	"The Descent of Winter" published in Ezra Pound's *Exile*. March 1928 meets Louis Zukofsky.
1931	Zukofsky guest edits the "Objectivist" number of *Poetry*, and includes Williams. With Flossie takes trip down the St. Lawrence to Newfoundland. Wins *Poetry*'s Guarantors Prize.
1932	Edits a revival of *Contact* with Nathanael West. Publishes *The Knife of the Times*, short stories.
1934	Publishes *Collected Poems, 1921–1931*, with The Objectivist Press, Preface by Wallace Stevens.

1935	Publishes *An Early Martyr and Other Poems* with Alcestis Press, 165 copies printed.
1936	Publishes *Adam & Eve & The City* with Alcestis, 167 copies printed.
1937	Begins publishing with James Laughlin's New Directions, starting with the first novel of the Stecher trilogy, *White Mule*.
1938	*Life Along the Passaic River* (stories) and *The Complete Collected Poems*.
1939	Ford Madox Ford starts Les Amis des William Carlos Williams. Sees Pound on his visit to the United States.
1940	Publishes *In the Money*, second novel of the Stecher trilogy.
1941	*The Broken Span* pamphlet, visits Puerto Rico.
1942	Meets Marcia Nardi, the "Cress" of *Paterson*.
1944	Publishes *The Wedge*.
1946	*Paterson (Book One)* published.
1948	Heart attack. Publishes *Paterson (Book Two)*, wins the American Academy of Arts and Letters' Russell Loines Award.
1949	*Selected Poems, Paterson (Book Three)*, death of his mother Hélène Williams. Son William Eric starts to take over the medical practice.
1950	New Directions publish *Collected Later Poems* and *Make Light of It: Collected Stories*. Wins National Book Award. Signs contract with Random House. First book-length study, by Vivienne Koch.
1951	Stroke. Publishes *Paterson (Book Four)* and *Collected Earlier Poems* with New Directions, *Autobiography* with Random House.
1952	Completes Stecher trilogy with *The Build-Up*. Serious stroke in August. Appointed as Consultant in Poetry to the Library of Congress but runs into opposition because of political pressure.
1953	Hospitalized for depression. Forced to give up Library of Congress appointment. Wins Bollingen Prize, shared with Archibald MacLeish.
1954	Publishes *The Desert Music, Selected Essays*.
1955	Publishes *Journey to Love*, undertakes reading tour across the country.
1956	Writes the introduction to Allen Ginsberg's *Howl and Other Poems*.

1957	Leaves Random House, *Selected Letters* published by McDowell, Obolensky.
1958	*Paterson (Book Five)* published, and *I Wanted to Write a Poem*. Third stroke.
1959	Publishes *Yes, Mrs. Williams*. The Living Theater produces *Many Loves* Off Broadway.
1961	Starts a sixth book of *Paterson* but has to give up writing because of strokes.
1962	Publishes *Pictures from Brueghel*.
1963	March 4, dies in Rutherford. MacGibbon & Kee contract to publish Williams in England. Williams posthumously awarded Pulitzer Prize and National Institute of Arts and Letters Gold Medal for Poetry.
1970	New Directions publish *Imaginations*, first reprinting of full texts of *Kora in Hell, Spring and All*, and "The Descent of Winter" since the 1920s.
1975	*William Carlos Williams Newsletter* (subsequently *William Carlos Williams Review*) begins publication.
1976	Florence Williams dies.
1983	To celebrate Williams's 100th birthday National Poetry Foundation publishes *William Carlos Williams: Man and Poet*, includes an interview with Robert Creeley and essays by Ginsberg, Denise Levertov, Pound, and Marjorie Perloff, among others.
1986	*The Collected Poems of William Carlos Williams, Volume I: 1909–1939* includes previously uncollected poems, as does *Volume II, 1939–1962* published in 1988.
1992	Inducted into The Poets' Corner of the Cathedral Church of St. John the Divine, New York City, October 25.

ABBREVIATIONS

A	*The Autobiography of William Carlos Williams*. New York: Random House, 1951.
ARI	*A Recognizable Image: William Carlos Williams on Art and Artists*. Ed. Bram Dijkstra. New York: New Directions, 1978.
CP1	*The Collected Poems of William Carlos Williams: Volume I, 1909–1939*. Ed. A. Walton Litz and Christopher MacGowan. New York: New Directions, 1986.
CP2	*The Collected Poems of William Carlos Williams: Volume II, 1939–1962*. Ed. Christopher MacGowan. New York: New Directions, 1988.
DL/WCW	*The Letters of Denise Levertov and William Carlos Williams*. Ed. Christopher MacGowan. New York: New Directions, 1998.
DS	*The Doctor Stories*. Compiled by Robert Coles. New York: New Directions, 1984.
EK	*The Embodiment of Knowledge*. Ed. Ron Loewinsohn. New York: New Directions, 1974.
FD	*The Farmers' Daughters: The Collected Stories of William Carlos Williams*. Norfolk, CT: New Directions, 1961.
I	*Imaginations*. Ed. Webster Schott [Contains *Kora in Hell, Spring and All, The Great American Novel*, "The Descent of Winter," and *A Novelette and Other Prose*]. New York: New Directions, 1970.
IAG	*In the American Grain*. New York: Albert & Charles Boni, 1925.
IWWP	*I Wanted to Write a Poem*. Ed. Edith Heal. Boston: Beacon Press, 1958.

Leibowitz   Herbert Leibowitz, *"Something Urgent I Have to Say to You": The Life and Works of William Carlos Williams.* New York: Farrar, Straus, Giroux, 2011.

Mariani   Paul Mariani, *William Carlos Williams: A New World Naked.* New York: McGraw-Hill, 1981.

ML   *Many Loves and Other Plays: The Collected Plays of William Carlos Williams.* Norfolk, CT: New Directions, 1961.

P   *Paterson.* Ed. Christopher MacGowan. New York: New Directions, 1992.

P/W   *Pound/Williams: Selected Letters of Ezra Pound and William Carlos Williams.* Ed. Hugh Witemeyer. New York: New Directions, 1996.

SE   *Selected Essays of William Carlos Williams.* New York: Random House, 1954.

SL   *The Selected Letters of William Carlos Williams.* Ed. John Thirlwall. New York: McDowell, Obolensky, 1957.

SSA   *Interviews with William Carlos Williams: "Speaking Straight Ahead."* Ed. Linda Wagner. New York: New Directions, 1976.

STS   *Something to Say: William Carlos Williams on Younger Poets.* Ed. James E.B. Breslin. New York: New Directions, 1985.

VP   *A Voyage to Pagany.* New York: Macaulay, 1928.

WCW/EW   *The Letters of William Carlos Williams to Edgar Irving Williams, 1902–1912.* Ed. Andrew J. Krivak. Madison, NJ: Fairleigh Dickinson University Press, 2009.

WCW/JL   *William Carlos Williams and James Laughlin: Selected Letters.* Ed. Hugh Witemeyer. New York: Norton, 1989.

WCW/LZ   *The Correspondence of William Carlos Williams and Louis Zukofsky.* Ed. Barry Ahearn. Middletown, CT: Wesleyan University Press, 2003.

YMW   *Yes, Mrs. Williams: A Personal Record of my Mother.* New York: McDowell, Obolensky, 1959.

I

CHRISTOPHER MACGOWAN

Introduction: the lives of William Carlos Williams

William Carlos Williams might have led the life of a small-town doctor – one whose career spanned some important advances in medicine and whose practice was impacted by two world wars, a deadly influenza epidemic, and a depression so severe that many of his patients could not afford to pay him – ending with a few years of retirement from medicine after successfully handing over his practice. Williams did lead this life. But at the same time he published more than forty books, and was part of a New York avantgarde that included such figures as Marcel Duchamp, Alfred Stieglitz, Wallace Stevens, and Marianne Moore. He knew Hilda Doolittle before she became H. D., and had a lifelong, if sometimes turbulent, correspondence with Ezra Pound. His work was well known to the expatriates who frequented Sylvia Beach's bookshop in Paris in the 1920s well before his own visit there in 1924. He was friends with painters Charles Demuth, Marsden Hartley, Charles Sheeler, and Ben Shahn, and purchased Demuth and Hartley's work when their buyers were few. He knew and corresponded with novelists Ford Madox Ford and Nathanael West, with critic Kenneth Burke, and poet Louis Zukofsky. He won the first National Book Award and a posthumous Pulitzer Prize; was a member of the Academy of Arts and Letters; was a mainstay for years, along with Pound, of James Laughlin's New Directions; and in his last decade was the subject of pilgrimages to his suburban New Jersey house by such figures as Jack Kerouac, Allen Ginsberg, and Gregory Corso. He corresponded with Denise Levertov, Robert Creeley, and Robert Lowell, was required reading at Charles Olson's Black Mountain College, and remains today an acknowledged influence upon many contemporary poets.

Williams was fortunate in some of his early contacts during his student years at the University of Pennsylvania, the years when he met Pound, H. D., and Demuth. He was also spared the intellectual isolation of so many American poets of the previous generation thanks to the reductions in the cost of paper and printing that made possible such little magazines as *Poetry* and *The Little Review* in Chicago, *The Egoist* in London, and the magazines that Williams himself would help edit, *Others* and *Contact*. Thanks to such little magazines the latest examples of modern writing and debate on two continents could be delivered to any subscriber's mailbox. The physical location of Rutherford, New Jersey, where Williams lived his whole life, also contributed to the fusion of his two careers. Rutherford is a half-hour train or bus ride from New York City. As in Williams's day, the city's skyscrapers are still visible on the horizon across the New Jersey meadowland swamps, despite the encroachment of a century's development. The resources of the city, its galleries, performances, and avant-garde salons were available to him any afternoon or evening when there were no office hours. Important too was the sophisticated, multicultural background of Williams's family. His brother Edgar went on to become a notable architect and urban planner, a recipient of the prestigious Prix de Rome. His Puerto Rican mother had studied painting in Paris, and his English father's sales position involved extended trips to Latin America. Spanish and French, as well as English, were spoken in the home and Williams published translations in both languages.

Williams determined early on a career that would unite his medical and writing interests. There were a few periods in the years that followed when he would regret the time and energy that medicine took away from his writing: the interruptions, the middle of the night phone calls, and even the medical bureaucracy that he had to work within. But much more often he recognized that his role as a doctor gave him the access to lives that would otherwise remain unknown and unrecorded. Readers familiar only with the anthology pieces on "things," a red wheelbarrow or a dish of plums, may be surprised at the dramas of ordinary lives that fill Williams's poems, stories, and novels.

Williams's earliest writing ambitions were conventionally literary and centered on theater. Writing plays would remain an interest, from his involvement with the University of Pennsylvania's Mask and Wig Club and plays put on locally in Rutherford, to later plays – one of which, *Many Loves*, ran successfully off Broadway when produced by Julian Beck and Judith Melina's Living Theater in 1959. But with his efforts to get a play produced in New York coming to naught, poetry increasingly gained Williams's attention. He liked to remember that Whitman was a first influence, but an early, unpublished epic, "Philip and Oradie," owes more to his admiration for Keats. Williams paid for his first book of verse, *Poems*, to be published in 1909, and arranged for its distribution through a local stationary store. The poems display a familiar late Romantic style that piles up inversions, and features such mainstays of magazine verse at the turn of the century as fruitful bees, a southern land of plenty, and twittering "nestlings." Poetry must be "poesy," while a shady tree by a river is "a leafy bay." Pound, now starting to make important literary connections in London, sent Williams a frank response upon receiving a copy, telling his friend that he needed to modernize himself – and sending the first of what would be more than forty years of reading lists. These lists were initially crucial for Williams, but eventually he found them wrong-headed and patronizing. Such a list from Pound would appear as one of Paterson's found objects four decades later.

Over the next few years, as Williams established his medical practice, married, and started a family, he did modernize his poetry. Pound helped again by steering his poems toward publication in London, and putting him in touch with the Grantwood, New Jersey, colony of artists, who included Man Ray, and most importantly Alfred Kreymborg – whose contacts introduced Williams to the avant-garde literary and visual arts world in New York and Chicago. Soon Williams was involved in *Others*, and published regularly in *Poetry* and other little magazines.

At first Williams's move in a modernist direction largely echoed Pound's own development. *The Tempers* (1913), published in London with Pound's help, mirrors Pound's pre-imagist work, although a poem like "Hic Jacet," despite its Poundian title, shows something of Williams's future direction – in being the result of his careful observation and his medical work in the local community. However, when in 1912–1913 Pound and H. D. began to explore the possibilities of imagism, Williams saw the potential for his own work. His sympathies were with those writers and critics calling for an American art that was more than just an offshoot of European tradition, but that at the same time met international standards of achievement. Imagism threw out many of the conventions of this tradition, particularly, for Williams, the English poetic tradition. Imagism seemed modern and efficient in its economy, just as America was modern and efficient. It was contemporary in its focus on the immediate moment, and its pictorial focus urged the reader to look carefully at his or her surroundings. These features became key characteristics of Williams's work in his subsequent writing, developed and adapted through the decades that followed, and tied to the key concept of "contact" – the title of the magazine he would edit with Robert McAlmon in 1920 and later in another version with Nathanael West in 1932. From this position Williams could set his work against the international modernism of Pound, H. D., and – newly arrived in London – T. S. Eliot. Thus when Pound abandoned imagism after a couple of years to return to the broader historical and social concerns of *The Cantos*, Williams's poetry remained largely pictorial, local, and concerned with immediate experience. His 1920 "Prologue" to *Kora in Hell* became a declaration of independence and an important statement of his poetics. In this essay he takes on not only Pound, but H. D., Eliot, and even Carl Sandburg and Wallace Stevens.

In 1917 the two titles that Williams debated for his volume *Al Que Quiere!* indicated the two directions in which he felt pulled. The eventual title, which Williams translated as "to him who wants it," acknowledges the small audience inevitable for avant-garde writing, while his alternative, "The Pleasures of Democracy," invites a much wider reading public. Williams wanted both titles, but his publisher objected. This tension, illustrated best through the contrast of content and form, proved fruitful to Williams for the rest of his career. But that wider reading public was slow in coming, and to increase Williams's sense of isolation the center of gravity for modernist experiment shifted east when first Duchamp and the other European modernists seeing out the world war in New York returned to France; they were soon joined by Gertrude Stein's "lost generation" of expatriates who flocked to Paris. Pound urged Williams to join them rather than be buried in a provincial New Jersey suburb; meanwhile the success of Eliot's *The Waste Land* defined the modernist poem as international, allusive, and unremittingly complex. Much of Williams's work in the 1920s had to be published in Europe with small expatriate outfits. In the 1930s his new collections appeared from craft presses in even smaller print runs. The wider readership eventually started to come with the appearance of James Laughlin, founder of New Directions, who took up publishing Pound and Williams in the later 1930s, and saw Pound win the Bollingen Prize in 1949 and Williams win his National Book Award the following year.

Williams experimented with ways to expand the possibilities of imagist strategies beyond the short poems for which the movement is best known. These included the prose/poetry sequence *Spring and All* in 1923, the diary format of "The Descent of Winter" in 1927 – both containing useful statements on Williams's poetics – and the ten-poem sequence "Della Primavera Trasportata al Morale" in 1930. These works retain the immediacy of the moment without forfeiting the complexities of a longer form. He was also interested, as early as the 1920s, in writing a long poem, although a number of false starts preceded his coming up with the collage-like format of *Paterson* in the early 1940s. The poem is based on both the history and the contemporary condition of the small industrial city to the north of Rutherford and just west of New York City, whose nineteenth-century wealth was based on the water power from its famous Falls – the second deepest, after Niagara, east of the Mississippi. As the poem records, Alexander Hamilton had seen the potential of exploiting the falls a century earlier. Williams's concept evolved as he published the first four volumes individually from 1946 to 1951, and then a fifth, not part of the original plan at all, appeared in 1958. *Paterson* was the poem that finally won Williams readers and critical attention. Once the beautifully printed limited run of each book sold out, New Directions published cheap reprint editions that gathered together the individual volumes as they appeared.

Both Pound and Williams tested the loyalty of publisher Laughlin in different ways: Pound with his anti-Semitic comments and the arguably treasonous wartime radio broadcasts that led to his arrest, while Williams let himself be tempted away to commercial publisher Random House in the first half of the 1950s by one of Laughlin's own former employees. This defection was the result of Williams's festering sense that his readership and income would be greater with a wider distribution of his books, a concern particularly important once he retired from his medical practice. New Directions published two volumes gathering forty years of his poems, but Williams wasn't finished yet. Despite increasing health problems he still had ten years and three new collections to come.

In the 1950s Williams began to be discovered by a new generation of poets. Among those acknowledging his influence were Allen Ginsberg – three of whose letters appear in *Paterson* – Denise Levertov, Robert Duncan, Robert Creeley, Charles Olson, Robert Lowell, Amiri Baraka, Frank O'Hara, and Kenneth Koch. These poets, with their own diverse interests, saw Williams's work as offering possibilities outside of the dominant, carefully crafted mode endorsed by the New Critics. Williams managed for a short time in the middle of the decade to give readings and talks around the country, but by the late 1950s he became increasingly housebound, and recurring strokes made composition, typing, and reading difficult. The Pulitzer Prize for his last volume, *Pictures from Brueghel*, which also collected the two volumes from the Random House years, was awarded posthumously.

Critical commentary on Williams was helped by New Directions making available much of Williams's more radical prose and poetry of the 1920s in the volume *Imaginations* (1970). Previously the full texts of *Spring and All* and "The Descent of Winter" had only been available for the most part in rare book rooms. Emily Mitchell Wallace's meticulous *Bibliography* (1968) allowed scholars to track down Williams's numerous contributions to the little magazines, while Paul Mariani's detailed biography, *A New World Naked* (1981), provided a well-researched and detailed account of the poet's life. The *William Carlos Williams Newsletter* (now the *William Carlos Williams Review*), founded by Theodora Graham in 1975, provided an opportunity for specialized discussion of the poet, and early issues documented the poet's unpublished papers and correspondence in major research libraries nationwide. (The most extensive collections are in the Poetry Collection at SUNY Buffalo and Yale's Beinecke Library.) The work of the

Williams Review was supplemented importantly by the various conferences and publications of the National Poetry Foundation at the University of Maine, Orono.

This *Cambridge Companion* covers the major directions of scholarship on Williams over the more than fifty years since his death, and points toward the continuing areas of discussion in contemporary critical debate. Eric White begins the essays by looking at the importance of the little magazine world to Williams, and argues for Williams's expansive sense of the "local" in his use of the term. Glen MacLeod describes Williams's relationships with the writers, artists, and communities most central to his work in the first twenty years of his career. The importance of the avant-garde visual arts to Williams, and their role in his concept of a poem's design, is explored by Peter Halter. Lisa Steinman takes a fresh look at *Spring and All*, a text that has received significant attention from scholars in recent years. Milton Cohen takes Williams's career into the 1930s, looking at the way that Williams's political positions sometimes put him at odds with magazines and editors with whom he might be expected to be in sympathy. Alec Marsh explores Williams's prose writing, including his experimental writing of the 1920s and the *White Mule* trilogy that he began in the late 1930s, while the themes and compositional history of *Paterson* and the varied critical responses it has produced are the subject of Erin Templeton's essay. This broadly chronological survey of Williams's career ends with Cristina Giorcelli's discussion of the 1950s poetry.

The essays that then follow are devoted to some of the central issues in recent Williams scholarship. Ian Copestake's essay puts Williams's position in the context of earlier American writing, and examines Williams's treatment of history in *In the American Grain*. Kerry Driscoll explores the sometimes controversial topic of Williams and women, arguing that there were some important changes in his thinking about gender following his correspondence with Harriet Gratwick. Williams's multicultural background as it appears in his work, and his sometimes conflicted sense of ethnic identity, is the subject of Julio Marzán's discussion. Hugh Crawford looks at the role of Williams's medical career in his poetry and prose, with particular attention to the short stories posthumously collected as *The Doctor Stories*. Finally John Lowney discusses Williams's legacy, his influence on the younger generation of the 1950s and on into the twenty-first century.

Inevitably, given space limitations, some aspects of Williams's career and some additional approaches to his work can only be suggested in the Further Reading section of this volume. Williams's role as a correspondent is one such area. John Thirlwall's 1957 *Selected Letters*, although weighted more toward the latter part of Williams's career, is a useful starting point, but individual volumes of correspondence with such figures as Ezra Pound, James Laughlin, Louis Zukofsky, Kenneth Burke, Marcia Nardi, and Denise Levertov have become available, and no doubt future collections will appear. Williams's role as a dramatist would be worthy of an essay, as would further discussion of his editorial work on the little magazines he was associated with, especially *Others* and the two incarnations of *Contact*. Some recent commentators are finding Williams's work important in the areas of environmental and disability studies. In addition, in recent years there have been a number of books aimed at introducing Williams's life and work to younger readers. This latter development is an appropriate extension of Williams's work as a pediatrician – another instance of the coming together of two lives that Williams, in most moods, never saw as separate.

2

ERIC B. WHITE

William Carlos Williams and the local

Across the arc of his long career, William Carlos Williams remained stimulated by the localities he worked and lived in. Rutherford and the surrounding environs of New Jersey and New York provided the focal point through which the doctor-poet appraised the seismic cultural shifts taking place during the first half of the twentieth century, in America and beyond. Nevertheless, he also insisted that localities cannot be viewed in isolation: knowing what was distinctive about his own location depended heavily upon his ability to refer to other places, peoples, and times. For example, in his late 1920s work *The Embodiment of Knowledge*, he argued that for all artists "the local" consists of the "material before [them]" (*EK* 23). The crucial point for Williams was that a poetics of the local did not imply a constriction, but rather, a necessary focalization of effort. As such, the local should not be "confuse[d]" with "the narrow sense of parochialism," because "the local in a full sense *is* the freeing agency to all thought, in that it is everywhere accessible to all" (*EK* 23).

From his earliest self-published poems through to *Paterson*, Williams consistently viewed the local as a dynamic crucible of modern experience. In this sense, Williams's investment in local culture was essential to his literary modernism, not a paradoxical quirk of it. Equally, his locally sourced modernist poetics were necessarily formed in dialogue with avant-gardes based overseas, since it was only by accessing those heated exchanges that he could fully comprehend the onset of modernity in his own backyard. As art and ideas circulated between continents during the peak years of literary modernism, Williams argued that the unique and untranslatable site-specificities of artists' localities were best expressed by creative interpretations. His cultural localism and literary modernism emerged from this matrix of "translocal" interactions, and in seminal works such as *Al Que Quiere!*, *Spring and All*, "The Descent of Winter," and sections of *Paterson*, he argued that only through such processes could a "national" literature truly begin. Williams's localist project ultimately proposes a method of making art that

8

involves, as he insisted in *Paterson*, "an/ interpenetration, both ways" of the locality and its wider contexts – a process which is constantly evolving and subject to endless revision (*P* 4).

Pragmatism and the local

In 1920 the American pragmatist philosopher John Dewey famously declared that "the locality is the only universal" point of reference for artists – an axiom that Williams was fond of quoting.[1] Although rarely given credit for it, Williams was among the key pragmatist thinkers to theorize and test the relational possibilities of the local.[2] Rather than a cohesive philosophical system, pragmatism is generally agreed to be a practice-based epistemology with an empirical emphasis.[3] Pragmatists have an intellectual investment in testing philosophical ideas through their relevance to everyday experience. Because of this, local spheres of activity are particularly important to formulating and testing their hypotheses. This is because localities tend to be concentrated forms of broader categories of geographical place, that is, the physical contours of the real world that Michel de Certeau argues "impl[y] an indication of stability" in a given site, and which pragmatists consider to be theatres of lived experience.[4] However, Dewey, like Williams, usually thought of geographical "place" in relation to cultural "space," where human activity invests a site with meaning over time. As de Certeau explains, "*space is a practiced place*. Thus the street geometrically defined by urban planning is transformed into a space by walkers."[5] Yet for pragmatists, neither of these terms was specific enough. For this reason Dewey and Williams turned to the more circumscribed vocabulary of "the local," which combines the stability and recognizability of place with the contingencies of space within a discrete, boundaried area over specific durations of time.[6] By extension, localism, though often dismissed as a form of inward-looking parochialism, or a narrower expression of uncritical nationalism based on a reification of tradition and the immutability of local culture, was in Dewey's and Williams's estimation quite the opposite. For Dewey, localities and their inhabitants were "constantly emergent or in flux," modifying each other "continuously in transactive processes."[7] Accordingly, the version of cultural localism that Dewey proposed in his 1920 article "Americanism and Localism" for *The Dial*, which Williams embraced in his own little magazine *Contact*, refuted such static affirmations of identity. Instead, their versions of localism emphasized how the unique environments of specific sites continually interacted with contingent external forces to modify populations and places they inhabited over time, and how artists might tap into those experiential processes.

More recently, the "spatial" and "transnational" turns in American literary studies have drawn attention to the ways in which circulations of populations, ideas, and interests across the globe shape cultural and national identities (and, in turn, the ways in which such movements problematize the restrictive paradigms of nationalism and the nation state as bases for such identities).[8] The local and its variants have gradually emerged as effective sites for contesting traditional notions of space–time dialectics and the identitarian geopolitics of nationhood across several fields of study. In this respect, Williams anticipated trends in some fields of contemporary scholarship which, in the words of the cultural historian James Clifford, have come to view "human location as constituted by displacement as much as by stasis."[9] It is fitting, then, that Williams's poem "To Elsie" served as a catalyst for Clifford's own book *The Predicament of Culture*, which offered an early version of what Clifford later termed the "translocal": a form of "cosmopolitanism" that "requires a perpetual veering between local attachments and general possibilities."[10] Adapting this term for literary studies, Jahan Ramazani has formulated "a *translocal poetics* as an alternative to understandings of the relation of poetry to place as either rooted or rootless, local or universal," which "highlights the dialogic intersections ... of specific discourses, genres, techniques, and forms of diverse origins."[11] Although Williams is often aligned with a culturally nationalist project – even a rigidly "nativist" one, which rejects identities perceived as alien[12] – his Deweyan cultural localism insisted that static, centrally or regionally imposed identities were anathema to the transactional, provisional experiences that formed for him the basis of his locally sourced art.

Nevertheless, the stubbornly fixed features of localities were deeply important to Williams. For him, the *trans*local remained forever in creative tension with what might be called the *cis*local. As numerous studies of transatlantic literature remind us, the prefix "trans" means "across," "beyond," or "on the opposite side," while its antonym "cis" means "on this side of."[13] So in addition to the widely used term translocal, we can use "cislocal" to refer to an experience of the local that, more often than not, remains rooted and identifiable with a particular geographical place for a sustained duration of time. Williams struggled to reconcile these two aspects of locality in most of his major works, but they remained inseparable for him. It was a tension that he both acknowledged and revelled in.

"To make a start,/ out of particulars": the early poetry

Williams's early poems establish local sites and characters in the suburb of Rutherford, New Jersey, as the focal points around which the rhythms of town life revolve. Upon closer inspection, however, it is surprising how frequently Williams turns his attention to zones of transition that link places and communities, such as ports, stations, and harbours, as well as streets, rivers, and skies. These zones are often interspersed with references to foreign lands, other cultures, and cross-cultural exchanges. Combined, these references built up the relational matrices of local experience that became the bedrock of Williams's poetics. In his self-published 1909 collection *Poems*, early glimpses of these strategies emerged in "A Street Market, N.Y., 1908." The poet watches "Far tribes there mingle free" as New World free enterprise dissolves Old World conflict "in glittering brilliant show."[14] The poem focuses on the potential of American capitalism to transform commercial transactions into cultural ones, and is appropriately "rich" with pecuniary metaphors and adjectives (indeed, the speaker seems dazzled by the experience). Nevertheless, his references to money also hint (perhaps unintentionally) at less successful aspects of the marketplace; "thick souls ebb and flow" could refer to cycles of boom and bust as well as a bustling market, and "Eyes that can see" were once "Blind to a patent wide reality" – his use of "patent" suggesting that a rosy vision of the marketplace has been contrived, packaged and sold under licence for profit, as well as describing a clear and obvious fact. Typically, Williams's enthusiasm for commerce and industry as a harbinger of modernity was accompanied by a deep distrust of the systems that powered them – especially when those systems were rigged by federal, state, and municipal governments.

By 1914, Williams had made a potent connection between the exploitation of the working classes, "Those toilers after peace and after pleasure," and the ways in which resilient local communities could resist the adverse imposition of larger economic interests (*CP1* 29). He dedicated one section of his 1914 long poem "The Wanderer: A Rococo Study" to the silk workers' strike of 1913. In "Paterson – The Strike," he descends "shivering/ Out into the deserted streets of Paterson" (*CP1* 30) to witness the "brutality" and hardship imposed by the ruling classes on the workers (*CP1* 31; also see notes p. 490). Yet again, Williams immerses himself in the raw spectacle of industrial unrest in the city's commercial district, absorbing its corporeal "savagery" which "[tossed him] as a great father his helpless/ Infant till it shriek with ecstasy" (*CP1* 30–31). But unlike his experience in "A Street Market," Williams is more aware here that his senses have been overwhelmed, and he detaches himself from the scene of the strike to get a "clearer" perspective by connecting with its wider geographical settings (*CP1* 31). Accordingly, the next section, "Abroad," gestures beyond Bergen and Passaic Counties, which "The Wanderer" (the Passaic river) links to New York Harbor and the Atlantic via Newark Bay. Here, Williams ascends the "Jersey mountains" and "the great towers" of the city, introducing aerial perspectives that help the poet traverse not only the boundaries of land, sea, and air but also the terrain of his own memory (*CP1* 32). On this imaginative flight,

> . . . the great towers stood above the meadow
> Wheeling beneath, the little creeks, the mallows
> That I picked as a boy, the Hackensack
> So quiet, that looked so broad formerly:
> The crawling trains, the cedar swamp upon the one side –
> All so old, so familiar – so new now
> To my marvelling eyes as we passed
> Invisible.   (*CP1*, pp. 32–33)

In this passage, rivers, roads, and harbours connect localities to one another, while depictions of seagulls, "crawling trains," and self-propagating vegetation ("waving grass," "precipitous bramble banks," and vines) all evoke processes of travel and translocation (*CP1* 32–33). The cislocal features of site – rooted landmarks that vary little over time – form counterparts to these translocal points of reference, and are suggested by "the cedar swamp," a zone where time and locality congeals and stagnates, while skyscrapers, "the great towers of Manhattan," form monuments to, and archives of, modernity, reflecting the modern cityscape back at itself (*CP1* 27). Each feature speaks to the co-constructing tensions between the translocal and the cislocal, which themselves become metaphors for the interior processes that create Williams's own perceptions of his locality. His memories from childhood become aligned with "mallows," flowers of the marsh-land, while "crawling trains" gesture simultaneously towards the industrial modernity of the city, and to the primordial zone of "the cedar swamp." Thus, all that was "so old, so familiar" becomes "so new now," as static ridges become "shifting hills" (*CP1* 32–33). Localities, like identities, negotiate and modify both past and present – observer and observed – and are sites where memory forms a continual dialogue with anticipation in order to condition the poet's reactions to place in an endless, self-perpetuating cycle.

Williams expanded and refined the first version of "The Wanderer" to serve as the final piece in his third collection of poems, *Al Que Quiere!* (1917), which also expanded and refined his explorations of locality. Whereas "The Wanderer" explored urban working-class populations in aggregate, the other poems in the collection (such as "Gulls," "Tract," "January Morning," and "Dedication for a Plot of Ground") are more concerned with "townspeople" at the familial or community level. This shift corresponds with Williams's own transition from an imagistic concern with "place" to his localist engagement with "space." His townspeople are crucial to the process of making his town (as de Certeau phrased it) *"a practiced place,"* in which populations' activities invest sites with cultural energy and significance. By rooting his practice of place as well as poetry and medicine in the tumultuous ordinary lives and domesticities of the towns and cities he circulated in, his work took a distinctively spatial turn.

"Tract" is perhaps the most famous example of Williams's "townspeople" poems. Pedagogical yet dialogic, it revolves around human mortality and the objects that attach a life to a place:

> I will teach you my townspeople
> how to perform a funeral –
> for you have it over a troop
> of artists –
> unless one should scour the world –
> you have the ground sense necessary.   (*CP*1 72).

The poem is emphatic and jocular in its rejection of artifice and ceremony, and as critics have long argued, "Tract" is Williams's attempt to convey a materialist poetics to his own community as well as to a broader readership. However, the "townspeople" should not be read as a mere metaphor for that imagined community of readers. The tense negotiations involved in crafting a local poetics begin for Williams, in practical terms, at the ground level, perhaps because the risk of failure is great. As Williams explains to an "old woman" in section XV of "January Morning," "I wanted to write a poem/ that you would understand ... But you got to try hard" (*CP*1 103–04). The implication is that most people *won't* try hard, but Williams refuses to modify his stance, not only because of his avant-garde position (which he likens to the behaviour of "young girls" who "run giggling/ on Park Avenue after dark/ when they ought to be home in bed"), but because doing so would be condescending to the very people who inspire his poetry (*CP*1 104). The truculence of "Tract" and "January Morning" are not a means of distancing his "townspeople," but of provoking a meaningful dialogue with them, and thus a means of approaching them intellectually as equals.

In "Dedication for a Plot of Ground," Williams performs the ritual that he rehearsed in "Tract," and challenges his townspeople to reconsider the terms with which they assign cislocal characteristics to a given site. In this poem, Williams creates a sense of region built from multiple networked localities that eventually extends to sense of national identity, in which a plurality of communities build, inhabit, and continue to modify the environment and each other over time: "dedicated to the living presence of/ Emily Dickinson Wellcome," his paternal grandmother "who was born in England," Williams describes her harrowing immigration to "New York" via "the Azores," and subsequent relocation to "St. Thomas,/ Puerto Rico, San Domingo" (*CP1* 105–06). "This plot of ground" in West Haven, Connecticut faces "the waters of this inlet," Long Island Sound, beyond which is the Atlantic Ocean (*CP1* 105). The location maintains her connection to the Atlantic, and through it, the locations that she clung to on her travels before settling in (and for) her final resting place in America. Those transatlantic and circumatlantic voyages, actual and imaginative, are distilled by Williams into a stark description of the mundane details and locations of a tough life now spent. "She grubbed this earth with her own hands," he writes of her "plot of ground," but the final two-line strophe alludes to the richness of a life that Williams's "Dedication" hitherto merely signposts: "If you can bring nothing to this place/ but your carcass, keep out" (*CP1* 106). Here, the poet demands that his readers retrace the multiple cultural inheritances of the complex identity interred in this American soil. *Al Que Quiere!* – with its Spanish title, multilingual poem titles, and references to the multi-ethnic and immigrant communities Williams visited on his medical rounds – constantly alludes to the translocal and transnational roots of American culture encapsulated in his "Dedication for a Plot of Ground." These strategies reveal how Williams cultivated a rhizomatic conception of locality from which the poet's imagination radiated.

Contacting America

In terms of both its subjects and its poetics, Williams's remarkable development from the uneven journeyman poetics of *The Tempers* to the brash modernism of *Al Que Quiere!* owes a great deal to his involvement in the transatlantic little magazine networks emerging in the 1910s. These titles included *Poetry* and *The Little Review*, based in Chicago, *The Egoist*, based in London, and most importantly *Others*, which was originally located in Williams's own backyard in Ridgefield, New Jersey. Unfortunately, *Others* had collapsed in the summer of 1919 (an event which Williams himself helped bring about), and his relationship with the editors of *The Little Review*, the magazine that he shifted his allegiance to, grew ever more fractious as the decade waned. The rapid ascent of the well-funded but Eurocentric journal *The Dial* in the US literary scene also made Williams pessimistic about the ability of American little magazines to foster critical environments in which locally sourced avant-gardes might flourish. So he decided to create his own.

Contact was a specialized literary and art magazine dedicated to exploring "the essential contact between words and the locality that breeds them."[15] Both Williams and his co-editor Robert McAlmon had monitored Dewey's articles in *The New Republic* since the late 1910s, but when Dewey finally entered a discussion about "Americanism and Localism" in *The Dial*, it galvanized their own purpose. Critiquing Joel Oppenheim's article "Poetry – Our First National Art," Dewey proposed a version of cultural localism as an experiential alternative to the vague and sometimes incoherent versions of "Americanism" proffered by literary nationalists, including Oppenheim.[16] According to Dewey, "Americanism" and "localism" were not synonymous terms. In fact, he insisted on their distinctiveness, since "the country is a spread of localities, while the nation is something that exists in Washington and other seats of government" (685). Like Williams, he argued that any collective sense of American identity must emerge gradually via centripetal exchanges of local experience – from interactions within and between America's diverse neighbourhoods and the print cultures they fostered – rather than any abstract, centrifugally transmitted sense of national identity.

Williams especially was convinced that if American artists properly apprehended their localities, then they would eventually overcome the popular compulsion to manufacture a "national art." "America is far behind France or Ireland in an indigenous art," he argued, because "Americans are still too prone to admire and to copy the very thing which should not be copied, the thing which is French or Irish alone, the thing which is the result of special local conditions of thought and circumstance."[17] The reason for this American inferiority complex was a systematic failure to engage with the local: those who did not know their "own world, in whatever confused form it may be, must either stupidly fail to learn from foreign work or stupidly swallow it without knowing how to judge of its essential value."[18] Over four issues *Contact* developed its localist vanguard, but suffered a setback when McAlmon joined the wave of American artists expatriating themselves to Europe in spring 1921. There would be one further issue of *Contact* in June 1923, but by then Williams had completed most of his major critical treatises on "the local" (apart from his extended essay on Edgar Allan Poe for *In the American Grain*). When this final issue of *Contact* appeared, *Sour Grapes* (1921) had long since been published and *Spring and All* had been sent to Paris for publication in McAlmon's fledging fine press imprint Contact Editions, where it appeared in autumn 1923. Given the specialized publishing context of *Spring and All*, Williams probably assumed that its limited readership would be familiar with his arguments about localism. This probably explains why in *Spring and All*, he performed his localist poetics rather than explaining them further. In fact, in its sustained address to the "imagination," the prose sections of *Spring and All* are more concerned with "the universal" than "the local," as the contingencies of local space are broadened to abstract discussions of "place."

In *Spring and All*, Williams defined the "imagination" as "a force, an electricity or a medium, a place" (*CP1* 235). In this collection, Williams seeks to translate his localist programme more directly into the transnational language of the arts (this project was already present in *Contact*, but the magazine's audience was primarily a cadre of fellow American avant-gardists, rather than the international audience McAlmon's Contact Editions targeted). By 1923, Williams believed it self-evident that the trans-atlantic imaginary emerged from the local and the contingent, and argued that "whether it is the condition of a place or a dynamization its effect is the same" basic expression of a poetics of contact (*CP1* 235). These translocal poetics enabled Williams to identify avant-garde practices of foreign painters such as Juan Gris and Marcel Duchamp as exemplars of "the modern trend" (*CP1* 194). Duchamp's ready-made methods, which he had already praised in *Kora in Hell* (1920), involved "detach[ing]" everyday objects "from ordinary experience" and reattaching them "to the imagination" (*CP1* 197). Crucially, Williams is not using "ordinary experience" as a pejorative here: imaginative contact with this quotidian arena is precisely where the local imagination becomes universal. Carefully balancing irony and exuber-ance, thrill and risk, *Spring and All* revelled in the modern experience of rapid translocation that Duchamp's ready-mades evoked, ascending from statistics (mortality rates: "Somebody dies every four minutes/ in New York State") to poetics ("To hell with you and your poetry") to "the next solar system" in the space of the opening five lines (*CP1* 231–32). Of course, these examples form hyperbolic condensations of the local and the universal, but they make an entirely serious point about the ways in which modernist poets mediated the staggering shifts of temporal and geographic scales made possible by new technologies and cultural frames of reference.

"[I]ntense vision of the facts": modernity and the local in "The Descent of Winter"

In the mid-1920s, Williams's own transatlantic travels emphasized how rapidly perceptions of time and space were changing in the Machine Age, with important consequences for his poetics. "The Descent of Winter" brought these cultural transformations into sharp relief. Begun aboard the *SS Pennland* in September 1927 on his return from Europe, where he had left his wife behind to care for their sons in a Swiss boarding school, "The Descent of Winter" represented another attempt by Williams to embody New World modernism by exploring its discrete corners. Like

Spring and All and his improvisational writing, "The Descent of Winter" captured the mercurial flux of his thought in scattershot bursts of prose and controlled late imagist poetry in a carefully structured textual schema. As its original title "Notes in Diary Form" suggests, the diary entries that organize the collection provided Williams with a clear sense of chronological progression through his New Jersey localities. And like *Kora in Hell*, "Descent" uses a figure with which to anchor his collection, a gesture which also anticipates *Paterson* in its use of a persona to connect and narrativize the New World. As Paul Mariani explains, "[t]he hero of his American portrait would be a little Polish girl, born in [Fairfield New Jersey] in his absence" named Dolores Marie Pischak (Mariani 263). The sound of her name, as Mariani notes, evokes the rushing flow of the Passaic River, but it also suggests the flow of immigrants into America. Hence, there is no single line of "descent" in "The Descent of Winter:" history, heredity, lineage, and the water rushing over Paterson Falls are as much at issue as the inevitable cycles of the seasons suggested by the title.

When Williams states in his entry for "10/23" that "I will make a big, serious portrait of my time," he approaches the task in a rather literal way. He inscribes the material building blocks of a mosaic – the "brown and creamwhite block of Mexican onyx" – with "a poorly executed replica of the Aztec calendar on one of its dicefacets" and the words "Puebla, Mexico, Calendario Azteca." By making this connection, Williams links geology, contemporary geography, and ancient methods of timekeeping to the commercially driven culture of present-day America via the tourist economy. This creates a vision of "America some years after the original," portrayed, significantly, by a die, which suggests a culture created from games of chance and speculation (*CP1* 295). Accordingly, themes of economics and mass production dominate the prose improvisation for "10/27." Opening with a reference to the current president, Calvin Coolidge, the section concludes in a ditch by the side of the road, and takes in a dazzling panorama of a city's commercial districts along the way. As Marjorie Perloff observes, "[i]n this surreal cityscape, objects in shop windows, seen from what is evidently the window of the poet's moving car" achieve an intentional "blurring of focus," which enables Williams to emphasize "the mobility and mystery of the city."[19] There is also a new urgency in his pairing of the electrical and botanical displays, and the ways in which they are mediated: in this locality, windows and other glass cases become as important as the people and things they contain. Williams initially identifies "lights like fuchsias" that line the streets, before traffic signals become "cherry-red danger and applegreen safety," thereby supplanting the earlier simile with a sensory fusion of signifier and signified (*CP1* 296). The correlation runs deeper as he puns on the dual meaning of "bulb," from which electric lights and flowers both produce their displays. This tactic updates a strategy he used in his 1913 poem "Contemporania." In that poem, he claimed kinship with leaves and plants because together they served as "Framing devices, flower devices" and worked symbiotically, aesthetically "peopling/ The barren country" (*CP1* 16). "Descent" reasserts the centrality of such "framing devices" in pragmatist figurations of the local. The lights infuse the urban locality with living energy and order, just as plants and townspeople had done consistently for Williams throughout his early oeuvre. New technologies transformed the ways in which places became practised and spatialized into vibrant modern localities, and "Descent" registers those changes emphatically.

Williams's juxtapositions of the natural world and urban localities continue in "11/2," in which he pairs "Dahlias" with a pedestrian asking for directions. The name of the street she is searching for in Rutherford, "Washington Avenue," also gestures towards the national and international geopolitical scales of the next poem, "A Morning Imagination of Russia" (*CP1* 303). Significantly, the poem shares the same date entry with the poem beginning "Dahlias," "11/2," which suggests how intersecting national, historical, and local frames of reference converge in the poet's imagination, and through a shared temporal context. Rather than a poem of sociopolitical resistance in the vein of "The Wanderer," "Morning Imagination" is an extended exercise in translocal affective contact with a medic on the other side of the world. Although the subject of the poem has been absorbed into the state's infrastructure, he remains, like Williams, a diagnostician and healer, but also a conduit of history and force for potential development in his own locality and beyond. Indeed, the common currency enabling these imaginative exchanges between Russia and America is the humane, healing "touch" that concludes the poem. As Brian Bremen notes, this is "that 'tactus eruditus' that Williams mentions in the 'Della Primavera [Trasportata al Morale].'"[20] "The Descent of Winter" gestures towards this "erudite touch," and the broader "problems of individualism, capitalism, American identity and historical development" it is meant to address, which Williams explored more fully in "Della Primavera's" onset of spring.[21] Nevertheless, in "Descent," and especially "Morning Imagination," Williams's "erudite touch" becomes an urgent, localist invocation of contact, rather than any coherent statement about international politics. Russia becomes the territory of his imagination, just as Dolores Marie Pischak is its child, and, in "Descent" both are cogent points of reference in the translocal framework because of that common descent: "Russia is every country, here he must live, this for that, loss for gain. Dolores Marie Pischak" (*CP1* 306). In this configuration, the "local soviet" Williams mentions serves as a political embodiment of that nodal locality Dewey spoke of, channelling and framing the forces that flow from the individual, to the neighbourhood, to the regional, national, and even universal scales, embodied in a single figure, the child of his imagination.

"The Descent of Winter" is a cultural critique that insists upon the temporality of place and the spatiality of time. As sweeping socio-economic and political forces inscribed themselves on the communities that Williams served and traversed, the new visual languages they created increasingly bound those groups together. In "Descent," Williams identified continuities between advertising culture, urbanization and technological innovations and the natural world. In "11/1," for example, the illumination provided by the night sky ("The moon .../ and the Pleiades") heightens the sense of optical distortion created by an "illumined/ signboard" advertising bread (CP1 302–303). It frames "ecstatic, æsthetic faces/ . . . leaping/ over printed hurdles" owned by "two/ gigantic highschool boys/ ten feet tall" (CP1 303). The rural setting allows the images on the advertisement to dominate the landscape, which frames them completely, exaggerating the inflated scale of the commercial landscape further still. "Descent" also emphasizes how industrial modernity distorts the non-urban world at the ecological level. Williams revisits that "river of my heart polluted" (CP1 308) that he originally explored in "The Wanderer" while also pointing towards its unifying potential in *Paterson*: its toxicity is a component of his experience of modernity, and therefore must be accounted for in his evocation of the local. The "stream" of the Passaic creates a geographical feature that is simultaneously translocal and cislocal, and that infuses its framing devices with potential: its "Ajax Aniline Dye Works" serve as an outpost for the commercial and industrial outlets that pepper the text and gesture towards the global forces shaping this New Jersey town, while "An old farm house in long tangled trees, leaning over it" evokes the stubbornly rural roots that govern local customs. Here, in "my own county, its largest city, my own time," Williams's locality radiates from his imagination, which he embodies in Dolores Marie Pischak: "O future worlds," he declares, "This is her portrait" (CP1 296–97).

"[T]he edge of the gorge": towards *Paterson*

Of course, "The Descent of Winter" is not a portrait of a person, per se – rather, it is an evocation of a locality, and another articulation of Williams's cultural localism. As the anthropologist Arjun Appadurai has argued, locality is "constituted by a series of links between the sense of social immediacy, the technologies of interactivity, and the relativity of contexts."[22] The connective channels that Williams relentlessly traces out in "Descent" are expressed not only in his self-conscious attention to circulations of electricity, traffic, water, and communications, but also to the erratic flow of his own language. In the multiplicity of its voices, "Descent" is not bound to a single personality – not even the author's. However, Williams had attempted to synthesize the single subject and the local in his 1927 poem "Paterson." In this *Dial*-award-winning poem, Williams cast Dr. Paterson as an organizing presence in the city that he shares his name with:

> Say it! No ideas but in things. Mr.
> Paterson has gone away
> to rest and write. Inside the bus one sees
> his thoughts sitting and standing. His thoughts
> alight and scatter –
>
> Who are these people (how complex
> this mathematic) among whom I see myself
> in the regularly ordered plateglass of
> his thoughts, glimmering before shoes and bicycles – ?
> They walk incommunicado, the
> equation is beyond solution, yet
> its sense is clear – that they may live
> his thought is listed in the Telephone
> Directory –   (CP1 264).

"Paterson" catches Williams's cultural localism at a crossroads: the poem emphasizes spatial and temporal framing using the language of the modern cityscape, and the problem of articulating identity in a heterogeneous nation of fellow commuters. But it also documents his mounting frustration with the task of correlating the local and the national with discrete encounters to create a provisional sense of an emerging "American" identity. Accordingly, and despite multiple opportunities for interpersonal "contact," the townspeople of Paterson "walk incommunicado." The "regularly ordered plateglass" through which Dr. Paterson glimpses them grants him endless opportunities for cultural diagnostics, and yet "the/ equation" that will render them comprehensible to him "is beyond solution." Nevertheless, "its sense is clear," and his ongoing detachment from his fellow commuters results in a commitment to identify with them, "that they may live." For in them, Williams writes, "I see myself." However, "his thoughts" are constantly interrupted and mediated by modern technology. Indeed "his thought" in the abstract "is listed in the Telephone/ Directory," and becomes yet another "idea" contained figuratively in a "thing" that documents the networked individuals of his city. Williams's point is that electronic communication and rapid transit disrupt as well as facilitate human interactions. Although "the Telephone/ Directory" and its demographic "equation[s]" accurately document a major cross section of Paterson's inhabitants, its omissions and taxonomic arrangement further alienate Mr. Paterson from the "sense" of those lives, resulting in further entropy.

Across failing telephone lines and language barriers with "doctors who can't speak proper english [sic]," and over the din of traffic and roar of the falls "pouring in above the city," Williams shouts rather than "says" his constant refrain: "Say it! No ideas but in things" (CP1 263–65). "Paterson" intersperses this slippery materialist dictum among the familiar localist portraits and travelogues that define Williams's early work – but it also plays an important role in connecting his cultural localism with a new symbolic system. Significantly, the "no ideas" axiom crops up in his description of the Olympian figures painted by the father of "Alex Shorn," "a boot-black" decorating the interior of his house with mythological scenes (CP1 264). Here, through the tentative language of pastiche, Williams introduces the groundwork for what Perloff describes as the epic "superstructure" of *Paterson* before she cites Robert Lowell that Williams's allusions signal a sustained engagement with "symbolic man and woman" conforming loosely to Hegelian notions of "*thesis* and *antithesis*" in a "struggle towards synthesis – marriage."[23] In this sense, *Paterson* represents Williams's drift towards the systems of symbolic order favoured by the New Critics. Published in 1946, in the aftermath of the Second World War, the opening sections of *Paterson* propose "To make a start,/ out of particulars/ and make them general," by starting in Rutherford and moving out from the local into the wider world. Williams immediately acknowledges and celebrates the fraught nature of the task of "rolling/ up the sum, by defective means" (P 3). The promise of a poetic synthesis of the local and the "universal" – "*by multiplication a reduction to one*" (P 2) – suggests his proposal for a kind of syncretic nationalism, on the one hand, and a valediction for the difficult, polyvalent subjects that he explored at the peak of his localist modernist project in the 1920s, on the other. The "*reduction to one*" also refers to the unifying persona of Paterson himself, "one man – like a city" (P 7). Here, Williams supplants his favoured metonyms with an epic simile, of the kind he explicitly rejected in "The Descent of Winter." And yet, from its very inception, Williams's recalcitrant localism, and the calculated irony that was at times its hallmark, chips away at his attempts in *Paterson* to forge a grand narrative, a "GRRRREAT HISTORY of that/ old time Jersey Patriot/ N. F. PATERSON!" (P 15).

Not only does Williams's intertextuality in *Paterson* interrogate and ironize his historical source material and quotations – it also continually draws attention to the raw materials of language and, ultimately, his cultural localism. For example, the epigraph eloquently announces this evolving poetics of contact, beginning characteristically with a disembodied colon, inviting readers to forge those connections with what he once called the smallest "particles of language" (*IAG* 221):

> : *a local pride; spring, summer, fall and the sea; a confession; a*
> *basket; a column; a reply to Greek and Latin with the bare hands;*
> *a gathering up; a celebration;* (P 2).

Williams's use of connective punctuation marks link geography, seasons, culture and language in crafty ways, suggesting at once the problems and possibilities of creating the "distinctive terms" for a new locally sourced poetics (*P* 2). As "*a reply to Greek and Latin with the bare hands*," it also announces a cumulative expression of Williams's cultural localism, which emerged as a response to the broader geographical, chronological, and cultural contexts from which his local language derived. In passages such as these, his old pragmatist emphasis on process and transactional exchange militates against his urge to compress, reduce and unify. In this sense, *Paterson* provides yet another iteration of a continuing and unfinished project, "*an identification and a plan for action to supplant a plan for action*" (*P* 2). Williams's localist impulse does not achieve a final expression in *Paterson*, but is resuscitated to exist in tension with an epic schema that threatened to destabilize his messy, difficult, and brilliant encounters with the local, which in their articulation made his ascent into the annals of literary history so singular.

NOTES

1. John Dewey, "Americanism and Localism," *The Dial* 68.6 (June 1920): 684–88, 687.
2. Williams's early "Philosophical Essays" (*EK* 153–91) and prose manuscripts (ca. 1919–21) discovered by Randy Ploog and myself confirm that his engagement with pragmatist conceptions of the local emerged alongside, rather than as a response to, work such as Dewey's. See "The Early Career of William Carlos Williams: A Critical Facsimile Edition of His Uncollected Prose and Manuscripts," *William Carlos Williams Review* 30.1–2 (2013): xi–119, 92–116.
3. The principles of pragmatist philosophy were first articulated by Charles Sanders Pierce and William James in the late nineteenth and early twentieth centuries, and developed by thinkers such as John Dewey. Contemporary proponents include Jürgen Habermas, Susan Haack and Richard Rorty.
4. Michel de Certeau, *The Practice of Everyday Life*, trans. Steven F. Rendall (Berkeley and London: University of California Press, 1984), 117.
5. Ibid.

6. See Eric B. White, *Transatlantic Avant-Gardes: Little Magazines and Localist Modernism* (Edinburgh: Edinburgh University Press, 2013), 12–13.

7. Malcolm P. Cutchin, "John Dewey's Metaphysical Ground-Map and Its Implications for Geographical Inquiry," *Geoforum* 39 (July 2008): 1555–69, 1565.

8. As Paul Giles has usefully summarized, the "spatial turn poses a particular challenge to an established tradition of American literature that ... was gripped by temporal perspectives;" in "Transnationalism and Classic American Literature," *PMLA: Publications of the Modern Language Association of America* 118.1 (2003): 62–77, 63.

9. James Clifford, *Routes: Travel and Translation in the Late Twentieth Century* (Cambridge, MA: Harvard University Press, 1997), 2.

10. James Clifford, *The Predicament of Culture: Twentieth-Century Ethnography, Literature, and Art* (Cambridge, MA: Harvard University Press, 1988), 4.

11. Jahan Ramazani, *A Transnational Poetics* (Chicago: University of Chicago Press, 2009), xiv, 43.

12. For a nativist reading of Williams, see Walter Benn Michaels, *Our America: Nativism, Modernism, and Pluralism* (Durham, NC and London: Duke University Press, 1995).

13. My use of the prefixes "trans" and "cis" derives from David Armitage's taxonomy of transatlantic studies, in which the "Trans-Atlantic" approach is "the history of the Atlantic World told through comparisons" and the "Cis-Atlantic" approach focuses on "particular places as unique locations," in "Three Concepts of Atlantic History," in David Armitage and Michael J. Braddick, eds., *The British Atlantic World, 1500–1800* (New York: Palgrave Macmillan, 2002), 16–21, 15. The third "Circum-Atlantic" approach is "the history of the people who crossed the Atlantic, who lived on its shores and who participated in the communities it made possible" (16).

14. William Carlos Williams, "A Street Market, N.Y., 1908," in Virginia M. Wright-Peterson, ed., *Poems* (Urbana and Chicago: University of Illinois Press, 2002), 18–19, 18.

15. William Carlos Williams, "Further Announcement," *Contact* 1 (December 1920): 10.

16. James Oppenheim, "Poetry – Our First National Art," *The Dial* 68.2 (February 1920): 238–42.

17. William Carlos Williams, "Comment," *Contact* 2 (January 1921): 11–12, 12.

18. Ibid.

19. Marjorie Perloff, *The Poetics of Indeterminacy: Rimbaud to Cage* (Princeton, NJ: Princeton University Press, 1981), 146.

20. Brian Bremen, *William Carlos Williams and the Diagnostics of Culture* (New York: Oxford University Press, 1993), 72.

21. John Beck, *Writing the Radical Center: William Carlos Williams, John Dewey, and American Cultural Politics* (Albany: State University of New York Press, 2001), 79.

22. Arjun Appadurai, "The Production of Locality," in *Modernity at Large: Cultural Dimensions of Globalization* (Minneapolis: University of Minnesota Press, 1996), 178.

23. Perloff, *The Poetics of Indeterminacy*, 148–149.

3

GLEN MACLEOD

Williams and his contemporaries

William Carlos Williams's general approach to life and literature has been aptly characterized as "conversational" (Whitaker 1–10). His mixed family heritage (English, Puerto Rican, French, Jewish) and volatile personality are reflected in the multiple voices and viewpoints of his poems. As his friend Marsden Hartley remarked, "[H]e is perhaps more people at once than anyone I've ever known – not vague persons but he's a small town of serious citizens in himself" (qtd. in Whitaker 1). This tendency toward multiple perspectives was strengthened by his work as a pediatrician and family doctor which brought him into daily contact with people of different types and backgrounds. He thrived on human interaction in his writing as well, relying on conversation with fellow writers and artists to help him define his own literary position. Art, for Williams, was always something of a group activity or team sport. His poem "Sub Terra" (1917) expresses his desire to be part of such a community:

> Where shall I find you,
> you my grotesque fellows
> that I seek everywhere
> to make up my band?   (CP1 63)

He thought of the modernist movement in these terms, as an ongoing dialogue with his contemporaries – sometimes supportive, sometimes contentious – that would stimulate his own creativity and help bring about the poetic renaissance he envisioned.

The most important of these contemporaries was Ezra Pound whom Williams met in 1902 when both were undergraduates at the University of Pennsylvania (P/W 3). Williams was dazzled by the young Pound, describing him as "the livest, most intelligent and unexplainable thing I'd ever seen, and the most fun" (A 58). In retrospect, he recognized this new friendship as the turning point in his career: "Before meeting Ezra Pound is like B.C. and A.D." (IWWP 5). Despite some serious disagreements and periods of coolness, the two men remained friends for the rest of their lives. At Williams's death Pound could write, "He bore with me sixty years, and I shall never find another poet friend like him" (*P/W* 319).

Although Williams was two years older, he was impressed by Pound's already vast knowledge of literature, found his quick intelligence and brash self-confidence entertaining, and thrived on their creative dialogue. However, from the start he was also keenly aware of Pound's deficiencies. Williams's careful scientific side, cultivated by his medical training, had little patience with Pound's showy aestheticism, and his democratic sympathies were offended by Pound's elitism. Pound maintained the tone of Williams's teacher long after Williams had become a mature artist himself who could clearly see Pound's own blindnesses. Nevertheless, Williams was devoted to his old friend and depended on him for bracing, honest criticism – the sort of criticism he got when he sent a copy of his first book, *Poems* (1909), to Pound in London. Pound flatly dismissed its stale romanticism, commenting bluntly, "Your book would not attract even passing attention here .... You are out of touch" (Paige 8). And although such frankness surely stung, Williams welcomed it as a challenge and a stimulus: "When I write badly, sock me, I like it" (*P/W* 136). He also returned the favor, regularly objecting to Pound's poetic posturing and misguided ideas; most notably, he denounced in letters and in print Pound's increasingly pro-Fascist and anti-Semitic views in the 1930s.

Pound and Williams promoted each other's work whenever possible. Williams included Pound's work in publications he edited, reviewed Pound's *Cantos* favorably as they appeared, and gave a positive notice even to *Jefferson and/or Mussolini* (1936). Pound arranged for the publication of Williams's *The Tempers* (1913), included his poem "Postlude" in the groundbreaking anthology *Des Imagistes* (1914), and generally used his influence to advance Williams's reputation among the transnational avant-garde. On Pound's essay, "Dr. Williams' Position" (1928), Williams wrote gratefully, "Nothing will ever be said of better understanding regarding my work than your article in The Dial" (*P/W* 95).

Both Pound and Williams hoped for a modernist Renaissance based on a fresh, clean, stripped-down use of ordinary language. As Pound put it – and Williams would agree – there should be "no Tennysonianness of speech; nothing – nothing that you couldn't, in some circumstance, in the stress of some emotion, actually say" (Paige 49). The imagist movement (1913–1914), associated most centrally with Pound and Hilda Doolittle (H. D.), stressed sharpness of observation, economy of phrasing, and organic rhythm – all virtues that Williams sought in his own poetry throughout his career.

The chief disagreement between Pound and Williams, never resolved, was over whether the revolutionary modernist movement was to be fundamentally local and American or cosmopolitan and European. Pound moved to London in 1908 and thereafter made his home in Europe (not counting several brief visits to the United States and his incarceration in St. Elizabeths Hospital from 1945 to 1958). Like Henry James before him, Pound believed that the thin cultural atmosphere of America could not support serious artistic growth. He scoffed at Williams's provincialism, badgering him to move to Europe to be at the cultural center of things. But Williams had early committed himself to life as a busy doctor, husband, and father in Rutherford, New Jersey, the town where he was born. Always suspicious of Pound's cultural pretensions, he was determined that his own poetry would be grounded in his specifically American experience and crafted from the raw material of American vernacular speech. When Pound mocked him as a country bumpkin, Williams rejoined that Pound, in becoming an expatriate, had cut himself off from his vital roots, dooming his poetry to a bloodless cosmopolitanism – sophisticated but academic, lacking any vital connection to real life.

Williams was not, of course, as parochial, uncultured, or narrowly patriotic as Pound liked to claim. He had received part of his high school education in Switzerland (1897–1898); studied pediatric medicine for six months in Germany (1909–1910), with a stop in London to visit Pound and meet W. B. Yeats; spent six months in Europe again in 1924, meeting such pioneers of international modernism as James Joyce, Ford Madox Ford, Constantin Brancusi, and Philippe Soupault; and visited there again briefly in 1927 when he met Gertrude Stein among others. He published regularly in European periodicals like *the transatlantic review, transition*, and *Broom*. Williams's emphasis on "the local" must be understood – as he understood it – in this international context (as Eric White points out elsewhere in this volume).

What Williams chiefly objected to in Pound's poetry was his "constant . . . cribbing from the Renaissance, Provence and the modern French." Such borrowing, he thought, was "rehash, repetition." It was not *new* (contrary to Pound's dictum, "Make it new!") and it was not fundamentally American, except in the pejorative sense that Americans had always been accused of being mere imitators of Europe (*I* 24). Williams accused both Pound and his close associate T. S. Eliot of being "Men content with the connotations of their masters" (*I* 24). But he reserved his sharpest barbs for Eliot, calling him "the worst possible influence in American letters" and repeatedly expressing his "contempt for and distrust of T. S. Eliot and all he does and says" (*SL* 226; *CP2* 453). Of Eliot's "The Love Song of J. Alfred Prufrock" (1915) he remembered: "I had a violent feeling that Eliot had betrayed what I believed in ... my contemporaries flocked to him – away from what I wanted" (*IWWP* 30). Even more devastating for Williams was the enormous success of Eliot's *The Waste Land* (1922). He called it "the great catastrophe to our letters" because it "gave the poem back to the academics . . . . It wiped out our world as if an atom bomb had been dropped upon it" (*A* 146, 174). Williams knew he could not compete with Eliot's erudition and superior craftsmanship. He resented his elitism, his privileged closeness to his old friend Pound, and the way these two Europeanized expatriates drew all attention to London as the center of modern poetry in English, sidetracking Williams's hopes for a specifically American modernism. "I felt at once that [*The Waste Land*] had set me back twenty years, and I'm sure it did" (*A* 174). *Spring and All* (1923) with its high-spirited mixture of prose and poetry, its railing against "THE TRADITIONALISTS OF PLAGIARISM," (*CP1* 185) is in part Williams's answer to the cultivated gloom of *The Waste Land*.

Another of Williams's contemporaries who followed Pound to London was H. D. Pound had introduced her to Williams in 1904 when all three were students in Philadelphia (she at Bryn Mawr). He was clearly drawn to H. D. with her unusual beauty and youthful, somewhat otherworldly spirit. Together they took long walks near her family's home in Upper Darby. He wrote to his brother Edgar on May 6, 1906, "Do you know Bo I'm dead in love with that girl. She isn't good looking and she isn't graceful; she isn't a beautiful dresser and she cannot play any music, but by Gee! she is a fine girl and she can have me alright" (*WCW/EW* 100). Her letters to him from this time convey a self-deprecating, playful, affectionate attitude toward this handsome, talented man who was three years her senior. Williams was doubtless flattered by her attention, yet kept a certain distance because he knew she was Pound's "girl." When, in 1911, she too abandoned America for London, Williams must have felt a complicated sense of betrayal as well as some jealousy toward both of them. The emotional dynamics of this literary triangle help to explain the bitterness that colors his later accounts of H. D., the most important of which is in the "Prologue" to *Kora in Hell* (1920).

The "Prologue" collected, as Williams said, "All my gripes to other poets, all my loyalties to other poets" (*IWWP* 30). His gripe about H. D. centers on an episode in the summer of 1916 when Williams submitted his long poem "March" to *The Egoist*, then co-edited by H. D. Since Williams last saw her, she had been living abroad for five years, had married the poet Richard Aldington, had lost a child, and had become a respected poet in her own right, a leading figure in the imagist movement with which Williams himself was aligned. She was no longer the unassuming college girl he had known in

Pennsylvania. He must have been surprised by the mature and self-assured tone of H. D.'s editorial letter (included in the "Prologue") which explained her substantial cuts in the poem. She praised his allusions to past art – the pyramids, Ashur-ban-i-pal, and Fiesole – but asked him to eliminate "the hey-ding-ding touch" which detracted from the "sacred" nature of poetry. Although he accepted virtually all her editorial changes, he was obviously nettled by this interchange, using it to characterize his basic differences with H. D. For him, modern poetry was anything but "sacred"; in fact, the offending passages of "March" had been a deliberate (if flat-footed) effort to disrupt the serious tone of the poem, to avoid "the desolation of a flat Hellenic perfection of style" – an obvious swipe at H. D.'s imagist poems (*I* 12–13). This uncomfortable exchange put a strain on their relationship. Williams's friendship with H. D. did not recover for many years.

Committed to remaining in the United States, Williams most wanted to feel part of a community of artists and writers such as Pound enjoyed in London. His interest in painting led him to the artists associated with Alfred Stieglitz's gallery, especially Marsden Hartley, Charles Demuth (a friend from his college days), and Charles Sheeler; and with the salon of Walter Conrad Arensberg, particularly the Frenchmen Marcel Duchamp, Jean Crotti, and Albert Gleizes. (For his interactions with contemporary painters, see the essay in this volume by Peter Halter.) One way he developed connections with his literary contemporaries was through little magazines such as *Poetry, The Little Review, The Dial, The Egoist, Broom*, and *the transatlantic review*.

The most important of these magazines, for Williams, was *Others*. He claimed that it "saved my life as a writer" (*A* 135). Its editor, Alfred Kreymborg, had previously been editing a short-lived magazine called *The Glebe* (1913–1914) when Ezra Pound sent him the manuscript of *Des Imagistes*, urging him to publish it. At the same time Pound suggested that Kreymborg get in touch with his friend Williams. Kreymborg dutifully published the anthology as *The Glebe*'s fifth issue (February 1914), but he did not meet Williams until 1915 when he was launching his new magazine, *Others*. The two quickly became friends and Williams began publishing poems in the magazine, doing editorial work, and generally helping in any way he could. In the process he became a loyal and enthusiastic member of "the *Others* group" whose best-known figures were, in addition to Williams and Kreymborg, Maxwell Bodenheim, Man Ray (who was then writing poetry), Mina Loy, Marianne Moore, and Wallace Stevens. "Whenever I wrote at this time, the poems were written with *Others* in mind," he recalled years later (*IWWP* 19). His dream of a community of poets was realized, for a time.

Maxwell Bodenheim was known as the Bohemian poet of Greenwich Village. Williams admired Bodenheim's poetry and was one of the first to befriend him when he moved from Chicago to New York in 1915, even allowing him to stay with his family briefly when he was homeless. Bodenheim became closely associated with *Others*. His poems appeared in it regularly, and he was on such good terms with both Kreymborg and Williams that the December 1916 issue was devoted to poems by only those three poets. Williams considered Bodenheim a "heroic figure" who lived wholly in his imagination, "an Isaiah of the butterflies" (*I* 27). His poem "M.B." (*CP1* 72) is about Bodenheim and the "Prologue" to *Kora in Hell* begins with an epigraph taken from Bodenheim's poem "Chorus Girl" (*I* 6). Bodenheim enjoyed his greatest fame in the 1920s and early 1930s when he published a number of scandalous, best-selling novels as well as six volumes of poems. At the same time he became notorious for his drunken antics. By the time he became a homeless alcoholic in the late 1940s – and was murdered in 1954 by a mentally ill man – Williams had lost touch with him.

Mina Loy's "Love Songs," featured in the first issue of *Others*, were a *succès de scandal* with their open sexuality ("Pig Cupid his rosy snout / Rooting erotic garbage") and modernist difficulty. Loy was English but had lived some time in Italy before coming to New York; she was said to have had an affair with the poet Filippo Tommaso Marinetti, founder of the Futurist movement. She was known for her great beauty, for her casually unconventional manner of living, and for her startlingly original poems. Williams consistently praised her poetry as well as her beauty. When they played husband and wife in Kreymborg's play *Lima Beans* with the Provincetown Players in New York in 1916, he got to kiss her during every performance – a memorable fact duly recorded in his *Autobiography* (139). Williams and his actual wife, Floss, would see a good deal of Loy in Paris during their six-month European stay in 1924.

"Marianne Moore was the only [American poet] Mina Loy feared," Williams claimed (*I* 10). Perhaps this is because the two women were opposites in many ways. Unlike Loy's cheerful unconcern for convention in art and life, Moore's poetry and personality were grounded in a firm moral sense. Williams recalled her saying, "My work has come to have just one quality of value in it: I will not touch or have to do with those things which I detest" (*I* 10). Yet she was universally revered among the *Others* crowd for her kindness and humor as much as for her idiosyncratic, inimitable poems. Williams published a poem about her in 1920 ("Marianne Moore," *CP1* 129–130). In essays, he commended her poetry's "cleanliness, lack of cement, clarity, gentleness," her "fastidious precision of thought," and her ability to strip language of all stale associations: "With Miss Moore a word is a word most when it is separated out by science, treated with acid to remove the smudges, washed, dried and placed right side up on a clean surface" (*SE* 123, 128). He praised her generosity of spirit, her delight in the abundant variety of experience, contrasting it pointedly with the pinched, disconsolate vision of T. S. Eliot's *The Waste Land* and "The Hollow Men": "Nothing is hollow or waste to the imagination of Marianne Moore" (*SE* 292). He summed up his admiration for Moore simply in 1948: "I don't think there is a better poet writing in America today" (*SE* 293). She admired him in return, always reviewing his work with sympathy and keen perception. She praised *Kora in Hell*, for instance, for its "[c]ompression, color, speed, accuracy, and that restraint of instinctive craftsmanship which precludes anything dowdy or labored" (Moore 56). He accepted her censure of his flippancies as he could not from H. D. – though he firmly rejected her criticism of the lesbian episode that begins *Paterson 4*.

Another New York-centered poet with whom Williams developed a lasting friendship during the *Others* years was Wallace Stevens. *Others* published such important early Stevens poems as "Peter Quince at the Clavier," "Thirteen Ways of Looking at a Blackbird," and "Le Monocle de Mon Oncle." By the time Stevens moved to Hartford for a new job in the insurance business, in May of 1916, he was considered one of the *Others* group and he was particularly close to Williams. The two had much in common, including the fact that both had full-time jobs outside of writing – Williams as a doctor, Stevens as lawyer and insurance executive. Both were necessarily committed to writing poetry in America (not Europe) and amidst the pressing demands of a professional career. After Stevens's move to Hartford, the two men continued to see each other occasionally, often at the "salon" of Walter Conrad Arensberg, a close friend of Stevens from Harvard. Up to 1921, when Arensberg moved to California, Stevens would take the train to New York several times a month to visit Arensberg's apartment, to see his growing collection of modern art, and to enjoy mingling with the avant-garde painters and poets, including Williams, who gathered there. After 1921, Stevens and Williams sometimes kept in touch by exchanging letters. More importantly, they maintained a kind of continuing dialogue by responding to each other's poems in print, a custom begun when Stevens used Williams's poem "El Hombre" (1916) as the epigraph for his own "Nuances of a Theme by Williams" (1918), criticizing Williams's poem by drawing out its colder, less romantic nuances. So Williams responded to Stevens's "Hibiscus on the Sleeping Shores" (1921) with "This Florida: 1924" (1932); and Stevens's "Stars at Tallapoosa" (1922) might have inspired Poem X of *Spring and All* (later titled "The Eyeglasses") (1923).

Williams aired some of his creative differences with Stevens in the "Prologue" to *Kora in Hell*. He thought Stevens was too self-disciplined and recommended that he "loosen the attention." More particularly, he decried Stevens's fondness for what he called "associational or sentimental value" – presumably referring to Stevens's invocations of distant or exotic places (Java, Lhasa, China) or things (girandoles, passion flowers, pagodas), or his use of foreign (especially French) words and phrases. To Williams, this lingering romanticism seemed merely escapist, a shirking of the modern poet's more difficult task which was to seek fresh contact with "those things which lie under the direct scrutiny of the senses, close to the nose" (*I* 14). Stevens, for his part, disagreed with Williams over the relative importance of form and content: "[Williams] is more interested in the way of saying things than in what he is saying" (Stevens 544). Hugh Kenner called this remark "one of the most extraordinary misunderstandings in literary history," but Williams himself would sometimes have agreed with Stevens's assessment (Kenner 55). In the Preface to his *Selected Essays* he wrote: "It is not what you say that matters but the manner in which you say it; there lies the secret of the ages" (*SE* n.p.). Williams was gratified that Stevens agreed to write the Introduction to his *Collected Poems 1921–1931* (1934) but irritated when Stevens described his aims as "anti-poetic." Although Stevens presented this observation as a carefully qualified compliment, Williams took it as a challenge to his central tenet that anything is potentially poetic. Perhaps their most dramatic poetic disagreement involved Stevens's "Description Without Place" (1945). The point of Stevens's poem, as he put it, is that "we live in the description of a place and not in the place itself" (Stevens 494). Williams took this, correctly, as a direct challenge to his career-long commitment to the primacy of place in poetic creation. His poem "A Place (Any Place) to Transcend All Places" (1945) is a spirited rejoinder to Stevens.

E. E. Cummings was another New York poet whom Williams knew and admired. Cummings was younger (b. 1894) than the other poets discussed here and did not move to New York until after World War I. But when he did, he made up for lost time. In January, 1920, his first set of poems appeared in *The Dial; The Enormous Room* (his memoir of his imprisonment in France as a suspected spy) was published in 1922; and *Tulips and Chimneys*, his first book of poems, came out in 1923. Williams recognized Cummings as a kindred spirit with his novel, idiosyncratic uses of language, and praised him generously, linking him with Pound as "the two most distinguished American poets" of the time (*WCW/JL* 56). He valued Cummings's staunch individualism as a bracing feature of the New York art scene. But he never developed a close friendship with the younger poet, finding him rather aloof and "solitary," not the gregarious type (*SE* 264–65). He included one of Cummings's poems in *Paterson V* as part of an excerpt from an interview with Mike Wallace in which Williams rejected it as poetry. Cummings returned the favor by charging Williams twenty-five dollars to reprint it (*P* 304).

One young contemporary with whom Williams did form a close, lasting friendship was Robert McAlmon. The two met in 1920 when McAlmon was twenty-four and Williams thirty-six. Despite the age difference they bonded immediately and were soon planning a new little magazine, *Contact*, partly to fill the gap left by the failure of *Others* in 1919. *Contact* was devoted – as the manifesto in its first issue announced – to "the essential contact between words and the locality that breeds them, in this case America" (quoted in Mariani 175). It was under-financed and cheaply produced, never had more than about two hundred subscribers, and did not last long: four issues appeared in 1920–1921, a fifth in 1923. (Williams revived it briefly in 1932 with Nathanael West as co-editor.) But its literary quality was remarkably high under the circumstances: its short run included work by Williams, McAlmon, Pound, H. D., Marianne Moore, Wallace Stevens, Mina Loy, and others. Ironically for a magazine devoted to "the local," many of these American writers were then living abroad, including (after 1921) McAlmon himself. And although Williams felt abandoned by McAlmon especially, he could take some consolation from the fact that McAlmon's Paris-based *Contact Editions* published his volume *Spring and All* in 1923. Despite his nativist theories, Williams found himself inevitably involved in transnational modernism.

In the years immediately following World War I, Williams was troubled to see his New York group rapidly dissipating. American writers and artists were flocking to Europe – to Paris in particular – to take advantage of the lower cost of living there and to be part of the upsurge of creative energy in the French capital. *The Little Review* moved its headquarters from New York to Paris in 1923. Even Alfred Kreymborg had gone to Rome to edit a new magazine called *Broom*. Pound and McAlmon were both urging Williams to come to Paris, if only for an extended visit. So, in 1924, Bill and Floss Williams embarked on a six-month trip to Europe where they would mingle with the international avant-garde. The writers and artists Williams met during this trip were important to him for the rest of his literary career. He and Floss traveled in France, Italy, Austria, and Switzerland – a journey that he fictionalized in his novel *A Voyage to Pagany* (1928) – but he was most influenced by the creative ferment of Paris. There he saw old friends and acquaintances such as H. D., Bryher, Mina Loy, Man Ray, Robert McAlmon, and Ezra Pound and made new ones including James Joyce,

Djuna Barnes, Ernest Hemingway, Sylvia Beach, Ford Madox Ford, Peggy Guggenheim, Nancy Cunard, and Constantin Brancusi.

Among the French writers Williams met in 1924 were the poets Louis Aragon and Philippe Soupault, both associated with Dada (now moribund) and the emerging surrealist movement. He became friendly with Soupault immediately and this direct, personal contact surely validated, for him, his close (but typically ambivalent) relation to both movements. Williams had known Marcel Duchamp and other key figures of New York Dada during his time with the Arensberg circle in the 1910s; and his own experiments in automatic writing, beginning with *Kora in Hell* in 1917, aligned him with the dadaists, as he was well aware: "I didn't originate Dadaism but I had it in my soul to write it. *Spring and All* shows that" (*IWWP* 48). This temperamental affinity also drew him to Surrealism. He translated Soupault's surrealist novel *Last Nights of Paris* in 1929. And he became involved with Surrealism in its American phase during World War II when the leading figures of the movement – including André Breton, the "pope of Surrealism" – were living in exile in New York.

Among the English-language writers he met in Paris, probably the most important for Williams personally was Ford Madox Ford. Ford was then editing the short-lived but now legendary *transatlantic review* which was publishing parts of Joyce's *Finnegans Wake* (then known as "Work in Progress") as well as work by Hemingway, Gertrude Stein, Jean Rhys, and other important modernists. Williams's poem "Last Words of my Grandmother" and one chapter of his book-in-progress, *In the American Grain*, appeared in *the transatlantic review*. Ford, ten years older than Williams, liked to champion the work of younger "experimental" writers. Williams was grateful for Ford's interest and they exchanged a few letters in the following years, but the two did not become close until the late 1930s when Ford was living in New York. During that time Ford visited Williams in Rutherford and made the extraordinary gesture of founding "Les Amis de William Carlos Williams," a group that met occasionally to have dinner and to read from Williams's work. After Ford's death in 1939, Williams wrote the elegy, "To Ford Madox Ford in Heaven." His 1950 review of Ford's tetralogy, *Parade's End*, calls it "the English prose masterpiece of [its] time" (*SE* 316).

Williams met James Joyce at the same party (given by Robert McAlmon) where he first met Ford. He and Floss spent two evenings during their stay in Paris in the company of Joyce and his wife Nora. Joyce's *Ulysses*, serialized in *The Little Review*, had become a *cause célèbre* in 1920 when the issue containing the "Nausicaa" episode was confiscated as obscene by the US Post Office. In the subsequent trial *Ulysses* was banned in the United States and

Joyce became a modernist hero. Copies of *Ulysses*, smuggled into the country, were prized possessions, symbolizing the struggle for freedom of expression against the oppressive forces of bourgeois conformity, the literary equivalent of Prohibition. (Williams himself owned a smuggled copy of *Ulysses* [*Descriptive List* 38].) Williams defended Joyce's "obscenity" as simple truthfulness, comparing him to Rabelais, the Catholic priest who treated the coarser aspects of life with broad and indulgent humor: "We should praise his humanity and not object feebly to his fullness, liars that we are . . .. To please God it is that he must look through the clothes" (*SE* 77–78).

Williams saw Joyce, the Irish Catholic outsider, as a natural ally, alienated from English literature and criticism as Williams felt himself – and all authentic American literature – to be. Joyce's intense focus on Ireland paralleled Williams's efforts to find the universal in his local American environment. At the time the two writers met, Joyce was publishing parts of *Finnegans Wake*. Williams praised its difficult, original use of language as a significant advance over *Ulysses*, an attempt to "break [words] up to let the staleness out of them" (*SE* 76) – a formulation that could apply to his own poetry.

Another Parisian writer famous for her experiments with language was Gertrude Stein whom Williams met on his brief final visit to Europe in 1927. Although she lived abroad, Williams thought of Stein as typically American because her outlook was "democratic, local (in the sense of being attached with integrity to actual experience)" (*SE* 118). He admired her originality and her controlled use of words *as* words: "Stein has gone systematically to work smashing every connotation that words have ever had, in order to get them back clean" (*SE* 163). To describe her method in these terms aligns her with Pound, an ironic juxtaposition because, as Williams says, "The two detest each other" (*SE* 162). He refers to Stein's "rout of the vocables" in *Paterson V* (219) and "Tribute to the Painters."

The last of Williams's important and lasting literary friendships from the first twenty years of his career was with Louis Zukofsky whom he met in 1928. (His important friendships with Kenneth Burke and James Laughlin would come later.) Zukofsky had an introduction from Pound, and Williams immediately welcomed him as a kindred spirit of a new generation. They remained friends until Williams's death in 1963. Mark Scroggins has aptly characterized their influence on each other: "From Williams, Zukofsky learned the virtues of keen observation of the everyday; from Zukofsky, Williams learned to shape his often amorphous verse into more sharply chiselled measures." This Poundian emphasis on "sharply chiseled measures" was a constant theme in their correspondence and one that defined, for Williams, the leading aim of the "Objectivists" – a diverse group named by Zukofsky in his "Objectivists" number of *Poetry* (February 1931) and *An "Objectivists" Anthology* (1932). The most important members of the group are generally taken to be (in addition to Williams and Zukofsky) Charles Reznikoff, Carl Rakosi, George Oppen, Lorine Niedecker, and Basil Bunting. In Williams's words, "[Objectivism] recognizes the poem, apart from its meaning, to be an object to be dealt with as such," emphasizing "how it has been constructed" (Preminger 582).

Although Zukofsky was twenty years younger than Williams, theirs was not the master–disciple relationship one might expect. In some ways their interaction mirrored the early exchanges of Williams and Pound – before Pound's fascist sympathies and anti-Semitic rants had alienated the doctor from Rutherford – with its open, no-holds-barred criticism on each side. Williams wrote to Zukofsky in 1943, "I'm pulling no punches. Same to you. Perhaps by kicking the bloody shit out of each other, if we're able, we may get a hell of a lot further than we ever have in the past" (*WCW/LZ* 332). Williams came to depend on Zukofsky's criticism, regularly sending him manuscripts of both poetry and prose to edit. The most dramatic and best documented example is Williams's 1944 volume, *The Wedge*. Zukofsky suggested major changes to Williams's original manuscript and Williams adopted nearly all of them, eliminating at least a third of the book (all of the prose and a good many poems), revising and rearranging much of the rest. He dedicated *The Wedge* to "L.Z." Zukofsky was advising Williams as late as 1961 about the poems of *Pictures from Brueghel* (1962) (see *CP2* 506n.).

Williams's long friendship with Zukofsky sustained and challenged him throughout his later career. It might be said to typify his relations with his literary peers. He needed close companionship with fellow writers, and he liked to think of writing as a collaborative enterprise. As he once put it to Zukofsky, "I never care who writes anything so long as it gets written" (*WCW/LZ* 251). Williams's active involvement with his contemporaries was grounded in this intense, almost impersonal, commitment to poetry as a communal ideal.

Works cited

The Complete Prose of Marianne Moore. Ed. Patricia C. Willis. New York: Viking Penguin, 1986

"Descriptive List of Works from the Library of William Carlos Williams at Fairleigh Dickinson University." *William Carlos Williams Review* 10.2 (Fall 1984): 30–53.

Ezra Pound and William Carlos Williams: The University of Pennsylvania Conference Papers. Ed. Daniel Hoffman. Philadelphia, PA: University of Pennsylvania Press, 1983.

Kenner, Hugh. *A Homemade World*. New York: Knopf, 1975.

Pound, Ezra. *Selected Letters of Ezra Pound, 1907–1941*. Ed. D.D. Paige. New York: New Directions, 1950.

Preminger, Alex, Frank J. Warnke, and O. B. Hardison, Jr., eds. *Princeton Encyclopedia of Poetry and Poetics*. Princeton, NJ: Princeton University Press, 1965.

Scroggins, Mark. "A Biographical Essay on Zukofsky," *Modern American Poetry*, http://www.english.illinois.edu/maps/poets/s_z/zukofsky/bio.htm. Web.

Stevens, Wallace. *Letters of Wallace Stevens*. Ed. Holly Stevens. New York: Knopf, 1966.

Whitaker, Thomas R. *William Carlos Williams*. Rev. ed. Boston, MA: Twayne, 1989.

4

PETER HALTER

Williams and the visual arts

A decisive phase in William Carlos Williams's formative years began in 1913 when the budding poet discovered, and got involved in, the New York avant-garde. Forty years later, Williams in his *Autobiography* closely connects this crucial period with the famous "Armory Show," the huge exhibition that for the first time introduced the American public to such movements as Post-Impressionism, Fauvism, Cubism, and Futurism, side by side with a comprehensive show of progressive American art:

> There was at that time a great surge of interest in the arts generally before the First World War. New York was seething with it. Painting took the lead. It came to a head for us in the famous "Armory Show" of 1913. I went to it and gaped along with the rest at a "picture" in which an electric bulb kept going on and off; at Duchamp's sculpture (by "Mott and Co."), a magnificent cast-iron urinal, glistening of its white enamel. The story then current of this extraordinary and popular young man was that he walked daily into whatever store struck his fancy and purchased whatever pleased him – something new – something American. Whatever it might be, that was his "construction" for the day. The silly committee threw out the urinal, asses that they were. The "Nude Descending the Staircase" is too hackneyed for me to remember anything clearly about it now. But I do remember how I laughed out loud when first I saw it, happily, with relief. (*A* 134)

Although this passage is muddled in terms of historical accuracy – Williams conflates the Armory Show of 1913 with the 1917 Exhibition of the Independents[1] – it reveals much about Williams's frame of mind at the time that he came into contact with the New York avant-garde art and what it was that he found so tremendously stimulating. More than anything else it seems to have been a dadaist spirit of irreverence and revolt, which radically challenged and debunked the high-minded seriousness then dominating the world of art and culture. What was crucial for Williams was the sense of a tremendous liberation that resulted from a radical break with the past and all of its accepted criteria. "Here was my chance, that was all I knew. There had been a break somewhere, we were streaming through, each thinking his own thoughts, driving his own designs toward his self's objectives" (*A* 138).

Williams's favorable response to modernist painting and the avant-garde can also be related to his personal background. As a young art student, his Puerto Rican mother had studied at an art school in Paris but had lost all hopes of a career when she had to give up her studies for lack of money. "Her interest in art became my interest in art," Williams later said (*IWWP* 16), and more than once he also mentioned that for several years he "was still undecided whether or not [he] should become a painter" (*A* 52). The other family member who was important in this respect was his brother Edgar, who shared Williams's love for the arts (and continued painting watercolors for all his life). In addition, there were Williams's lifelong friendships with Ezra Pound and the painter Charles Demuth. At the time of the Armory Show, Pound was in London and Demuth in Paris, and both were in close contact with the local art scene and informed Williams about what was going on in the avant-garde. In Paris, Demuth had become a good friend of Gertrude Stein, and he had met Duchamp, Picasso, Braque, Matisse, and the other Fauves. After his return from Paris in late 1913, Demuth's first-hand knowledge of the Parisian and European art scene would prove invaluable for Williams. Demuth took him along to the Arensbergs and introduced him not only to the New York avant-garde but also, in due time, to Marsden Hartley and Charles Sheeler, both of whom then also became Williams's lifelong artist friends.

In 1915, Williams got in touch with Alfred Kreymborg at the instigation of Pound, and he immediately became an important member of the group of artists and writers that had set up their summer place in Grantwood near Richfield on the New Jersey Palisades. In the summer of 1913, the young painters Man Ray and Samuel Halpert had found what Williams described as "several wooden shacks there in the woods": "Several writers were involved, but the focus of my own enthusiasm was the house occupied by Alfred and Gertrude Kreymborg to which, on every possible occasion, I went madly in my flivver to help with the magazine [*Others*] which had saved my life as a writer" (*A* 135).

Others was as short-lived as most avant-garde magazines of the period – its final issue was edited by Williams in 1919. But the group of writers and artists around Kreymborg did not just dissolve; they now met in New York, often at Walter and Louise Arensberg's, who had accommodated Duchamp and where one would frequently find, among others, Picabia, Gleizes, Edgard Varèse, Charles Demuth, Mina Loy, and Wallace Stevens.

It was difficult for Williams to understand, and assess, the new movements and the various theories behind them, but it was still possible to be boosted by the basic attitude of defiance and liberation that informed so much work of the avant-garde. In addition, it was important that avant-garde art, as Williams and his artist friends saw it, did not just break with "stereotyped forms" and conventions but turned to many aspects of the contemporary world – such as the modern industrial and urban environment – that traditional art had completely bypassed or even purposely ignored. Williams therefore sought to be part of a similar revolution in poetry that not only left behind "the deadness of copied forms" (SE 218) but also promised to open up entirely new spheres by a dramatic widening of subject matter. When he began writing, the world as he knew it rarely appeared in the art and poetry he had grown up with – for instance, neither the world of the poor Italian and Eastern European working-class immigrants that stretched to the east of his home-town Rutherford nor the masses of destitute people that Williams had encountered during his internships in New York hospitals played a role in contemporary writing. All of this was "unsuitable" subject matter, rejected as banal, trite, vulgar, or meaningless.

In those decisive years in the mid-1910s, Williams came to the conclusion that turning to those neglected aspects of the contemporary world as part of a "local assertion" (A 138) necessitated not only to find new adequate poetic forms but also to reject traditional notions of beauty. As he saw it, most of these notions relied on an obsolete dualistic scheme of values in which the refined was set against the gross, the beautiful against the ugly, the extraordinary against the banal and the meaningful against the meaningless.

For Williams, one possible strategy of countering these traditional views consisted in taking traditional literary forms, such as the pastoral, and giving it new meaning by turning it upside down:

Pastoral

When I was younger
it was plain to me
I must make something of myself.
Older now
I walk back streets
admiring the houses
of the very poor:
roof out of line with sides
the yards cluttered
with old chicken wire, ashes,
furniture gone wrong;

the fences and outhouses
built of barrel-staves
and parts of boxes, all,
if I am fortunate,
smeared a bluish green
that properly weathered
pleases me best
of all colors.

                No one
will believe this
of vast import to the nation.   (CP1 64–65)

By replacing the rural and bucolic world of the traditional pastoral with that of the urban poor, Williams writes veritable counter-pastorals; at the same time he retains some of the standard elements of the classical form. Thus Peter Schmidt points out that Williams opens "Pastoral" with a condensed version of the classical debate between the values of city and country, with the poet abandoning the prospects of a career in favor of a more contemplative life in the country.[2] As in many traditional pastorals, the poet finds sustenance and beauty in a world that most of the "leading citizens" (CP1 70) despise or ignore. In Williams's urban pastoral, however, the world of high culture is replaced by low culture, or even by junk. The bulk of the poem is dedicated to a loving enumeration of this junk, which, for the speaker, has its own beauty and its own magic.

Williams's assessment of these values gains wider meaning when seen as part of the rejection of the genteel poetic tradition by the poets (and artists) of the *Others* group. Van Wyck Brooks was one of the earliest critics who saw the "new poetry" of the New York avant-garde in this larger context. He noted that these young poets consciously fought against the common notion that only "Highbrow" culture was valuable and that "the only hope for American society lay in somehow lifting the 'Lowbrow' elements in it to the level of the 'Highbrow.'"[3]

While the poets around Kreymborg were still fighting for a marginal recognition – "we were destroyers, vulgarians, obscurantists to most who read," Williams recalled in his *Autobiography* (148) – they were grateful for the support they gained through the enthusiasm of the French dadaists for America's technological culture. Of special importance were some notorious statements of Marcel Duchamp, who had been a celebrity from the very first moments he arrived in New York in 1915. In several interviews he championed all things new – and thus all things American – because, for him, America *was* the new. He declared that "we must learn to forget the past, to live our own lives in our own time." He also praised New York as "a complete work of art"; the city, as he said, was the perfect embodiment of the "scientific spirit" of the twentieth century and of American vitality as opposed to European decadence.[4]

Duchamp's most radical gestures in this context were his so-called "ready-mades," industrial objects such as his bicycle wheel, bottle rack, snow shovel, or urinal. All of these ready-mades, as he declared, were works of art once he had moved them from their original context to the artist's studio or gallery and given them a title and a signature. Duchamp denied that these objects had any aesthetic merit in themselves, but many of those who, like Williams, were highly stimulated by the ready-mades immediately discovered their aesthetic potential. Williams's description of Duchamp's *Fountain* in his autobiography as "a magnificent cast-iron urinal, glistening of its white enamel" (134) is revealing in this respect.

Williams's own procedures in "Pastoral" and many other poems are closely related to those of Duchamp, irrespective of the important differences in intention and attitude. Duchamp emphasized – and radically redefined – the artist's role, suggesting that art works are the result of choice rather than craft or artistic genius. Williams, in turn, emphasizes the appeal, aesthetic or other, of the found object. Thus "Pastoral" contains a veritable list of *objets trouvés* whose utter insignificance (or ugliness) from a conventional point of view clashes with the high value placed upon them by the speaker.

"Pastoral" is the first of many poems – among them "The Red Wheelbarrow," "The Great Figure," "The Right of Way," "Perfection," or "Between Walls" – in which the random constellation of *objets trouvés* is of "supreme importance" (*CP1* 206). And although Williams, unlike Duchamp, never downplays artistic method or poetic craft, he makes it clear that there is a decisive element of chance in all of these poems. Thus the speaker in "Pastoral" has to be "fortunate" on his walks to find the "fences and outhouses" or "furniture gone wrong" "smeared a bluish green / that properly weathered / pleases me best / of all colors." ("Fortunate" of course also wryly suggests that the poet has to go out of his way and walk the back streets of the "unfortunates" to discover the riches of their backyards.)

*

Among the artists and critics forming the New York avant-garde of the 1910s and 1920s, Williams, Demuth and Marsden Hartley were perhaps those most keenly interested in, and stimulated by, the close collaboration between literature and the visual arts. Moreover, all three of them, in their own ways, tried to contribute to an indigenous American art. At the same time they were critical of all those who blindly embraced all things American and technological, particularly if enthusiasm for American art entailed belittling or ignoring what was happening in Europe.

Thus both Demuth and Williams, like Hartley, felt that one could learn much from the Europeans when it came to developing an art form that would no longer try to "copy" reality but transform it in works that were always recognizable as art – poems that were made, construed, by words on the page, as paintings were made by means of paint on paper or canvas. At the same time the two friends were agreed on the need to dramatically expand the range of "suitable" subject matter. Thus next to his delicate flower studies Demuth also produced a great number of watercolors on such topics as vaudeville and the night life of the *bohème* in the big cities, and most of his works in oil and tempera done in the 1920s and early 1930s were on urban and industrial subjects – factories, grain elevators, frame houses, or roof tops with water tanks and lightning rods.

In the 1920s, Demuth also painted a series of "poster portraits," as he called them, conceived as homages to his artist friends. The most famous of these is the painting *I Saw the Figure 5 in Gold*. It is based on Williams's poem "The Great Figure," which Williams, as he later recalled in his autobiography, wrote on his way to Marsden Hartley's studio, where he would sometimes drop in "for a talk, a little drink maybe and to see what he was doing":

> As I approached his number I heard a great clatter of bells and the roar of a fire engine passing the end of the street down Ninth Avenue. I turned just in time to see a golden figure 5 on a red background flash by. The impression was so sudden and forceful that I took a piece of paper out of my pocket and wrote a short poem about it. (*A* 172)

The Great Figure

Among the rain
and lights
I saw the figure 5
in gold
on a red
firetruck
moving
tense
unheeded
to gong clangs
siren howls

and wheels rumbling
through the dark city.   (CP1 174)

Williams's poem evokes the enthusiasm of the Futurists for the dynamic chaos of the modern metropolis. Like "Overture to a Dance of Locomotives" or "Rapid Transit" it evokes the teeming life force sought and celebrated by the Futurists in the big cities. But in spite of its obvious affinities to the Futurists and their praise for all things technological and urban Williams's poem is more complex in attitude. Whereas the Futurists saw modern urban space as the epitome of collectivity and mass identity, Williams still retains the individual in a central role. In the poem, it is the isolated "I" with his particular sense of beauty who recalls a thrilling moment "unheeded" by all the others around him. As the golden figure 5 rushes by on the firetruck, it produces an intense moment of revelation. The golden figure is transformed from a mere number into one of the new heraldic signs that are part of the new and different beauty of the modern world.

The moment, however, is not only one of elation but also anxiety. That the firetruck with its golden 5 rushes by "tense" and "unheeded" suggests that the poem, for Williams, is also about the isolation of the artist who feels marginalized or even completely ignored in "an America inimical to its vital, creative talents."[5] In this context, it also makes sense that it is this particular poem that Charles Demuth chose for his tribute. *I Saw the Figure 5 in Gold* pays homage to Williams for taking up a subject – the modern city – that the American modernists regarded as quintessentially American.

In his painting, Demuth emphasizes the sudden dramatic appearance of the golden figure 5 out of night and darkness by painting it three times. While the largest 5 seems to float right in front the viewer's eyes, the second and third recede into the background and draw the eye to the center with the stylized red firetruck. The three 5's thus create both a dramatic sense of motion and a strong sense of spatial depth. Moreover, in order to enhance the striking effect of the golden 5, Demuth laid out the second of the three numbers in gold leaf and thus turned it literally into a figure 5 in gold. By means of this collage item he introduced an additional tension, since the sense of depth and motion is partly blocked by the middle 5, which draws the eye to the picture plane on which the gold leaf is glued, and thus to the painting as a *tableau-objet*, to use the cubist term.

Demuth may also have responded to the anxiety of the isolated avant-garde artist that underlies Williams's poem. He not only pays homage to his friend by the illuminated signs "Bill" and "Carlo[s]" in the night sky but also by the words "ART Co" on the firetruck, as well as by co-signing the painting both with his own initials and those of his friend. With "art Co.," Demuth may well have suggested to his friend that they were not alone but united in a common cause – that they were all part of what Demuth and his friends saw as the American Scene. "The Great Figure" is not only quintessentially modernist in subject matter – "What, for instance, could be more lost, more uncorrelated, a closer Contact, a greater triumph of anti-Culture, than this poem?" wrote Kenneth Burke in 1922[6] – it also shows that by the early 1920s Williams had definitely come into his own as a modernist poet. The typical Williams poem written after 1916/1917 combines the imagist technique of utmost concentration on one or a few images with short, terse run-on lines that direct the reader's attention to each successive detail. Moreover, of crucial importance in all of these poems is enjambment. Williams had learned from the visual arts that he could "design" a poem, and that enjambment was an important part of this concept. The tension between lineation and syntax could be exploited in a great number of ways: As of old, line units could coincide with sense units, but phrases or clauses could also be splayed, even to the point where lines comprised no more than a single word. Moreover, Williams realized that to visually organize a poem also involved rhythm and, along with it, the entire aural dimension of poetry. Line ends could go along with natural pauses or deliberately go against them, and they could function as moments of rest or moments of disorientation, to name only a few of a wide range of possible effects.

*

In the years after 1916, Williams not only came to realize that for his poetics the visual dimension – "the poetic line, the way the image was to lie on the page" (*A* 138) – was of utmost importance; he also discovered that to arrange them in little stanzas of two, three, or four lines greatly improved them in terms of stability and order. One of the rare instances in which he reflects on this aspect of his poetry occurs in *I Wanted to Write a Poem*, where the seventy-three-year-old Williams says in conversation with Edith Heal:

> Free verse wasn't verse at all to me. All art is orderly . . .. As I went through the poems I noticed many brief poems, always arranged in couplet or quatrain form. I noticed also that I was peculiarly fascinated by another pattern: the dividing of the little paragraphs in lines of three. I remembered writing several poems as quatrains at first, then in the normal process of concentrating the poem ... the quatrain changed into a three line stanza, or a five line stanza became a quatrain, as in:

The Nightingales

Original version	Revised version
My shoes as I lean	My shoes as I lean
unlacing them	unlacing them
stand out upon	stand out upon
flat worsted flowers	flat worsted flowers.
under my feet.	
Nimbly the shadows	Nimbly the shadows
of my fingers play	of my fingers play
unlacing	unlacing
over shoes and flowers.	over shoes and flowers.

See how much better it conforms to the page, how much better it looks? (*IWWP* 65-66).

That Williams would insist on the decisive difference between non-stanzaic poems in "free verse" – which, as he says, "wasn't verse at all to me" – and "orderly" stanzaic poems shows how important the discovery of the stanzaic or patterned poem was for him. Williams must have realized not only "how much better it look[ed]" but also that this type of poem allowed him to introduce the stanza as a second major unit beyond the line, which interacted in multiple ways with the other units in terms of contrast and progression. Thus in "The Nightingales" the elimination of one line is clearly an improvement, and this beyond the fact that the poem indeed looks much better on the page. What is decisive is that it now consists of two stanzas that can be directly juxtaposed. Both stanzas present a few objects in front of the speaker, arranged from top to bottom, and these objects are introduced in the order in which the eye of the speaker takes them in. In this respect, the relationship between the two stanzas is crucial because the second stanza repeats the first with a slight but important difference, and it is in this difference that the poem comes alive, that it works.

In both stanzas the objects are presented in terms of layers or levels. In the first stanza, the speaker focuses on two levels: the shoes and the carpet beneath them with its "flat worsted flowers." In the second stanza, the perspective is essentially the same, but now the view is somewhat enlarged since the stanza does not start with the shoes but with what appears *above* the shoes, namely the poet's fingers, or, more precisely, "the shadows / of [his] fingers play[ing] . . . over shoes and flowers" (*CP1* 169).

This small shift brings about an imaginative transformation of the entire scene. It is only now that the title makes sense, as we realize that the shadows of the fingers are the shadows of the nightingales shooting back and forth across shoes and flowers. By this shift the mundane little indoor scene is transformed into an imaginative scene that, by way of the title, evokes Keats's famous "Ode to a Nightingale." Williams boldly sets up his own (American) poetry – dedicated for the most part to completely "unpoetic" subject matter – as a counterpart to the great European heritage. Thus the flowers in Williams's poem are not part of a pastoral setting but are part of the floral design of a machine-made carpet or rug; and the nightingale, finally – which is not only the romantic bird *par excellence* but a species that does not exist in America – only makes it into the poem by way of the poet's imaginative "reading" of the shadows of the fingers playing over shoes and flowers, a reading that is as original as it is rooted in precise observation.

*

In the prose parts of *Spring and All*, which contain Williams's most extended discussion of his modernist poetics, there are several passages on his favorite cubist painter, Juan Gris, whose aesthetics Williams obviously sees as a counterpart to his own. Gris, writes Williams, paints "things with which he is familiar, simple things – at the same time to detach them from ordinary experience to the imagination":

> Here is a shutter, a bunch of grapes, a sheet of music, a picture of sea and mountains (particularly fine) which the onlooker is not for a moment permitted to witness as an "illusion." One thing laps over on the other, the cloud laps over on the shutter, the bunch of grapes is part of the handle of the guitar, the mountain and sea are obviously not "the mountain and sea," but a picture of the mountain and the sea. All drawn with admirable simplicity and excellent design – all a unity. (*CP*1 197–98)

Compare this comment on Gris to poem XXII of *Spring and All*, later titled "The Red Wheelbarrow":

> so much depends
> upon
>
> a red wheel
> barrow
>
> glazed with rain
> water
>
> beside the white
> chickens (*CP*1 224)

Like Gris, Williams takes up things with which he is familiar, simple things, to detach them from "ordinary experience." Here, too, we have a few things that the reader is not even for a moment permitted to "witness as an illusion." Words here evoke objects with utmost clarity, but the words do not become invisible behind these objects but remain present as material units, each one next to, or set against, the other: "Red" against "wheel," "wheel" against "barrow," "rain" against "water," "white" against "chickens." In such a poem, one is also aware of words *qua* words because in some cases they first denote one thing and then, when we move on to the next line, something else. Thus "a red wheel" becomes "a red wheel / barrow," and "rain" becomes "rain / water." "White," in turn, which is a free-floating color word when we first come across it, suddenly transforms into the white of "white / chickens." Words are objects here, elements in a linguistic system in which they assume varying functions and maintain a separate reality all by themselves.

Williams also makes the reader aware that words are objects or things in an even more literal respect: they are black letters on a white page, words that can be moved around on the page so as to form a pattern and become part of a design. Late in his life, looking back, Williams said in an interview with Walter Sutton:

> as I've grown older, I've attempted to fuse the poetry and painting to make it the same thing ... [T]o give a design. A design in the poem and a design in the picture should make them more or less the same thing.   (*SSA* 53)

Thus in "The Red Wheelbarrow" Williams, by means of typographical arrangement, turns a single sentence of sixteen words into a poem with four identical stanzas. Each of these stanzas has four words, three on the first and one on the second line. In addition, the single words that make up the second lines are all disyllabic ("upon," "barrow," "water," "chickens"), whereas the words that come at the end of the first lines are all, with the exception of the introductory first stanza, monosyllabic with a long vowel or diphthong ("wheel," "rain," "white").

Apart from this intricate visual and aural design there is of course what we could call the "architectural" design of the poem on the macro level of the four stanzas: After an opening "meta-poetic" stanza the few details of the scene focused on are taken up in the order in which, one by one, the eye takes them in. In cinematographic terms, the focus is first on the red wheelbarrow by means of a semi-long shot, then zooms in, as it were, to a close-up of surface and texture (which includes the tactile or haptic sense) before it finally moves to the white chickens and thus enlarges the view again.

*

"Designing" a poem was not limited to strict stanzaic forms of the kind used in "The Red Wheelbarrow." If enjambment could be exploited in multiple ways, so could the visual effects of the various arrangements of words, lines, and stanzas. Thus, over the years, Williams developed countless ways of exploiting the visual dimension of poetry. Several of the formal discoveries associated with this technique – such as the stanzaic form – are not widely used before the 1920s, but the poem "Canthara" (*CP1* 78) shows that Williams successfully employed visual effects as early as 1917:

> The old black-man showed me
> how he had been shocked
> in his youth
> by six women, dancing
> a set-dance, stark naked below
> the skirts raised round
> their breasts:
>> bellies flung forward
> knees flying!
>>> – while
> his gestures, against the
> tiled wall of the dingy bath-room,
> swished with ecstasy to
> the familiar music of
>> his old emotion.

Visually, there are three lines that deviate from the norm of left-hand alignment. The first of these, line 8, marks the climax of the dancing, and it not only stands out by being indented but also by the fact that it is used iconically, in the sense that the line not only *says* "bellies flung forward" but also *visually represents* the forward movement in the way in which the line appears almost literally flung to the right.

Part of the overall design of this poem resides in the way in which it is rhythmically structured by enjambment. The first seven lines are all violently enjambed, which emphasizes the old man's urge to tell – and show – what he had once witnessed in his youth. This contrasts with lines 7–9, in which we come to the climactic moment of the dance. These three lines are all end-stopped, and thus lack the dynamism of all the preceding lines. What is at first surprising makes perfect sense on second thought: now that the dance reaches its climax we are invited to enjoy the iconic rendering of movement – to enjoy the moment when the lines themselves begin to dance.

In "Canthara," Williams also uses the visual dimension to structure the poem as a whole. Strictly speaking, the poem consists of one stanza only, but by means of the isolated word "while" Williams visually and thematically sets off the last six lines against the preceding nine lines. All by itself and preceded by a dash, "while" marks a clear pause and signals that what follows differs and is yet connected to what came before, temporally as well as psychologically. Both the first and the second part of the poem describe the old man as he, highly excited, tells about, and simultaneously enacts or performs, the dance of the six women. But whereas the first part is centered on the old man's dancing, the second part focuses on "his old emotion." The fact that these three words that conclude the poem are also moved to the right can be read iconically, too: the last line not only refers to the "old" emotion brought back from a remote past but is literally set apart – and thus at a remove – from the preceding lines.

Thus Williams also visually emphasizes the difference between the story as it is told and the story as it is reenacted in the dance: the moral outrage that the old man shows at the beginning is not much more than social veneer. In the dancing – the language of the body – the professed feeling of shock quickly gives way to a deeper and much more genuine emotion of sheer delight, revealed in gestures that "swished with ecstasy to / the familiar music of / his old emotion."

*

Poems like "The Red Wheelbarrow" clearly show Williams's indebtedness to theories of art as construction that played an important role in post-impressionist and early modernist art. Williams, like his friends Charles Sheeler – and Charles Demuth, to whom he dedicated *Spring and All* – frequently referred to architecture and to bricklaying when he stressed the importance of design in both poetry and the visual arts, and Juan Gris defined painting as *une sorte d'architecture plate et colorée*. Williams's own constructivist art theory found its most famous expression in his definition of the poem as "a small (or large) machine made of words" (*CP2* 54).

Constructivist theories played an important part within the paradigmatic change in early modernism from realism and its goal of an ever-refined rendering of the surface of things to an art that was concerned with the *essence* of inner and outer realities. Concurrent with this change was the belief that art works should not hide their traces but, on the contrary, foreground their own specific character as artifacts, made things.

Of equal importance for modernist art were theories of expression. They, too, had been gaining wider currency since the late nineteenth century and had become popular with Kandinsky's *Concerning the Spiritual in Art* (1912), excerpts of which Williams must have read shortly after its publication.[7] All viable art, Williams came to believe in those years in the wake of Kandinsky, is concerned with exploring the visual dynamics inherent in the disparate forms that we are surrounded by. Good art makes us aware that, as the psychologist and art theorist Rudolf Arnheim put it, "all form is primarily visual action."[8] Williams explicitly thematized this conviction (and how it affects what we see) in a number of poems, such as

"To a Solitary Disciple," "Spring Strains," "Portrait of the Author," and "Raindrops on a Briar," but it also underlies many others. One of them is "The Locust Tree in Flower" (second, "redesigned" version, *CP*1 379–80):

The Locust Tree in Flower

Among
of
green

stiff
old
bright

broken
branch
come

white
sweet
May

again

The intricate design of the poem draws the reader's attention to the fact that it is "crafted" – made, or constructed – in more than one sense. Like so many other Williams poems, it is iconic in the sense that it imitates, in the shape of poem and title together, the locust tree (which, particularly on sandy soil, often grows bare on the lower branches and only retains a green "roof" at the top of a long, slender stem).

The poem, moreover, is not only iconic on the visual level; it also imitates the sequential act of perception in its arrangement of words: It imitates, in other words, how the speaker's eye, while looking at the flowering tree, goes from detail to detail, back and forth between dead wood, green leaves, and clusters of white flowers, before it shifts, in the concluding part, to a higher level of abstraction in its invocation of spring: "come // white / sweet / May // again."

Beyond its iconic dimension, the poem immediately draws attention to its construction by the way it starts with two prepositions that are mutually exclusive within the poem's single sentence. The first of these prepositions ("Among") connects things spatially, whereas the second preposition ("of") relates them on the level of derivation, origin or source. The first of these prepositions therefore points to the co-presence of old growth and flowering tree, whereas the second preposition connects these details on the level of time or causality and thus brings in the cyclic nature of organic life, as well as the fact that everything exists in both space and time. In this context, it is far from accidental that the poem comprises a total of thirteen lines, with the first twelve of them grouped in four stanzaic units of three lines each. The poem thus alludes to the four seasons, and it is appropriate that the last – and separate – line of the concluding invocation of spring consists of the word "again."

At first sight, "The Locust Tree in Flower" seems to consist of a random accretion of words that don't make sense because they are robbed of the meaning that they get from their specific place within a conventional syntactic frame. In fact, the string of words in the poem functions not unlike the pieces of a puzzle that the reader has to sort out. In this it represents a type of poem that recurs throughout Williams's career, one that assigns to the reader the role of a co-creator who has to find out how the details "mounted" in the text could cohere. Many of the poems in *Spring and All*, for instance, fall into this category, but by means of such devices as line breaks and (absent) punctuation, Williams opens up many other poems to multiple interpretations and directs the reader's attention to not only what words mean but also *how* they mean.

Last but not least, Williams makes use of many of these devices in *Paterson*, where he lifts them to yet another level. *Paterson* could be called a large-scale collage, in which Williams's poetry is interspersed with various kinds of prose writing, ranging from historical documents to contemporary material, including letters sent to him by fellow poets. Both in terms of style and authorship, therefore, *Paterson* is heterogeneous rather than homogeneous, composed of parts that are multiple and assembled rather than unified and fully integrated. Once again the notion of the found (with its different concept of artistic creation), which, decades ago, Williams had first come across in Duchamp's ready-mades, proves to be central for the "design" of his epic poem.

In *Paterson*, however, this concept of art as construction or large-scale montage stands in a partly unresolved relationship to a more traditional notion of organic unity in which all individual parts receive their meaning only within the totality of the unified whole. It is this traditional concept that Williams had in mind when he originally conceived of *Paterson* as a poem in four parts. After finishing Book IV, however, Williams decided to write yet another part, Book V, which allowed him to move beyond the original concept and thus to open up his poem once again. In Book V, reflections on the importance of art play a central role. In the passages devoted to painting, however, the emphasis is now on the old masters, ranging from the anonymous artists of the Cloisters's unicorn tapestries to Dürer, Leonardo, Bosch, Botticelli, and, above all, Pieter Brueghel the Elder. Thus Section III opens with a poem devoted to Brueghel's *Nativity*, anticipating the cycle of ten poems that Williams published in 1962 in *Pictures from Brueghel*.

In all of these poems, Brueghel is celebrated as yet another master who "saw it all" (*CP2* 394) and therefore never separated the high from the low, the spiritual from the mundane. Moreover, Brueghel, like the other "old masters" evoked in *Paterson V*, is not contrasted with the great modernists but seen as part of a line that "perhaps" goes as far back as "the abstraction / of Arabic art" (*P* 220). Like them, Brueghel saw that "the / imagination must be served" (*P* 225) in paintings that take us beyond an art of mere mimesis.

It is not surprising, therefore, that one of Williams's most succinct statements on his own poetry as an art of construction reflects not only the aesthetics of modernist painting that so profoundly influenced him but also what Williams found and admired in Pieter Brueghel, namely an art that combined a passionate sincerity of vision with a compelling rigor of design:

> When a man makes a poem, makes it, mind you, he takes words as he finds them interrelated about him and composes them – without distortion which would mar their exact significances – into an intense expression of his perceptions and ardors that they may constitute a revelation in the speech that he uses. It isn't what he *says* that counts as a work of art, it's what he makes, with such intensity of perception that it lives with an intrinsic movement of its own to verify its authenticity.   (Introduction to *The Wedge, CP2* 54)

NOTES

1. Williams's wife Florence was convinced that he never attended the 1913 exhibition: "Bill did not attend the first Armory Show, though he always insisted he did. He went to the second one [of 1917], where he read along with Mina Loy and others. He wasn't himself when he swore he'd been to the first one so I gave up trying to convince him." [Florence Williams, quoted in Edith Heal, "Interview with Flossie," *William Carlos Williams Newsletter*, 2.1 [Fall 1976]: 11.]
2. Peter Schmidt, "Some Versions of Modernist Pastoral: Williams and the Precisionists," *Contemporary Literature* 21.3 (1980): 395–99.
3. Van Wyck Brooks, *America's Coming-of-Age* (rev. ed. Garden City, NY: Doubleday, 1958), 83.
4. "A Complete Reversal of Art Opinions by Marcel Duchamp, Iconoclast," *Arts and Decoration* 5 (September 1915): 427–28.
5. Christopher J. MacGowan, *William Carlos Williams's Early Poetry: The Visual Arts Background* (Ann Arbor, MI: UMI Press, 1984), 93.
6. Kenneth Burke, "William Carlos Williams: Two Judgments," in *William Carlos Williams: A Collection of Critical Essays*, Ed. J. Hillis Miller (Englewood Cliffs, NJ: Prentice-Hall, 1966), 50.
7. See Mike Weaver, *William Carlos Williams: The American Background* (Cambridge: Cambridge University Press, 1971), 37–39.
8. Rudolf Arnheim, *Toward a Psychology of Art: Collected Essays* (Berkeley and Los Angeles, CA: University of California Press, 1966), 74.

5

LISA M. STEINMAN

"No confusion – only difficulties" in Williams's *Spring and All*

Spring and All had few readers when it was first published by Robert McAlmon's Contact Publishing Company in Paris in 1923. Only about 300 copies were printed, and most of those were not distributed.[1] Later the same year, Williams reprinted nine of the poems from the volume (with one poem and terminal punctuation added) in a small pamphlet, *Go-Go* – the second in the serialized *Manikin*, published in New York by Monroe Wheeler. *Go-Go* had a print run of only 150 copies and so, again, a small readership.[2] Some of the twenty-seven poems that first appeared in the Contact edition are also included – with or without titles – in Williams's 1934 *Collected Poems*, the 1938 *Complete Collected Poems*, and the 1951 *Collected Earlier Poems*. The mixture of prose and poetry that formed the 1923 Contact version of *Spring and All* was not widely available until 1970 in a New Directions volume entitled *Imaginations*.[3]

At least three questions about *Spring and All* arise once one knows its publication history and has some experience with the difficulty of reconstructing and explaining the complexities of this history. First, there is the question of to what exactly one refers when one writes "*Spring and All*." Second, there is the question of how to characterize the mixture of and relationship between the prose and poetry in the Contact volume. Finally, there is the question of why – given that the original *Spring and All* had so few readers in 1923 and was not reprinted as a whole until almost fifty years later – so many critics since 1970 have lauded *Spring and All* as Williams's best or most interesting work?[4]

These questions are not easily settled, but it does cast light on the text to ask them in tandem. That said, it may avoid confusion to begin with the first question. Asking to what one refers when one writes "*Spring and All*" is not a question about the genre or nature of the volume published by McAlmon in 1923, but rather a question about what happens when the context in which something is read changes. For example, can one accurately say that the well-known and often reprinted "The Red Wheelbarrow" first appeared in *Spring and All*, when the poem in the Contact edition had no title except the Roman numeral "XXII" and was followed by four pages of fragmented prose statements or short paragraphs? Or rather, four pages follow poem XXII in the smaller-sized Contact edition; not quite three pages follow in the edition now most often cited, namely the first volume of the 1986 *Collected Poems of William Carlos Williams*, which is to say that even these two versions are not precisely the same.

This may seem like a trivial distinction, but how long one reads before finding what looks like a poem does affect a reader's response, especially since the work itself raises questions about what poetry is and what it offers readers, questions to which I will return. First, however, I want to continue sketching the more general question, one that has increasingly interested twenty-first-century critics, namely in what sense is any poem changed by a changed context? Again taking "The Red Wheelbarrow" as an example, one can ask whether the poem that opens "so much depends" is the same when read in the 1923 *Spring and All* as it is when found in some of Williams's later collections of poetry or in a *Norton Anthology* or, for that matter, in 1933, in two other anthologies: *Fifty Poets: An American Auto-Anthology* edited by William Rose Benét and *Active Anthology*, edited by Ezra Pound?[5] It does not seem quite right to say what we read remains the same in all these contexts. Burton Hatlen has proposed that the poem changes when a title is added and especially when it does not conclusively end with terminal punctuation. Yet in the 1933 anthologies, the poem remains open-ended, without a final period, and even then the poem is arguably experienced differently than it is in the original. More recently, Gillian White, while not explicitly discussing poems by Williams, argues against what she calls the "dehistoricizing" of poems and suggests that any poem will be ontologically different in different contexts even if there are no changes in the actual text on the page.[6]

Certainly, readers' experiences change depending on the context in which they are reading. We might, for instance, read "The Red Wheelbarrow" trying to discern Williams's characteristic style and subject matter – or his development as a poet – when the poem is printed with other poems by Williams. For example, the vignette of ordinary objects, like the suggestion that the scene is important (with much depending on it), is similar to what can be found in a number of poems from Williams's 1917 volume *Al Que Quiere!*, such as "Pastoral," which implies that the aesthetic appeal of poor neighborhoods has "import," despite public opinion to the contrary (*CP1* 64–65).

Encountered in an anthology, however, such poems might seem more canonical, especially if read in a classroom. Yet in 1933, Benét's anthology probably cast the poem in a different light.[7] Although Alfred Kreymborg, Marianne Moore, and Wallace Stevens (other poets associated with modernist experimentation) were included, so too was the more traditional verse of Charles Erskine Scott Wood, Lizette Woodworth Reese, Edwin Arlington Robinson, Edgar Lee Masters, Robert Frost, and others; Williams's contribution appeared just before a piece by Alfred Kreymborg and just after a poem by Arthur Davison Ficke, a poet at that point known for his sonnets who in 1916 pseudonymously coauthored *Spectra: A Book of Poetic Experiments*, a book making fun of more experimental verse. In this context, it is not clear precisely how "The Red Wheelbarrow" would have struck a reader in 1933; it might have stood out as more "experimental" than work by some of the other more populist or Georgian poets Benét – not, himself, closely associated with modernism – invited to contribute. Or the chickens and farm implement might, in such a context, have made the poem seem more domesticated and populist than it would have seemed in Pound's *Active Anthology* from the same year, in which it was printed along with poems by Basil Bunting, Louis Zukofsky, Marianne Moore, George Oppen, and T. S. Eliot, among others more closely associated with modernism, and where Pound's introduction focused readers on writers "in whose verse [he thought] a development appear[ed] … to be taking place."[8]

This is not at the moment to argue that poem XXII is different from "The Red Wheelbarrow" as it was published in, for example, the fourth edition of *The Norton Anthology of Poetry* because the former is a more open poem, whereas the title and terminal punctuation, as well as the appearance of the text next to other texts that are obviously shaped like poems (left justified, with lines that do not reach the right margin), make the latter a poem that offers more closure.[9] Rather, I am here raising theoretical questions about, among other things, the role of readers and of history in defining what a poem – any poem – might be. At the same time, it is worth pointing out that how a reader might experience any poem differently in different contexts is underlined by the way Williams's redactions of *Spring and All's* poem XXII (retitling it "The Red Wheelbarrow," in some instances adding a final period) changes the experience of reading the text not simply because context always changes poems, but in a more self-conscious way. Indeed, Williams changed the text by the time *Go-Go* appeared in 1923, and then changed it again in 1933, so the instability of what was written is authorized, or at least orchestrated, by Williams, and thus not simply a matter of revisiting the text in light of newer theoretical ideas. This leads, then, to the second question with which I opened, namely what was *Spring and All* in 1923, for Williams or for his earliest readers?

In his *Autobiography*, looking back at his earlier work, Williams said about what he and others were writing: "What were we seeking? No one knew consistently enough to formulate a 'movement.' We were ... closely allied with the painters ... We had followed Pound's instructions" (*A* 148). Pound's sense of a needed reinvigoration of poetry (later associated with the injunction to "make it new") is arguably the main preoccupation of the beginning of *Spring and All*. The first six pages of the text are centrally concerned with the difference between the old world and the new and play with the possibility of destroying the old ("Kill! kill! let there be fresh meat") that the world might be "made anew" (*CP1* 179), even as the high poetic diction ("anew") suggests that the project of renewal is not so easily accomplished. The very title of the volume, at least on one reading, works similarly: it is not necessarily a cry of excitement – welcoming spring and everything spring implies – but may rather dismiss spring and all that kind of stuff. Williams's spring is also set against Eliot's 1922 *The Waste Land*, and against other literary springs invoked by Eliot, although the trope is one found frequently in earlier works by Williams such as the 1921 "St. Francis Einstein of the Daffodils" or the 1920 *Kora in Hell*. In *Spring and All*, not long before we read poem I, we are told: "It is spring: life again begins to assume its normal appearance as of 'today.' Only the imagination is undeceived" (*CP1* 182), suggesting that sheer presence or "the exact moment ... the only thing in which I am at all interested" (*CP1* 178), that which Williams seeks in *Spring and All*, is not easily achieved or maintained.

Nor was it solely Pound's "instructions" that raised the question of how to renew perception or the arts; the artist Charles Demuth's poem on Marcel Duchamp's "Fountain" (the urinal Duchamp signed "R. Mutt" and submitted to the 1917 Independents Exhibition) makes much the same point when Demuth writes of many would-be artists: "When they stop they make/ a convention./ That is their end"; the last line of the poem reads: "The going just keep going."[10] Numerous writers and visual artists at the time voiced a similar insistence on process (or, as Pound's anthology put it, "development"). And many of those painters and movements in the visual arts – including what came to be known as American Precisionism (*Spring and All* is dedicated to Demuth), cubism (Juan Gris is the visual artist mentioned most often in *Spring and All*), and dadaism (the end of *Spring and All* refers readers to "[Marsden] Hartley's last chapter" [*CP1* 235] on dadaism) – were important to Williams.[11] That creative pieces should not be static (as in Demuth's poem) and might change in new contexts (one of the issues raised by Duchamp's "Fountain") were topics of conversation in the circles in which Williams moved.[12] It seems that the apparently later theoretical questions I first raised already concerned Williams in 1923, although his concerns were voiced using a slightly different vocabulary than is found in twenty-first-century criticism.

This sharpens the question of how to read not excerpts from but the whole of the 1923 *Spring and All*, including its mixture of poetry and prose. There is, first, the problem of the relationship between the questions raised by Duchamp or Williams and now current theoretical questions; after all, the questions themselves are posed in different contexts. Nonetheless, the call for seeing "anew" in *Spring and All*, with its insistence on being in "the moment" – the first line voices a desire for something "of moment" (*CP1* 177) meaning both something of importance and something living or present – suggests that recontextualizing is part of seeing anew for Williams. There are also questions about whether the whole of *Spring and All* is thematically or theoretically focused, or whether it offers instead a series of disjointed moments, only some of which focus on presence or renewal. If the latter, is there a coherent purpose informing the disjointedness?

There have been various answers offered to these questions. Burton Hatlen, again, talks about the openness of Williams's "radically experimental text," and Christopher MacGowan succinctly characterizes the "thematically related, manifesto-like prose" that first seems as discontinuous as the poems, noting too that some critics have read the poems as "a loosely defined sequence, although [others] ... have argued that they are purposefully random."[13] Most approaches to the volume tend not to look for an overarching theme or progression – which presumably would not make the text "open" – but do note repeated themes, analogues, or influences in order to characterize what *Spring and All* is (or what it was in 1923). A number of discussions about the nature of Williams's project in *Spring and All* see the volume as involving or exploring some kind of duality, if not outright ambivalence, and the text clearly does offer multiple, not always compatible, suggestions about the relationship between poetry and prose, nature and art, the actual world and the world of the imagination, or between Europe and the United States.[14] All of these seeming dichotomies and ostensible confusion are discernable in the text, although it is less clear why this is so.

James Breslin and Burton Hatlen are among those who suggest that the mixture of prose and poetry reads as a continuous text, and so find coherence in the way the volume, even with all its apparent inconsistencies, is structured.[15] Hatlen, in particular, offers a number of compelling close readings to support his claim that *Spring and All* is most interestingly read as a sequence, not a random assortment of poems and prose passages; for example, he notes that poem XXI ends with the lines "so lascivious/ and still," while poem XXII (not, he argues, the same as the excerpted "The Red Wheelbarrow") follows immediately with the line "so much depends"; the two poems not only "mirror one another" formally, but operate "in some ways as a single poem" with the repetition of "so" and the way in which poems XXI and XXII in different ways emphasize what is "still."[16]

To extend Hatlen's reading, it is worth noting that dynamism, not stillness, is what the poems and the prose that precede poem XXII have associated with the imagination, which, after the first poems appear, is said to be "freed from the handcuffs of 'art'" (*CP1* 185), "art" presumably indicating received ideas of art rather than process-oriented modernist practices. Poem I presents a new world that "quickens" (a word that reappears a number of times, signaling both motion and birth); moreover, what we read is called "notes jotted down in the midst of the action" (*CP1* 183, 186). As the text continues, it seems that Williams underlines how his own activity needs to stay in motion, and how his "spring" – if it is not to become what he dismisses as "crude symbolism" (*CP1* 188–89) – needs to be not just new, but constantly renewed. Again, however, the text marks the difficulty of defining or maintaining whatever it is that makes art continue to be experienced as living. Poem V, for instance, focuses on images of motion and intensity (wind, "strident voices, heat/ quickened, built of waves") only to end "How easy to slip/ into the old mode, how hard to/ cling firmly to the advance – " (*CP1* 190–91); poem VI proclaims "No that is not it" (*CP1* 191) and toys with the idea that sounds and language ("I" becomes "the diphthong// ae"), not staged representations of an observing self or representations of the world, best mark the continuous imaginative process Williams celebrates.

Reading the progression of the text in this way oversimplifies it, but does suggest that *Spring and All* enacts a process of thought in motion about, among other things, what it is that art (not, in Williams's terms, "art") offers and requires. By the time poem XXII appears, Williams has considered disassociating the power of art from what he calls "illusion" and refigured what art offers as "A CREATIVE FORCE ... SHOWN AT WORK" (*CP1* 199, capitalized in the original), and as giving "value to life" by a "quickening of ... sense" (*CP1* 202). He further distinguishes between prose – "the fact of an emotion" – and poetry – "the dynamization of emotion into a separate form" – calling for a new world, a "separate form," tacitly a work of living art that deploys an "energizing" force (*CP1* 219–20). In short, one can read *Spring and All* as an enactment of thought about a variety of topics, including the nature of the imaginative activity the volume itself embodies. We are not given conclusions but shown ideas, images, and the linguistic forms that shape thought as constantly shifting, which is to say in motion.

This insistence on thought in motion does make Hatlen's point about the stillness in poems XXI and XXII puzzling. Why, given the text's overall emphasis on dynamic force and motion, does Williams underline the fact that poem XXII is a still life of sorts? The distinction the book makes previously between the vitality of poetry and the amassed facts – a "lump" (*CP1* 220) – of prose is also complicated just after poem XXII. The first short sentence following the last line of the poem is: "The fixed categories into which life is divided must always hold" (*CP1* 224). And yet the very categories of poetry and prose to which the prose has called attention now seem to be questioned. The lack of punctuation after the last line of poem XXII ("chickens") suggests the poem has not ended; the insistence on holding to "fixed categories," however, like the turn to unlineated passages, appears at the same time to suggest that we are no longer reading a poem, but prose: a different category. Yet if the sentence immediately following the image of the chickens affirms fixed categories, and is a syntactically complete sentence, the rest of the first block of prose reads: "These things are normal – essential to every activity. But they exist – but not as dead dissections" (*CP1* 224). Depending on what one takes the antecedent of "these things" to be – apparently "fixed categories" (perhaps more specifically prose and poetry) – the definition of "fixed categories" is again thrown into question by the not-so-fixed fragmented syntax and the double qualification ("but ... but"). Just before the four pieces that look like poems, titled XIX through XXII, Williams clearly associates prose with "statement[s]" and "facts"; poetry, with "movement" (*CP1* 219). Yet after we read what first seems a still life composed of wheelbarrow, rain water, and chickens, what looks like prose sounds both animated and open-ended. At very least, the emphasis on what is "still" in the poems and the disjointedness of the prose refigures what we are to understand as signifying "movement." Further, the salient distinction may not be between prose and poetry (although earlier in *Spring and All* it seemed to be) but between what is fixed and what is open to change, regardless of whether what is on the page appears to be poetry or prose.[17] The distinction first proposed is, toward the end, explicitly dismantled as Williams writes that there is "no discoverable difference between prose and verse ... and that both are phases of the same thing" (*CP1* 230). As centrally, it seems that even in what looks like prose, we are again invited to see, even to participate in, an act of the mind in the process of trying to figure out what counts as living knowledge, earlier associated with poetry as well as with the imagination and dynamism or energy.

There are a number of reasons poem XXII might first present itself as a still life, but surely one reason is to signify that what fuels thought or keeps art alive is not a matter of arriving at any settled conclusion. Nor can thought that is in motion be identified by predetermined stylistic features, such as the use of verbs or the description of motion, let alone by rhyme or poetic form. Something else is necessary. At times, *Spring and All* identifies that something else as the imagination. Yet another paragraph-like block of text that follows poem XXII reads in total: "It is the imagination that – " (*CP1* 225). This again suggests that what looks like prose can be open-ended but also that the nature and function of imagination are difficult to define. We are told it is "a force" (*CP1* 178) and that "on which reality rides" (*CP1* 225) but also "a cleavage through everything by a force" (*CP1* 225). By the end of the volume, Williams makes explicit that the unstable nature of the definitions he has offered is purposeful: "Sometimes I speak of imagination as a force, an electricity or a medium, a place. It is immaterial which" (*CP1* 235). The choice of the word "immaterial" is telling, again insisting that whatever animates or gives value to the world cannot be pinned down; what the book emphasizes is a continuous act of engagement – an activity – not an object of knowledge. And it is further suggested that any reading of *Spring and All* will similarly not arrive at any definitive conclusion but will shift as the various threads of thought and the issues thought about are approached, challenged, and reconfigured from different perspectives.

On the one hand, this is to return to my earlier suggestion that *Spring and All* anticipates ideas about the instability of texts, being both an embodiment of thinking and something like a kind of virtual reality *avant la lettre* by means of which readers can participate; indeed, by the second page, we are told: "I myself invite you to read and to see" (*CP1* 178). On the other hand, to say even this is to propose that *Spring and All* is more decorously staged than a characterization of it as thought in motion suggests. It does move from what can (and did) become a kind of slogan – "make it new" – to a self-conscious focus on process. Yet the text also moves between different registers and poses other questions. For instance, *Spring and All* refers to Prohibition (*CP1* 181) and to Woodrow Wilson (*CP1* 185), which is to say to the news – not the "new" – in 1923; it enters the realm of sociology with considerations of class and social welfare policies in poem XVIII, also known as "To Elsie"; it raises questions about jazz (*CP1* 216), about mass cultural forms from cinema (*CP1* 213–14) to baseball (*CP1* 233–34) to advertising (*CP1* 197, 200, 232); it enters debates on public education, echoing John Dewey's distinction between "inquiring" and "acquiring."[18] In short, although some critics claim that in *Spring and All* art is figured as having a primarily aesthetic function, most agree that the volume does not focus on aesthetic questions in isolation so much as on the relation between the arts and historical, sociological, or anthropological realities.[19]

The volume at times does claim that art is separate from life, citing Juan Gris's *The Open Window* to this effect:

> [Gris's painting,] though I have not seen it in color, is important as marking more clearly than any I have seen what the modern trend is: the attempt is being made to separate things of the imagination from life, and obviously, by using the forms common to experience so as not to frighten the onlooker away but to invite him   (*CP*1 194)

This leads directly, with only a comma at the end of the prose passage, into the one unnumbered poem in *Spring and All*, which opens "The rose is obsolete" – a poem arguably based on Gris's painting *Roses* (or *Roses in a Vase*) – and is followed by poem VIII, which (also lacking a final period) leads in turn into what seems like prose about familiar things that are nonetheless detached from ordinary experience.[20] The following prose paragraph returns to Gris's *The Open Window*: "Here is a shutter, a bunch of grapes, a sheet of music, a picture of sea and mountains (particularly fine) which the onlooker is not for a moment permitted to witness as an 'illusion.' One thing laps over on the other, the cloud laps over on the shutter" (*CP*1 197–98). Within a page, there is a discussion of how pictures have the "power TO ESCAPE ILLUSION and stand between man and nature as saints once stood between man and the sky – their reality in such work, say, as that of Juan Gris" (*CP*1 199). Gris reappears a last time in a discussion of "beauty," in which beauty is aligned with "a state in which reality plays a part" (*CP*1 204). I dwell on Gris's presence in *Spring and All* because he is the visual artist most often mentioned in the text, but also because it seems to be in part through Gris that Williams explores the question of what art has to do with the actual world: is it a separate reality (not life) as the first passage on Gris implies?[21]

It seems clear that for Williams in *Spring and All* art is not representation, not, that is, what he calls "illusion." Like the American Precisionists – first called the Cubist-Realists – most of whom Williams knew, Gris's painting deploys cubist technique such as overlapping planes, with the composition based on (for Gris) a mathematical grid, and yet – as Williams says – it also include forms "common to experience."[22] Williams's comments suggest too that the aesthetic pleasure afforded by the painting is something "in which reality plays a part." Williams seems to say that images or representations that are recognizable do matter, and at the same time he argues that vital pictures have reality because they are equal to other forms of the real rather than dependent on mimesis.

Gris's title surely thus appealed to Williams, with art not a mirror held up to nature but an open window. Yet Gris's merger of local, quotidian details with elements that insist the reality a viewer sees is that of the painting, not a copy of natural or domestic worlds, also speaks to Williams's project or at least his questions about what art offers. In *The Open Window*, the outside clouds overlap what appears to be an interior, if open, shutter; the design formed by blocks of print on paper are repeated and aligned with the design formed by the louvers on either side of the tilt bar on two shutters, bringing the design, not the objects portrayed, to the viewer's attention. Turning once more to poem XXII, one can see that there too the formal design of the poem vies with the scene described for a reader's attention: the first and last couplets each open with a line of three words forming four syllables; the middle two couplets with lines of three monosyllabic words. The second line in each couplet is composed of a single, disyllabic word. Sound also patterns the poem, with consonance, alliteration, and slant rhyme: "depends" echoes "chickens"; "so" echoes "barrow"; the modulated *a* sounds in "glazed," "rain," and "water" yield to the modulated *i* sounds in "beside," "white," and "chickens."

For a poem with only sixteen words, the texture formed by sound is striking. In this way, the poem calls attention to the materiality of language and may draw also on a piece by the other painter central to the volume, Charles Demuth. Exhibited in 1922 at the Daniel Gallery in New York, Demuth's *Spring* is a *trompe l'oeil* oil painting of swatches of cloth – literally, material – with different designs on each swatch. It first looks like a collage. As Henry Sayre has argued, the piece tropes on spring fashions and on the materiality of painting.[23] As in *The Open Window*, viewers are shown that how (and in what context) one sees affects what one sees. Both paintings, like Williams's book, play with form, question representation, and the material of art, but are not sealed off from the actual world on which they also comment.

Form or texture may play another role in both Gris's painting and *Spring and All*, as well. In *The Open Window*, the paint used for most of the interior scene is flat, largely without discernible brush strokes, but where a cloud overlaps a shutter there is an area of impasto, calling attention to the paint as paint. Indeed, it may be the mixture of techniques that is the most striking feature of the piece. Williams similarly textures language by including in *Spring and All* prose and poetry, numerous registers (philosophy, history, popular culture, aesthetics) and mixed diction – "the cat's nuts" (*CP1* 216) coexisting with "veritable" (*CP1* 226); "Pah!" (*CP1* 200) with "universality" (*CP1* 204).[24]

To note that *Spring and All* calls attention to the materiality of language is not, however, to say Williams's stylistic eclecticism is solely in the service of the aesthetic or of the new, any more than it is to say that in *Spring and All* the emphasis on thought in motion means Williams is not really thinking about social or political realities. As he says in poem VI, "energy *in vacuo/* has the power/ of confusion" (*CP1* 192); by the end of the prose that follows poem XXII he says: "There is no confusion – only difficulties" (*CP1* 226). Moreover, just how imagination, aesthetic pleasure, life, and gritty actuality are related remains for us a difficult question.

Certainly, one cannot extract single poems or sections to illustrate Williams's final position on the relationship of art and life, since in *Spring and All* thought is enacted in motion, not codified. For just this reason, I would suggest that *Spring and All* is not the same book it was in 1923. The very multiplicity of issues Williams sets in motion, including how context matters, surely accounts for much of the current and continued interest in *Spring and All*, opening the book to a variety of now-contemporary critical approaches, which place the volume itself in new contexts. Finally, it is tempting to say that his refusal to rest content with received opinion or come to conclusions means Williams was right on one count: art remains most alive when it continues to invite readers to grapple with difficult and moving questions – in both senses of the word "moving."

NOTES

1. See Emily Mitchell Wallace, *A Bibliography of William Carlos Williams* (Middletown, CT: Wesleyan University Press, 1968), 19–20. Paul Mariani, in *William Carlos Williams: A New World Naked* (New York: McGraw-Hill, 1981), 209, notes that McAlmon claimed most of the copies sent to America were confiscated by U.S. Customs.
2. Wallace, *A Bibliography of William Carlos Williams*, 21.
3. William Carlos Williams, *Imaginations*, ed. Webster Schott (New York: New Directions, 1970), 83–151; Frontier Press issued an unauthorized version of *Spring & All* the same year. Most recently, in 2011, New Directions published another edition. Williams himself switched the order in which "Quietness" (poem XXI in 1923) and "The Red Wheelbarrow (poem XXII) appeared in the 1938 *Complete Collected Poems* and again in the 1951 *Collected Earlier Poems* (see Wallace, *A Bibliography of William Carlos Williams*, 46, 81). Some of the prose was also reprinted without the poems both by Williams and after Williams's death (Wallace, *A Bibliography of William Carlos Williams*, 19–20); notes on where individual poems from the volume were reprinted (as well as the whole of *Spring and All*) appear in *The Collected Poems of William Carlos Williams*, Vol. I, ed. A. Walton Litz and Christopher MacGowan (New York: New Directions, 1986), 175–236, 500–1. Unless otherwise noted, citations from *Spring and All* are from this volume [hereafter, *CP1*]. Burton Hatlen's seminal article, "Openness and Closure in Williams' *Spring and All*," *William Carlos Williams Review* 20.2 (1994): 15–20, gives what is still one of the best accounts of the publishing history of *Spring and All* in its various incarnations.

4. See, for example, James E. Breslin, *William Carlos Williams: An American Artist* (New York: Oxford University Press, 1970), 50, 86; Marjorie Perloff, *The Poetics of Indeterminacy: Rimbaud to Cage* (Princeton, NJ: Princeton University Press, 1981), 110; Mariani, 191, 209.

5. William Rose Benét, ed., *Fifty Poets: An American Auto-Anthology* (New York: Duffield and Green, 1933), 61; Ezra Pound, ed., *Active Anthology* (London: Faber & Faber, 1933), 45.

6. See Hatlen, throughout, and Gillian White, *Lyric Shame: The "Lyric" Subject of Contemporary American Poetry* (Cambridge, MA: Harvard University Press, 2014), 33.

7. *Fifty Poets* let the poets pick the poem they most wanted "to represent" them, as the introduction notes (Benét, *Fifty Poets*, vii).

8. Pound, *Active Anthology*, 5.

9. Margaret Ferguson, Mary Jo Salter, and Jon Stallworthy, eds.,*The Norton Anthology of Poetry* (New York: W. W. Norton and Company, Inc., 1970), 1166. I choose the fourth edition because it first came out the same year that New Directions included the 1923 version of *Spring and All* in *Imaginations*.

10. Charles Demuth, "For Richard Mutt, " *The Blind Man*, 2 (1917): 6.

11. See Bram Dijsktra, *The Hieroglyphics of a New Speech: Cubism, Stieglitz, and the Early Poetry of William Carlos Williams* (Princeton, NJ: Princeton University Press, 1969); Henry M. Sayre, *The Visual Text of William Carlos Williams* (Urbana: University of Illinois Press, 1983); *Technology*, Christopher MacGowan, *William Carlos Williams's Early Poetry: The Visual Arts Background* (Ann Arbor: UMI Research Press, 1984); Lisa M. Steinman, *Made in America: Science, Technology, and American Modernist Poets* (New Haven: Yale University Press, 1987); and Peter Schmidt, *Williams Carlos Williams, the Arts, and Literary Tradition* (Baton Rouge: Louisiana State University Press, 1988), among others.

12. Demuth was close friends with Williams and Williams's *Autobiography* specifically mentions Duchamp and "Fountain," although he misremembers the urinal as having been rejected for the 1913 Armory Show rather than for the 1917 Independents Exhibition (Williams, *Autobiography*, 134–37).

13. Hatlen, "Openness and Closure in Williams' *Spring and All*," 15–16; Christopher MacGowan, *Twentieth-Century American Poetry* (Oxford: Blackwell, 2004), 48, 197.

14. See MacGowan, *Twentieth-Century American Poetry*, 198; Hatlen, "Openness and Closure in Williams' *Spring and All*," 17.

15. Breslin, *William Carlos Williams*, 78–79; Hatlen, "Openness and Closure in Williams' *Spring and All*," 15–16, 23–24.

16. Hatlen, 22–23. Focusing on the 1923 edition, Hatlen does not address the way Williams switched poems XXI and XXII in the 1938 *Complete Collected Poems* to avoid splitting the "better poem" across two pages (CP1 501).

17. For the text's continued attention to the distinction between prose and poetry, see also CP1 226, 229.

18. See Lisa M. Steinman, "William Carlos Williams: *Spring and All*," in *A Companion to Twentieth-Century Poetry*, ed. Neil Roberts (Oxford: Blackwell, 2001), 411.

19. See, for instance, Michel Oren, "Williams and Gris: A Borrowed Aesthetic," *Contemporary Literature*, 26.2 (1985): 197–211. Broader questions about the relationship in *Spring and All* between art and historical realities are raised by, among others, David Frail, *The Early Politics and Poetics of William Carlos Williams* (Ann Arbor: UMI Research Press, 1987), James Clifford, *The Predicament of Culture: Twentieth-Century Ethnography, Literature, and Art* (Cambridge, MA: Harvard University Press, 1988), John Lowney, *The American Avant-Garde Tradition: William Carlos Williams, Postmodern Poetry, and the Politics of Cultural Memory* (Lewisburg: Bucknell University Press, 1997), Justin Read, *Modern Poetics and Hemispheric American Cultural Studies* (New York: Palgrave Macmillan, 2009), and Joshua Schuster, "William Carlos Williams, *Spring and All*, and the Anthropological Imaginary," *Journal of Modern Literature*, 30.3 (2007): 116–32.

20. The connection between Gris's painting and "The rose is obsolete" was proposed first by Bram Dijkstra in *Hieroglyphics of a New Speech*, 173–6, contested by Henry M. Sayre in "Distancing 'The Rose' from *Roses*," *William Carlos Williams Newsletter* V.1 (1979): 18–19, and reargued by Peter Halter in *The Revolution in the Visual Arts and the Poetry of William Carlos Williams* (New York: Cambridge University Press, 1994), 74–80, 235–36. Although the poem is not numbered, it does fall between the poems numbered VI and VIII.

21. Williams could not yet have read Gris's writing on art (not published until 1924) nor could he have seen Gris's 1921 *The Open Window* in person, since it was not shown in the United States before *Spring and All* was published, and Williams did not travel abroad between 1920 and 1924, although the painting was reproduced in *Broom* I.3 (1922): 264, where Williams would have seen a black and white print of it.

22. Dijkstra points out the similarities between Gris's work and that of the American Precisionists (*Hieroglyphics of a New Speech*, 173). Karen Tsujimoto, *Images of America: Precisionist Painting and Modern Photography* (Seattle: University of Washington Press for the San Francisco Museum of Modern Art, 1982), 21–23, discusses why the Precisionists – not called such in their day, and not a coherent group with a manifesto or single style – were not analyzed systematically until the mid-forties when Milton Brown suggested they be called "Cubist-Realists," because of their synthesis of French cubism and American realism in Milton W. Brown, "Cubist-Realism: An American Style," *Marsyas* 3.5 (1943–1945): 139–60.

23. My argument borrows from Henry M. Sayre, "Avant-Garde Dispositions: Placing *Spring and All* in Context," *William Carlos Williams Review* X.2 (1984): 20–22.

24. Although he could not have seen the textured paint in the black-and-white reproduction in *Broom*, Williams may well have discussed Gris's work and technique with Demuth, who had admired Gris's work since 1914 (MacGowan, *William Carlos Williams's Early Poetry*, 103).

6

MILTON A. COHEN

Williams and politics

In sharp contrast to the rightist politics of other great modernist poets – Pound, Eliot, Frost, Cummings, and Yeats – William Carlos Williams all his life remained a forthright and unapologetic liberal, a small-d democrat but far enough left to describe himself as "pink."[1] Early on, empathy for ordinary people became the pole star that guided his political views, regardless of whether the wind blew strongly from the left, as it did in the 1930s, or from the right, as in the anti-communist late 1940s and 1950s. Even in the politically quiescent 1920s, when most of his contemporaries scorned politics, Williams was among the few who expressed his political liberalism in his poetry. In the wild oscillations of the intensely politicized 1930s and late 1940s–1950s, he paid a price for sticking to his liberalism: in the 1930s, communists that dominated such major literary magazines as *Partisan Review* publicly humiliated him (even though he supported many of their causes), and the red-hunting McCarthyites blocked his appointment as Consultant in Poetry to the Library of Congress in the early 1950s. Still, Williams persevered and refused to recant his positions.

Inseparable from his democratic credo was Williams's unshakable identity as an American (a topic discussed in other essays in this volume). Curiously, his English father may have influenced both attitudes but in opposing ways. William George Williams was a socialist who supported Henry George's single-tax movement, but his refusal to become an American citizen incurred his son's resentment and probably intensified Williams's own sense of Americanness (Leibowitz 49, 41).

A far stronger influence on Williams's egalitarianism was his medical career. In the scruffy industrial towns around Rutherford, New Jersey, where "Doc Williams" set up shop as a general practitioner and obstetrician, his patients were mostly working class and ethnic, often recent immigrants. These were the days when doctors routinely made house calls, and he knew their homes and their lives, their struggles to survive economically, especially during the brutal Depression, their diseases and disfigurements stemming from medical neglect and poverty.[2] Where middle-class radicals in the 1930s pontificated endlessly about the "proletariat," Williams dealt every day with ordinary, working-class people, not abstractions. And unlike Stevens, who lived essentially separate lives as poet and insurance executive, Williams's poetry and fiction, rooted as he believed they should be in the locality, drew on his patients' lives and ailments, as he observed them with a clinical but sympathetic eye:

> They call me and I go.
> It is a frozen road
> past midnight . . . .
> The door opens,
> I smile, enter and
> shake off the cold.
> Here is a great woman
> on her side in the bed.
> She is sick,
> perhaps vomiting,
> perhaps laboring
> to give birth to
> a tenth child. Joy! Joy!
> . . . .
> I pick the hair from her eyes
> and watch her misery
> with compassion.
> – "Complaint,"   CP1 153–54

Perhaps the last lines are unnecessary: compassion for this woman's suffering pervades this poem, intermingled with the doctor's sardonic irony in delivering her tenth child – no choir is singing "Joy to the World!" for this birth! – and in his unvoiced complaint about having to get up and go out into the freezing night to answer this call.

Williams's egalitarianism and nationalistic identity affected his poetic and political identity in another way. They placed him at polar opposites to the modernist elitism and internationalism of Ezra Pound, his sometime friend and constant correspondent, and T. S. Eliot, Williams's *bête noir*. Both Pound and Eliot despised liberalism and democratic leveling, which they believed also leveled the quality of art; both adhered to differing versions of hierarchical authority and control; and both employed learned and arcane allusions in their verse that made it virtually inaccessible to the common reader. About their extreme political differences, Williams debated with Pound (until he felt Pound was unreachable in his fanatical fascism[3]) and railed obsessively against

Eliot. But his determination not to return poetry to the classroom, as he put it,[4] to use plain American English in poems that were directly apprehensible and required neither endnotes nor reference books, was as much a political statement as it was an aesthetic one.

1920S

Williams's decision to remain in the United States (apart from two trips to Europe in the 1920s) was fraught with fears of becoming provincial as well as frustration about the country's lack of direction in the 1920s. Friends like Robert McAlmon and the ever-hectoring Pound lost few chances to remind him that the action was in Paris and that Williams was missing it living in New Jersey. Williams often feared that these claims were true, resenting the leaden weights – medical career and family – anchoring him to New Jersey. His philosophy of a poetry rooted in the locality thus made the most of necessity. And his poetry and prose in the 1920s sometimes directly addressed his concerns about his country: its hedonistic abandon, its reckless subservience to a booming economy and big-business pundits.

The poem that best captures this concern is "To Elsie," which appeared in the experimental *Spring and All* of 1923. While ostensibly about Elsie, who, with "broken brain," was placed by the state in the Williams household as a servant, the poem makes her mental and economic destitution stand for "the truth about us." That truth is memorably expressed in the poem's opening:

> The pure products of America
> go crazy –
> mountain folk from Kentucky
>
> or the ribbed north end of
> Jersey
> with its isolate lakes and
>
> valleys, its deaf-mutes, thieves
> old names
> and promiscuity between
>
> devil-may-care men who have taken
> to railroading
> out of sheer lust of adventure –
>
> and young slatterns, bathed
> in filth
> from Monday to Saturday

to be tricked out that night
with gauds
from imaginations which have no

peasant traditions to give them
character ....   – *CP*1 217

Reckless, exploitive men; ignorant, inarticulate, terrorized women; filth; crude sex exchanged for "gauds"; imaginations bereft of peasant traditions[5] – all combine to portray a free-wheeling, dirty world of sexual exploitation that lacks any sort of stabilizing standards.[6] Though this section of the poem addresses Appalachian poor whites, the poem's last lines expand the perspective to include "us" in the ubiquitous filth:

as if the earth under our feet
were
an excrement of some sky

and we degraded prisoners
destined
to hunger until we eat filth

while the imagination strains
after deer
going by fields of goldenrod ....

Without the presence of a vital imagination, the poem suggests, physical life reduces itself to the lowest common denominator. But who would rectify this fatal imbalance in America between the physical and the imaginative? Certainly not the country's leadership, where there is

No one
to witness
and adjust, no one to drive the car ...   (*CP*1 218–19)

The last image is especially apt not only for its American mechanical context (like railroads above), but also as a symbol of materialist acquisition in the booming 1920s. If the drivers (visionary leaders) and adjusters – the social planners – are missing, the car is sure to run off the road.

Social engineers and centralized planning were not lacking in one country Williams was curious about in the 1920s: Russia. In the same year that it announced its first Five Year Plan, 1928, Williams wrote a long evocation – or, as the title suggests, an "imagination" – of the new Soviet state, "A Morning Imagination of Russia" (*CP*1 303–06). In it, an unnamed, college-educated observer, in this new "red cold world of / the dawn," feels a liberating openness and rapport with peasants he had never known before. He is not afraid to work in the fields, picking herbs and learning from an old woman how to find wild ginger. Finally, he decides to listen at the local soviet and make up his own mind about the issues. The poem concludes with a sense of how shaky the Russian experiment is. Like a recovering patient in a hostile environment,

> We are convalescents. Very
> feeble. Our hands shake. We need a
> transfusion. No one will give it to us,
> they are afraid of infection.

Yet, the final lines are optimistic: "We have paid heavily. But we / have gotten – touch." Here, the speaker's voice abandons the more detached "he" for the involving "We," just as Williams does in "To Elsie." Only now, the sensuous imagination has been invigorated through a new social vision. To be sure, Williams's imaginative evocation is idealistic and naïve in emphasizing the individual's right to judge issues for himself in a state that, under Stalin, distrusted intellectuals and brutally repressed their annoying habit of thinking for themselves. Soon enough, Williams would discover for himself this intolerance in homegrown, literary expressions of communism.

A few leftist writers like John Dos Passos and Upton Sinclair shared Williams's interest in Russia in the 1920s; many more sided with him about an international *cause célèbre*, the last act of which was being played out in Massachusetts in August 1927: the scheduled executions of Nicola Sacco and Bartolomeo Vanzetti. Williams felt that these men, jailed on questionable evidence in 1920 for a payroll robbery and murder, had been unjustly accused, convicted, and sentenced to death because they were Italian immigrants and anarchists. Following delays and appeals of six years, a review committee, comprised of the presidents of Harvard and MIT and a former judge, confirmed the verdict. Williams was outraged; many years later he explained to John Thirlwall: "I believed that they had been double-crossed, that New England was ganging up on these men."[7] Although he did not join the writers who marched on the Massachusetts State House, he wrote an angry poem, "Impromptu: The Suckers" (*CP1* 270–72), anticipating the execution (which occurred shortly after). Interestingly, the poem continually refers to the prisoners as "Americans," not immigrants or foreigners, and assumes a bitterly ironic tone:

> It's no use, you are Americans, just the dregs.
> It's all you deserve ....
> You are inheritors of a great

> tradition. My country right or wrong!
> You do what you're told to do. You don't
> answer back the way Tommy Jeff did or Ben
> Frank or Georgie Washing. I'll say you
> don't. You're civilized.

And Sacco and Vanzetti are not the only American "suckers" – "scapegoats to save the Republic." The opening lines identify Americans in general, distracted from this injustice by "vile whiskey" and sex, as victims: "You too will always go up with the two guys, / scapegoats . . . ." Again in stanza four: "the / New England aristocracy, bent on working off / a grudge against you, Americans, you / are the suckers." And if Americans won't "answer back" to this grotesque abuse of power, what have they inherited from "Tommie Jeff" et al.? Perhaps Williams felt the poem was too angry, the irony too blatant. It did not appear until his 1941 book of poems, *The Broken Span* (*CP*1 513).

<h2 style="text-align:center">1930s</h2>

The tenor and intensity of political activity among writers and intellectuals changed dramatically in response to the Depression. Reacting to its scope and severity – to the closed factories, bread lines, soup kitchens, and men sleeping in parks and Hoovervilles – waves of writers, including many of the most influential, came to believe that in this time of distress, they had a responsibility to address and try to ameliorate social and economic conditions. Almost unanimously, these writers felt that the root of the problem was capitalism itself; that it must at the very least be radically reformed, or, better still, replaced by a new and promising economic system, communism. Almost overnight, Karl Marx replaced Freud as required reading.[8]

Though he had scarcely been apolitical in the 1920s, Williams was caught up in this new political fever, just as he experienced the Depression itself first-hand in the decline of his medical practice. Although he disagreed sharply and repeatedly with those who espoused communism, he expressed his own liberal-leftist views in numerous ways; and these views fluctuated over the decade. He co-edited the leftwing magazines, *Contact* and *Blast* (and even provided a home for the latter's indigent editors); he sent poems and essays to liberal and leftist magazines like *The New Republic, New Masses, Nation,* and *Partisan Review*; he gave speeches on behalf of Social Credit (a non-leftist economic philosophy he briefly shared with Ezra Pound and Gorham Munson); and he joined (and subsequently left) several leftist political groups and causes.[9] When the Spanish Civil War broke out in 1936, he actively supported the Loyalist side, writing poems and essays, translating Spanish poets, and organizing and chairing the Bergen County Medical Board to Aid Spanish Democracy. Finally and most important for posterity, political themes proliferated in his poetry and fiction in the 1930s – but themes that reflected Williams's idiosyncratic interests.

On several occasions, Williams asserted that he was not a Marxist and that he believed that American communists were thoroughly out of touch with the American temper he had described at length in *In the American Grain*. Personally and artistically, he refused to subordinate self-expression to party doctrine. As he wrote Marianne Moore in May 1934, "I won't follow causes. I can't. The reason is that it seems so much more important to me that I *am*" (*SL* 147). Moreover, in the communists' goal of revolution he feared a bloodbath (Mariani 348). But his broader views evolved about whether and to what extent writers should concern themselves with political causes. Initially a pure formalist, he declared to Kay Boyle in early 1932: "poetry is related to poetry, not to social statutes," (*SL* 131). A year later, in accepting the editorship of *BLAST*, a far-left literary magazine, he declared that the artist "must not under any circumstances debase his art to any purpose" – such as for communist propaganda. To do so, he would be "jettisoning his personal integrity as an artist."[10] But he also acknowledged in the same editorial that "present-day Communism" was "intellectually inescapable," and that, in a communistic state, the writer looks for new forms in "*social materials*" (qtd. in *ARI*, 78, 80, emphasis added).

These materials, even in non-communist America, were everywhere present in the painful realities of the Depression; and they appear with increasing frequency in Williams's poems up to about 1935–1936, but always with Williams's particular slants. In the "The Sun Bathers" of 1934 (*CP1* 371), the first two stanzas sound like the proletarian poems published in the Communist Party USA's literary magazine, *New Masses*:

> A tramp thawing out
> on a doorstep
> against an east wall
> Nov. 1, 1933:
>
> a young man begrimed
> and in an old
> army coat
> wriggling and scratching

A homeless tramp sleeps in the cold; a young man is dirty and miserable in a lice-infested, second-hand coat. The date, too, is significant: 1932–1933 was the pit of the Depression – and winter is coming on. But not quite yet. The title tells us, ironically, that these two are sun-bathers: the tramp is "thawing out." And where the conventional proletarian poem would now insert its message of outrage or hope that the revolution would abolish such misery, Williams shifts the poem's mood entirely in the final stanza:

> while a fat negress
> in a yellow-house window
> nearby
> leans out and yawns
>
> into the fine weather

"Thawing out" strengthens into "fine weather": warm sunshine imaged perhaps by the "yellow" house. And while the negress's diet may not be good, she's not starving, either. Nor is she toiling under a matron's pitiless demands, but yawning and leaning out of the window to enjoy the sunshine. Perhaps it's even her house! What begins as a stereotypically proletarian poem becomes Williams's particular kind of political poem: closely observed details that certainly reflect the time, but refuse to impose on it a trendy social message.

By the mid-1930s, as the Communist Party worldwide enjoyed record popularity in its call for a Popular Front against fascism, the urge to write political poems or essays affected many modernist poets, regardless of their politics. Pound's *Fifth Decad of Cantos*, Frost's *A Further Range*, Cummings's *no thanks*, Stevens's *Owl's Clover* – all reflect this urge, even when these poets were reacting against the prevailing leftist movement. Williams, too, published his most political book of poems in this period, *An Early Martyr* (1935), which contains such political poems as the title poem, "Item," "Late for Summer Weather," "Proletarian Portrait," "The Yachts," and "A Poem for Norman Macleod." In some of these poems, he succumbs to the temptation to become didactic and hortative – preachy. The title poem, "An Early Martyr" (*CP1* 377–78), for example, is a paean to a would-be Robin Hood of 1920, John Coffey, who was denied his day in court (at which he planned to make a political speech) and remanded to a mental asylum. Williams felt that, like Sacco and Vanzetti, Coffey had been "railroaded" by the law (377, 537), and urged his example to inspire others:

> Let him be
> a factory whistle
> That keeps blaring—
> Sense, sense, sense!
> so long as there's

A mind to remember
and a voice to
carry it on—
Never give up
keep at it!

But precisely what sympathetic readers should "keep at" is never specified beyond an implied striving for the same crude leveling Coffey himself sought.

The message of "Proletarian Portrait," on the other hand, seems all too clear. "A big young bareheaded woman / in an apron" takes off her shoe in public. "Looking / intently into it // She pulls out the paper insole / to find the nail // That has been hurting her." Direct action is the theme here; if a nail – or a boss – is hurting you, confront the problem directly, even if you must violate public decorum. Williams's title identifies the girl (whose apron shows she is fresh from someone's kitchen) as a "proletarian," and the political label, with its fashionable cachet at the time, gives the poem the obviousness of a propaganda poster. Not surprisingly, Ezra Pound disliked the poem for that reason. But it is possible that Williams intended the title ironically; note the grandiosity of an earlier title for this poem: "Study for a Figure representing Modern Culture" (540).

"The Yachts" (*CP1* 388–89) is the strongest poem of this book and Williams's most anthologized political poem. It is a curiously and unevenly divided poem, juxtaposing aesthetic and political views of the same objects: racing yachts. For eight stanzas, the poem is an aesthetic appreciation of these beautifully made yachts, which, like the well-made poems Williams admired, move with effortless grace and speed through their medium. Indeed, the sea, "lapping their glossy sides, as if feeling/for some slightest flaw," cannot sink them, for they are "the best man knows / to pit against [the ocean's] beatings." There is even a touch of envy, as the speaker notes that the yachts are "youthful ... free," and move with a grace that is "naturally to be desired."

Suddenly, with no transition, the ninth stanza transforms the perspective and attitude toward the yachts. We now see them from the water, amid a surrealistic "sea of faces ... an entanglement of watery bodies" struggling "in agony, in despair" to stay afloat:

Arms with hands grasping seek to clutch at the prows.
Bodies thrown recklessly in the way are cut aside . . ..

Broken,

beaten, desolate, reaching from the dead to be taken up
they cry out

The "skillful" yachts ignore their cries and "pass over" the victims.

Critics have long recognized that the last three stanzas present the yachts in a social context, as the playthings of the rich. Their luxury, the poem suggests, cannot exist without the drowning poor, to which the yachts – and their owners – are completely indifferent. Williams acknowledged that the poem is "a *very* vague imitation of Dante," a debt visible not in only the terza rima of the first two stanzas, but also in the horrific images of drowning bodies trying to save themselves.[11] Less obviously, several features of the first eight stanzas anticipate the shocking last three. Though man-made, the yachts, like great machines of a factory, dwarf the "ant-like" crew, which "crawls [over them] ... solicitously grooming them." They are indifferent to their servants, and pampered not only by the crew, but by racing in a "well guarded" arena (guarded not only by the land, but also perhaps by police to keep out the riff-raff). Like movie stars, they are "surrounded by/ lesser and greater craft which, sycophant, lumbering / and flittering follow them." All of these features make the yachts' indifference to the drowning poor somewhat less shocking.

But only somewhat. The poem's radical change of mode, from a semi-realistic narrative of action in stanzas 1–8 to the surrealistic, horrific scene of stanzas 9–11; its shift of perspective, from being on a par with the yachts (and beyond the ant-like crew) to being in the water with the drowning; and the speaker's accompanying shift of tone, from admiring the well-made yachts as art objects to implicitly damning them as toys of the remote rich – all these transformations continue to shock readers and daringly unbalance the poem. Twenty years after he wrote it, Williams called the poem's first section "a false situation which the yachts typify with the beauty of their movements" whereas "*the real situation* (of the poor) is desperate while 'the skillful yachts pass over'" (*CP*1 541, emphasis added). Although his empathy is obviously with the oppressed, and the poem implies a Marxist condemnation of the rich, Williams's perspective is not neatly Marxist. In an unpublished letter to Ezra Pound, he described the yacht race as a metaphor for Roosevelt's struggle against wealthy Republicans trying to block his New Deal programs, while the poor would ultimately be the losers (Mariani 370–71). His political perspective, therefore, is an unsettled mixture of liberalism and radicalism.

This same idiosyncratic politics informs the 1938 poem "The Poor" (*CP*1 452–53). The opening two lines would immediately disqualify it for inclusion in any radical literary magazine of the time: "It's the anarchy of poverty / delights me." Was one allowed to be "delighted" by any aspect of poverty in the 1930s? "[A]narchy" here means unexpected visual diversity in an age of increasing sameness: "among the new brick tenements" – all drearily alike, no doubt – the poem celebrates "the old/ yellow wooden house" (the same one as in "The Sun Bathers"?) that breaks up their monotony. The speaker discovers unexpected artistry: "a cast-iron balcony / with panels showing oak branches / in full leaf." Variety appears in "the dress of the children // reflecting every stage and / custom of necessity – " and in the houses of the poor: "Chimneys, roofs, fences of / wood and metal in an unfenced // age and enclosing next to / nothing at all." The people in this poem may be poor, but they are not *victims*: the children's motley clothing is not described as ragged or lice-infested; the fenced yards show pride of possession even if they enclose "next to nothing at all." And "unfenced age" sounds more like a swipe at a Marxist ideal (or was it New Deal leveling?) than a capitalist reality.

Finally, the poem focuses on one old man dressed comfortably – "in a sweater and soft black / hat" – who shows the same pride of place (even if it's a narrow place) by sweeping "his own ten feet" of the sidewalk. That he sweeps it in a wind that is "fitfully / turning his corner" and may therefore negate his efforts is no matter: the wind "has / overwhelmed the entire city." As with the economic disaster of the Depression, the whole city is affected; so one does the best one can. In retrospect, it is remarkable that *The New Republic* printed this poem in 1938: its anti-proletarian theme makes Williams sound like Frost, while its aesthetic delight in visual diversity links him to Cummings and recalls "The Sun Bathers."

Taken together, Williams's political poems of the 1930s resist categorical labels and are individual blends of the poet's liberal-leftism and aesthetic appreciation. If "Proletarian Portrait" and "An Early Martyr" are calls to action, and "The Yachts" conveys the Left's implacable hostility to the rich, poems like "The Sun Bathers" and "The Poor" (as well as "To a Poor Old Woman" and "Late for Summer Weather") refuse to stereotype the poor or to depict them as oppressed victims. That these political texts coexist with many imagistic poems from the same period shows that Williams's interest in political themes was not single-minded. And by the end of the 1930s, he was concerned with other poetic matters, namely his collage epic, *Paterson*.

Williams's fiction in this period reflects the same political qualities as his poetry: precise observation, empathy for ordinary, working-class people, and refusal to stereotype them by the prevailing leftist formulas. Because he found it difficult to publish his poetry in the 1930s, he turned to fiction, publishing two books of short stories – *The Knife of the Times* (1932) and *Life Along the Passaic River* (1938) – and the novel, *White Mule* (1937). The stories are often drawn from Williams's experiences doctoring, for example, the perennial problem of getting a recalcitrant child to swallow medicine in "The Use of Force."[12] Or they draw on his observations of the locale, for example, "Life Along the Passaic River," or capture the garage talk that ensues while "Doc" decides whether to splurge on new tires. In *White Mule*, the protagonists, Joe and Gurlie, are a working-class couple, but Joe, an *ex*-labor organizer, now owns his own shop and considers unions "a business like any other." Even more heretically, he becomes a strike-breaker and runs an open shop. One might have expected leftist critics to have damned the novel, but most praised it – as did apolitical critics – for its realistic dialogue and unsentimental characterization. Williams's critical reputation, in fact, steadily improved over the 1930s, particularly when his *Complete Collected Poems* appeared in 1938. Leftist critics who had earlier dismissed his poetry as a relic of the formalist 1920s, now recognized its capacity for growth and praised its empathy for and acute perceptions of everyday people and life.[13]

This growing critical esteem certainly did not apply to Williams's dealings with radical magazines in the 1930s or to his decisions to pull out of leftist causes he had just joined. Agile as a poet and fiction-writer, he was impulsive and maladroit in his everyday dealings with the Left. In particular, he had a knack for provoking condemnations with his blunt honesty and for stum-bling into cross-fires between the rival magazines, *Partisan Review* and *New Masses*. One example will suffice.[14] In April 1936, *Partisan Review and Anvil* (the two magazines had briefly merged) held a symposium on "Marxism and the American Tradition"; ten prominent writers, including Williams, were invited to respond. Obviously, the editors expected its leftist participants to affirm that Marxism did indeed fit well within the American tradition.[15] Though warned by a friend to be careful answering the survey, Williams expressed his view forthrightly and at length that "the American tradition is completely opposed to Marxism" (*SL* 157–58). To his surprise, *Partisan Review* printed his opinion, knowing the fur would fly. In the next issue, the editors summarized the storm of protest:

> The letters [responding to the Symposium] reflect a lively interest in the subject, which accounts, perhaps, for the spirited exceptions taken in most of them to William Carlos Williams' point of view. His "uninformed notions of Marxism and Americanism," to quote from one letter, are roundly condemned by most of the correspondents.[16]

Not content to summarize these slams, *Partisan Review* printed one letter against Williams, a long diatribe that insults not only his political sophistica-tion but his poetry. For good measure, the editors added their own disap-proval: "Needless to say, the editorial position of *Partisan Review* is utterly opposed to the direction of thought shown in Mr. Williams' contribution." But what really stands out in this heretic-burning is the bold-face title the editors gave to the brouhaha: **"Sanctions Against Williams."** Though "sanctions against" was probably intended to mean "disapproval of," the words and their prominence seem to call for punishment or retribution[17] – a shocking advocacy for a magazine purporting to stand for open-minded discussion. In any case, the magazine had singled out Williams, the dissenter, for abuse and ridicule. Williams was appalled by this response, but apparently undeterred: In the following year, he again became involved in a conflict with *PR*, tried to explain and justify his position in its pages, and again suffered a humiliating response.

The late 1940s and 1950s: the Library of Congress affair

As Williams devoted most of his poetic attention in the 1940s to his epic poem, *Paterson*, he wrote relatively few poems that could be considered political. Two notable exceptions, however, were "Russia" (*CP2* 144–47) and "Choral: The Pink Church" (*CP2* 177–80), appearing in 1948 and 1949 respectively.

"Russia," the more focused of the two, is a Whitmanesque plea to Russia and Russians to "come with me into / my dream" – a dream in which aesthetics and artists (Mayakovsky, Da Vinci) prevail, not politicians: "I do not call upon / a party to save me, nor a government / of whatever sort." But just as Auden despaired that "poetry makes nothing happen," the speaker realizes that he is "uninfluential"; thus, his dream is unworldly "folly," merely a contrasting "background / upon which" Russia, "idiot of the world," will build its empire. The concluding lines, however, are regrettably ambiguous: "background *upon which*" could be misread as the support or basis for Russia's empire-building. (Williams, of course, meant the opposite: his dreams are ineffectual and ignored, hence a contrasting background.) Moreover, the tone of a disappointed lover, spurned, who "dedicate[s]" his dreams to Russia and does "not/ resist you" conveys something less than strong condemnation. These elements left Williams open to the charge that he was soft on communism and supported Russian expansionism.[18]

Separated by two decades, "Russia" and the earlier "A Morning Imagination of Russia" are bookends to Williams's feelings about Russia. "Morning" expresses the poet's hopes for the new political experiment, "Russia" his forlorn despair that Stalinist Russia has disappointed those dreams and is now just another empire-builder.

About one prediction in "Russia" Williams was dead wrong. He assumes that the poem – "this paper" – will be "forgotten." It was not.

Just as he had misjudged the ideological intolerance and viciousness of leftist magazines in the 1930s, Williams also misjudged the anti-communist hysteria of the late 1940s and early 1950s. Or perhaps he simply ignored it.

Publishing "Russia" and "The Pink Church" at that time was tantamount to waving a red flag in front of a bull. And Williams had done more, publicly defending Ezra Pound during the Bollingen Prize controversy. When the bull inevitably charged, Williams was gored.

In September 1952, when it was announced that Williams had been appointed "Consultant in Poetry" to the Library of Congress, the Right struck. Virginia Kent Cummins, editor of *The Lyric* magazine and longtime foe of modernist poets, accused Williams of being a communist sympathizer, based on the poems "Russia" and "The Clouds" and on the many leftist causes he had supported in the 1930s (Mariani 651). Soon large-circulation newspapers picked up the story, the *Chicago Daily Tribune* calling "Russia" "the very voice of communism" (CP2 473). At the time, Williams was in poor health, having just suffered a second stroke, and received a three-month delay for beginning his official duties as Consultant. But before he could assume them, he was informed that the Librarian of Congress, Luther Evans, ordered that he must undergo a full investigation by the Civil Service Commission and the FBI. Cummins's accusations had done their work. When Williams's lawyer interceded, Evans revoked the appointment, citing not Williams's loyalty but his ill-health. The following year, however, Williams was again appointed, but Evans still insisted on the "loyalty and security procedures"; he then shelved the appointment. Evans's successor later wrote Williams that the Library of Congress had not even evaluated the FBI report and that, in any case, Williams's security status was not in question. Williams had the letter published in *The New York Times* to clear his name (Mariani 666–67).

Unlike so many writers whose loyalty had been challenged during the anti-communist hysteria, Williams never recanted his political poems of the late 1940s, nor his support of leftist groups and causes in the 1930s. Though he suffered from his lack of caution in challenging the political headwinds of his time and from others' willful misunderstanding of his work, he remained outspoken about his political beliefs throughout his life.

NOTES

1. In the late 1940s, Williams wrote to poet Babette Deutsch: "I AM a pink, plainly and finally. I am *not* a red" (qtd. in CP2 477). It says something about Williams's forthrightness and lack of caution that he uses the same word – "pink" – that anti-communist witch-hunters were using then to slur people and destroy their careers. Williams probably assumed that the FBI was not reading his mail.

2. See, for example, his brilliant story about a doctor's unsuccessful attempt to treat an indigent child's fatal infection: "Jean Beicke," in *Life Along the Passaic River*.
3. "I like him immensely as always ... [But] the man is sunk, in my opinion, unless he can shake the fog of fascism out of his brain ... which I seriously doubt that he can do" (letter to James Laughlin, 7 June 1939, in *SL* 184).
4. "Critically [in *The Waste Land*] Eliot returned us to the classroom just at the moment when I felt that we were on the point of an escape to matters much closer to the essence of a new art form itself – rooted in the locality which should give it fruit" (*A* 174).
5. This seems one of the few instances in which Williams sees Europe possessing something America might benefit from: a peasant culture. Yet that same culture mitigates against the social mobility that Williams saw as an essential quality of American life.
6. This socio-cultural critique, focusing on sexual exploitation, sounds remarkably similar to that of the poet Williams most despised: T. S. Eliot. Compare the sexual exploitations of "Lil," the typist, and the woman in the canoe in *The Waste Land*.
7. Qtd. in *CP1* 513. Cf., "the New England aristocracy" in the poem.
8. For a more detailed discussion of how writers underwent a kind of religious conversion to Marxism (in Malcolm Cowley's words), see Cowley, *The Dream of the Golden Mountains*, Chapter 4; Aaron, *Writers on the Left*, Chapter 6: and Cohen, *Beleaguered Poets and Leftist Critics*, Introduction.
9. Among the groups Williams either joined, attended meetings of, signed petitions of, or wrote essays for in the 1930s were the communist-sponsored League of American Writers, the American Federation of Writers, the American Writers Congress, the Committee for Cultural Freedom, the League for Cultural Freedom and Socialism, and the Committee of 400.
10. "Art and Politics: The Editorship of *BLAST*" (1933); rpt. in *ARI* 75, 78. The context of Williams's declaration reflects both the magazine's communist platform and readership: "This magazine holds that in order to serve the cause of the proletariat [the writer] must not under any circumstances debase his art ..."
11. *CP1* 541. Canto VII of the *Inferno* describes the wrathful in the river Styx struggling to pull themselves aboard the tiny skiff carrying Virgil and Dante. When he was in Paris, Williams may have seen Delacroix's magnificent rendering of this scene in the Louvre. *The Divine Comedy* uses terza rima throughout; Williams abandoned the rhyme scheme after two stanzas, but kept the stanzaic structure of three long lines.
12. Interestingly, this story is now frequently anthologized.
13. See, for example, Ruth Lechlitner's extensive survey of his work in *Poetry*, September 1939, 326–35.
14. For a detailed discussion of Williams's political travails, see Cohen, "Stumbling Into Cross-fires," *Journal of Modern Literature* 32 (Winter 2009): 143–59.
15. For example, the CP-USA's slogan of the same time: "Communism is 20th Century Americanism."
16. "Correspondence," *Partisan Review* III.4 (May 1936): 30.

17. Mariani, for examples, asserts "the editors were *calling for* "Sanctions Against Williams" (389, emphasis added). Leibowitz makes the same assumption (322).
18. Williams was much clearer about his anti-Stalinism in his letters. To Babette Deutsch he states: "I particularly detest ... the Dictatorship not of the proletariat but of such rats as Stalin and all his kind" (qtd. in *CP2* 477). See also his letter to Seldon Rodman about "Russia" (*CP2* 473).

7

ALEC MARSH

William Carlos Williams and the prose of pure experience

William Carlos Williams was two kinds of writer: the unpretentious presenter of "objective" local particulars and a breathless surrealist. His poetry ranges from the stark reportage of "The Raper from Passenack" (1935)[1] – to enigmas like "Crustaceous /wedge/ of sweaty kitchens" (*CP*1 211) in *Spring and All*. Williams could write "The Descent of Winter," an improvisatory poetry journal published in Ezra Pound's *Exile* # 4 in October 1928 and, that same year, the straight *A Voyage to Pagany*, his "first serious novel." Edith Heal called it "fictionalized recall"(*IWWP* 45, 47); we might call it "creative non-fiction." Underneath *Voyage's* conventional surface is a quest narrative of an American searching for the sources of imaginative power,[2] yet deeply distrustful of art, a familiar position for the culturally colonized American writer, who yearns like Emerson for an "original relation to the universe," not one inherited from the English fathers; including, in Williams's case, his own. An innocent artist abroad, "He wanted to write – that was all, and not to have written, but to be writing ... To be feeling it in his mind and his fingers as it flowed out" (*VP* 15) Williams wrote of his thinly disguised alter ego, Dev Evans.

To hear Williams tell it, it was all "writing" – the poetry, the prose, all one. "It *is* that prose and verse are both *writing*" he insisted with some frustration to Parker Tyler in a 1948 letter: "prose and verse are to me the same thing" (Williams's emphasis, *SL* 263). Both are writing, for sure, but they are not the same thing when written; Williams never could explain just what he meant.

There are two contradictory trends of Williams's prose: surrealism and realism. The first is his "own version of Dadaist 'automatic' writing'" (Schmidt, qtd. Boone 3)[3]; or, in accord with André Breton's 1924 definition of surrealism as "psychic automatism in its pure state, by which one proposes to express – verbally, by means of the written word ... the actual functioning of thought"(qtd. Peterson 34). Williams was very much aware of surrealism and surrealist writing: in 1929 he translated Philippe Soupault's *Last Nights of Paris*; from 1927 he read Eugene Jolas's journal *transition* with attention

(Tashjian 7); he knew personally many of the surrealists when they lived in New York, among them Picabia and Duchamp in the nineteen teens, and during the Second World War, another wave of surrealist refugees, including Breton himself. Williams can be considered "a Dada-Surrealist prose poet" (Peterson 34).

It is convenient if not quite true to claim that Williams's surrealist phase did not survive the 1920s. *A Novelette*, begun in January 1929 would be its last gasp in that account. But with Williams there are no well defined "phases." He began publishing "proletarian fiction" in the *New Masses*, a Communist organ, as early as 1926. In the thirties he wrote much politically engaged, realist prose – some fifty short stories, two novels, major essays – including "The American Background" (1934) – yet in the forties, *Paterson* (1946–1951) uses all of the avant-garde forms he explored in the 1920s and more. If, in the 1950s, working for the respectable Random House, Williams wrote a lot of straight prose – he finished the Stecher trilogy of novels, an autobiography and penned plays – he also conceived sprawling poetry, such as "The Desert Music" (1951) that can fairly be called "projective verse."

Williams's 1920s prose experiments

In the 1920s the dadaist-surrealist Williams wrote two significant experimental fictions; besides *A Novelette*, *The Great American Novel* has been read as a post-modern "anti-novel" *avant la lettre* (*I* 155). Pound, who would call Williams "the best prose writer and poet in America" (*P/W* 51) admired the piece, which was pulled together immediately after Williams had put down Joyce's *Ulysses*. His competitive instincts riled, Williams wrote Pound, who was looking for some prose for William Bird's Three Mountains Press series that would include Pound's mock-autobiography *Indiscretions* (1923), and most famously, Hemingway's *in our time* (1924): "Just finished Ulysses. . . . It encourages me to champion my own particular form of stupidity – or knowledge or intelligence or lackknowledge. It is the first of the return from the desert." He had "about fifty pages of prose bits" he had "spilled" in the last decade, "a miscellaneous lot" to be called "PROSE." (*P/W* 65). Despite this unpromising introduction, Bird published *The Great American Novel* in 1923.

Williams's response to Pound's acceptance indicates that Ezra vociferously approved Williams's prose, though he must have called the work "thoughtless" and "intuitive," terms that resonate throughout the critical reception of Williams's "fiction" – if that's what it is (*P/W* 66). Williams told Zukofsky that "Joyce had nothing to do with my development. Even when I seem to resemble him most (in The Gt. Am. Novel)" (*WCW/LZ* 77), but Chapter III of *The Great American Novel* is probably quoting Pound's response when it begins "It is Joyce with a difference." The difference being greater "opacity" (a quality Pound valued in Williams [See *I* 11]). "Less erudition, reduced power of perception" (*I* 167) – all this sounds like Pound. In any case Pound is nearby, for Williams quotes from another letter of response to *Kora in Hell* in the next paragraph; viz. that the French would be reminded of Rimbaud (see *P/W* 44). Certainly, Williams was measuring himself against Joyce, dreading the inevitable comparison; "In other words it comes after Joyce, therefore it is no good, of no use but a secondary local usefulness like the Madison Square Garden tower copied from Seville – it is of no absolute good. It is not NEW. It is not an invention" (*I* 168). He inoculates himself against the criticism he expects to get. If it's American, it's a copy, brashly inauthentic – a baroque Spanish tower on an arena – for "class"!

The resentment of the post-colonial writer is everywhere in Williams, never more flamboyantly than in this *Great American Novel*, a title to be read as a contradiction in terms. For great American literature cannot exist. The resentful ex-British colonial is a comforting pose for Williams: "I am far under them," he snorts, gesturing vaguely to cultural oppressors, "I am less, far less if you will. I am a beginner. I am an American. A United Stateser" he says bitterly, "Yes, it's ugly, there is no word to say it better" (*I* 175). Then he goes on a revealing rant, a veritable barbaric yawp: "For the moment I hate you, I hate your orchestras, your libraries, your sciences, your yearly salons, your finely tuned intelligences of all sorts. My intelligence is as finely tuned as yours but it lives in hell, it is doomed to eternal – perhaps eternal – shiftings after what?" (*I* 175–76). What indeed, if not cultural authority unavailable in these benighted States until the liberation of the American language from English cultural domination.

The value of Joyce, his "real, if hidden, service" is that "[h]e has in some measure liberated words. Freed them for their proper uses. He has to … a great measure destroyed what is known as 'literature.' *For me as an American* it is his only important service" (my emphasis *I* 169). Joyce's Irishness is crucial; when Williams speaks, as he frequently does, of "setting words free" he means to free them from the dead hand of the English colonizer.

The Great American Novel bristles with self-conscious competitive anxiety, against "literature," against his contemporaries, against the United States itself. The end of the work shows a nostalgia for an older frontier America, epitomized by Appalachia (although tellingly, this section is plagiarized [*P/W* 67])! But Williams turns to the dangers of industrial work (mercury, thermometer making) spending the last page on explaining "shoddy," a word that has slipped into American English as a synonym for cheaply made. Shoddy means a kind of recycled wool fiber cloth. We are told how shoddy army coats, cheap working men's shirts and even shoddy quilts are made. It's surely an allegory of an America addicted to sharp-practice and the production of clever simulacra; somehow, Williams's "novel" is implicated too. Its final words seem heavily ironic: "You've seen this fake oilcloth they are advertising now. Congoleum. Nothing but building paper with a coating of enamel" (*I* 227). Congoleum becomes the fitting symbol for our American "culture of purchase, a culture in effigy" (*SE* 147) – in short, our cultural simulacrum driven by money made from shoddy goods and imported store-bought traditions. This mélange became the America Williams celebrated, sardonically, in his great American novel.

A Novelette is far more "experimental." Written in the intervals between calls during a flu epidemic, it feels disjointed and frantically self-conscious – "Better to learn to write and to make a smooth page no matter what the incoherence of the day, no matter what erasures must be sacrificed to improve a lying appearance to keep ordered the disorder of the paperless actual," he mutters. Don't we see that "The compositions that are smoothed, consecutive are disjointed. They bear no relation to anything in the world or in the mind" (*I* 274–75). The disjointed quality of *Novelette* is in the service of a more accurate mimesis. Here Williams repeats Breton's belief in "psychic automatism" in the service of accurately representing the "actual functioning of thought."

Williams makes a show of his anti-symbolism; "End the obscure with the actual. End the obscure allusion, the involved symbolism. Here none" (*I* 292). But, just six pages later he devotes a magnificent paragraph to "the great mullein" epitomizing the "expression of melancholy ruin." Its "large outer leaves have faded and lost form, and become mere brown rags, like the tatters of miserable poverty, drenched in the rains of winter and draggled on the mud of the cold inhospitable earth" (*I* 298). Altogether, a beautiful paragraph in the best 19th Century style, as smooth as a page can be; and incidentally the most memorable paragraph in *A Novelette*.

Williams made a virtue of haste; he claimed he just reacted, bragging to Zukofsky,

> When I am busiest with my trade as a physician (consequently have the least time for writing) I have the swiftest, most abundant stimulus to write and get the most done ... It is the only way in which I can work with mad speed. It has to be and it is. It is lucky maybe – maybe I lack the inhibitions which would make me stop when I had done – and need a physical knife to cut me off from the paper (*WCW/LZ* 79).

This hasty quality is found in *A Novelette*, which takes "doctrinaire formula-worship" (*I* 279) as enemy number one. Even so, when it was sent off to Pound in 1932, Williams put it together with a miscellany of "Other Prose" giving a full sample of his familiarity with a variety of formulas. It's all prose and it's all *writing*, but it's not verse, and *A Novelette* and "The Accident" excepted, not even "creative writing"; nor are these "literary experiments." Taken together they show Williams as an anxious, earnest figure, saying in effect: "look at me being spontaneous." This earnestness informs his major modern work of the time, which from the improvisations of *Kora in Hell* (1920) to "From: A Folded Skyscraper" (1927) and "The Descent of Winter" (1928) featured hybrids of prose and verse, brilliantly fulfilled in *Spring and All* (1923), a lecture-demonstration considering mimesis and its problems. There, the prose lectures, while the verse demonstrates mimesis without representation – that's the idea. There is nothing Dada in the sequence, no matter its reputed debt to Apollinaire (Perloff 112). Actually, Williams is engaged in a classic metaphysical struggle to accurately register reality through the imperfect medium of language. He appreciates "the virtual impossibility of lifting [via writing] to the imagination those things which lie under the direct scrutiny of the senses" (*SE* 11).

Spring and All is far more derivative of Emerson, Whitman and William James than the French. Like later Williams, including *The Wedge* and *Paterson, Spring and All* is in what Richard Poirier called "the Emersonian Tradition"[4] which signally worried about that "original relation to the universe" demanded by Emerson at the opening of *Nature* a new "poetry and philosophy of insight" rather than "build[ing] the sepulchers of the fathers" (Emerson 7). He is seconded by Henry Thoreau on top of Mt. Ktaadn, notionally the first being ever there, who in the face of "primeval, untamed, and forever untamable *Nature*," cries out: "Think of our life in nature, –daily to be shown matter, to come in contact with it, rocks, trees, wind on our cheeks! the *solid* earth! the *actual* world! the *common* sense! *Contact*! *Contact*!" (Thoreau's emphasis 645–46), thereby anticipating Williams's keyword in a frantic attempt to experience existence unmediated by culture. "There is a constant barrier between the reader and his consciousness of immediate contact with the world" Williams complains (*CP1* 177), sounding the same note of impatience as Walt Whitman in *Leaves of Grass* when he laments the cold mechanics of printing that come between poet and reader (Whitman 69). Like Thoreau throughout *Walden*, Williams dares his reader to know "what he is at the exact moment that he is" (*CP1* 178). Thoreau-like he "improve[s] the nick of time" and like him wishes to "stand on the meeting of two eternities, the past and future" (Thoreau 336); the fleeting moment of being here now. But how to preserve that moment in writing? How to write, as Dev Evans wished, rather than "to have written"? How to be reading, not to have read?

Williams denied that he was in a long line of American writers[5] to whom this problem was as vital as it was to himself; besides, he knows that just because he is writing, he is already being written; that is, he is "plagiarizing" the thoughts of others. The only answer is to "destroy the world" (*CP1* 179); that is, to destroy culture and with it the dead language accumulated in literature: "the greatest characteristic of the present age is that it is stale – stale as literature – " (*CP1* 219). The only possible point to Williams's conceit of the annihilation of the human species and its eternal return is that culture, including literature, had disappeared.[6] Because "EVOLUTION HAS REPEATED ITSELF FROM THE BEGINNING" as the "perfect plagiarism," so "the imagination, drunk with prohibitions, has destroyed and recreated everything afresh in the likeness of that which it was. Now indeed men look about in amazement at each other with a full realization of the meaning of 'art' " (*CP1* 181). Only in its absence can we realize "the meaning of art"; only in its absence can art be made anew. But art can never be absent as long as there is language. So "The Traditionalists of Plagiarism" hold sway (*CP1* 182).

These wishes are not to be taken literally, any more than "we the people of the United States" [even this is a plagiarism] should go "to Europe armed to kill every man, woman and child in the area west of the Carpathian Mountains (also east) sparing none" (*CP1* 178). To imagine "the new world naked" is to regress to the state of what Freud calls "infantile wishing" and Williams calls "baby promises": "The man of imagination who turns to art for release and fulfillment of his baby promises contends with the sky through layers of demoded words and shapes" (*CP1* 188) – this, evidently, is the meaning of "excrement of some sky" in *Spring and All*. "The pure products of America" (*CP1* 217–18) are made crazy because language hides rather than reveals reality.

Like a bee trapped in a bottle, Williams's "gyrations" (*CP1* 209) throughout *Spring and All* are a series of attempts to write his way to the other side of language as though language too could just be new and never refer. No transcendentalist, he has "rejected religious dogmatism" (*CP1* 202) and, as a physician, Williams is an empiricist, so the only way out of the impasse of referentiality is to embrace "experience," to overcome his own subjectivity and somehow merge with the things, to complete oneself in them: "My whole life has been spent (so far) in seeking to place a value upon experience and the objects of experience that would satisfy my sense of inclusiveness without redundancy – completeness, lack of frustration with the liberty of choice; the 'things' which the pursuit of 'art' offers –"(*CP1*

202). Williams wants art to complete experience, not to represent it; he says later, "works of art ... must give not the sense of frustration but a sense of completion, of actuality – It is not a matter of 'representation' – much may be represented actually, but of separate existence" (*CP*1 204). By completing experience in the "imagination" the work of art achieves a "separate existence." The "proof" of "the work of the imagination [is] not 'like' anything but transfused with the same forces which transfuse the earth" (*CP*1 207). The earth, or mundane experience, is to be recorded "at the moment when the consciousness is enlarged by the sympathies and the unity of understanding which the imagination gives"; Williams wishes to perfect and to "practice skill in recording the force moving, then to know it, in the largeness of its proportions" (*CP*1 206). Here Williams touches what William James called "radical empiricism," like James, Williams is intent on capturing the "world of pure experience" as that pluralistic "blooming, buzzing confusion" that it really is (James 233).

James clarifies Williams. Like Williams an empiricist (and an MD) James's psychology is fundamentally concerned with mimesis because, like Williams, he understands that experience trumps ideas; our feelings mirror our reality. But, James writes, "even if feeling do[es] mirror the reality exactly, still it *is* not that reality itself" (James 75) – just what bothers Williams. Yet, "Experience molds us every hour and makes of our minds a mirror of the time-and-space connections between the things of this world" (James 76). These connections are not a one-to-one impress of the world onto our minds – a relation some philosophers have called truth. Rather, James says in a *New York Times* interview of 1907 "Mind *engenders* truth *upon* reality ... Our minds are not here simply to copy a reality that is already complete. They are here to complete it, to add to its importance by their own remodeling of it, to decant its contents over, so to speak, into a more significant shape" (James's emphasis 448). There is no evidence that Williams read this interview, but by calling James's "significant shape" the poem, we approach Williams from the proper pragmatic direction. "Poetry" Williams claims, is "new form dealt with as a reality in itself" (*CP*1 219). And James's sexual imagery speaks to the erotic charge Williams's enthusiasm for the real often carries.

So what does Williams think prose should do? "Prose: statement of facts concerning emotions, intellectual states, data of all sorts – technical expositions, jargon, of all sorts – fictional and other –" (*CP*1 219). This definition is why I call the prose sections of the poem lectures. "Prose, relieved of extraneous, unrelated values must return to its only purpose: to clarity to enlighten the understanding." Unlike poetry, "There is no form to prose but that which depends on clarity. If prose is not accurately adjusted to the exposition of facts it does not exist – Its form is that alone" (*CP1* 226). We may wonder if, in this case, the "prose" of *Spring and All* is prose at all. Clear it ain't!

Prose or poetry, Williams gravitates toward the mimetic problem: "the writer of imagination" does not wish to "disassociate" his words from "natural objects and specified meanings" but to "liberate" them "from the usual quality of that meaning by transposition into another medium, the imagination" (*CP1* 235). Later, Williams would reformulate the entire problem into the equivocal slogan: "No ideas but in things" a premise not nearly as materialistic as it seems.

Transposed into Jamesian terms, Williams's meaning clarifies. The pragmatist, James declares, "turns away from abstraction and insufficiency, from [merely] verbal solutions" and he "turns towards concreteness and adequacy, towards facts, towards action and towards power. That means the empiricist temper regnant and the rationalist temper sincerely given up. It means the open air and possibilities of nature, as against dogma, artificiality, and the pretence of finality in truth" (James 379). In Williams's words: imagination is "dynamiz[ed]" to "free the world of fact from the impositions of 'art' ... and to liberate the man to act in whatever direction his disposition leads" (*CP1* 235).

Williams's "careless" realism

When not a surrealist, Williams wrote a form of social realism, "tough and honest," as Robert Halsband observed, reviewing *Make Light of It: Collected Stories* in 1950. He qualified his praise somewhat, noting "if by a story is meant a plotted and structured narrative, then it would be difficult to find one in this collection" (Doyle 229). Babette Deutsch, a friend reviewing the same collection compared Williams to Chekhov: observing how the two physicians look "at the daily commonplace with the alert, amoral eyes of the doctor, both setting down their observations with rare fidelity to the facts" (Doyle 227). The heady compliment is double-edged, however, as "there is a gulf" betwixt the two; Deutsch notes in Williams a "carelessness not to be expected from one who writes such notable poetry. He will introduce irrelevant details, tack on superfluous content, dwell on trivia that have caught his fancy. Nevertheless, his ear for the vocabulary, the speech rhythms, the tone of voice of ordinary men and women, boys and girls, in the midst of situations important to them, makes these pages startlingly come alive ... " (Doyle 228).

Perhaps Williams's "carelessness" is his more faithful realism. These stories reveal his trust in ordinary speech and distrust of artfulness. When art meets life, we think, art must somehow impose itself to give raw experience some kind of dramatic shape. But Williams wishes to avoid shapely narratives, wanting to let things happen as they happened. A problematic approach at best, but part of the experiment of telling it like it really is. Speaking of the poetry, Paul Mariani argues that "the unfinished feel of some of his poems was there by careful attention to the overall design, not because of carelessness or insouciance" (Mariani 206) – ditto the prose.

In a chapter of *The Autobiography* called significantly, "The Practice," Williams dwells on his double practice as physician and writer, "that one occupation complements the other" (*A* 359).

> My business, aside from the mere physical diagnosis, is to make a different sort of diagnosis concerning them as individuals, ... And when one is able to reveal them to themselves, high or low, they are always grateful as they are surprised that one can so have revealed the inner secrets of another's private motives. To do this is what makes a writer worth heeding ... he has gone to the base of the matter to lay it bare before us in terms ... we cannot in the end escape. (*A* 358)

Williams searches for "the evasive life of the thing, to phrase the words in such a way that stereotype will yield a moment of insight. That is where the difficulty [of writing] lies. We are lucky when that underground current can be tapped and the secret spring of all our lives will send up its pure water." But that "seldom happens" because "our lying habits of everyday speech and thought are foremost, telling us that *that* is what 'they' want to hear" (*A* 358–59). The "underground current" is certainly an image of the unconscious mental life: James's famous "stream of thought," the "psychic transitions, always on the wing ... not to be glimpsed except in flight" (WWJ 44). James continues in another place concerning the truth: "we may glimpse it, but we never grasp it ... (WWJ 453). This same glimpse is found in Williams's *Autobiography*: "We catch a glimpse of something, from time to time, which shows us that a presence has just brushed past us, some rare thing – just when the smiling little Italian woman has left us. For a moment we are dazzled. What was that? We can't name it ... " (*A* 360).

This glimpse of being Williams tries to capture in his short fictions. It requires a delicate touch. Any self-consciousness on the part of the writer will kill it. The solution was to keep the stories as close to the actual as possible, not with self-conscious avant-garde tricks, but through a plain rendition of the moment that rare bird of Being brushed past.

In the thirties, when most of Williams's short stories were written, Williams was trying out an anti-"art" aesthetic, searching, as he wrote in an unpublished review of the Communist poet H.H. Lewis, for a "proletarian *style*" as a way of resisting "the older verse forms and practices" typified by Eliot

(*STS* 71). He appreciated Lewis's "fervid sincerity that flows in his blood" (*STS* 71). This aesthetic informs Williams's short narratives.

In December 1931, Williams wrote to Zukofsky asking about George Oppen's remark "about sincerity being not in the writer but in the writing." (*WCW/LZ* 118). In Williams's short stories, the word combinations that matter are *not* the doctor-narrator's words. Absolute faithfulness to one's perception means trusting *the language of the other*, not one's own. Williams's tales are almost entirely as acts of *listening*. They are interested in embodied speech – the speech of the people; it depends on them to tell the story. His imaginative contribution is to record with intense and sincere imaginative sympathy just as he does when listening to a patient. Diagnosis is effected by listening – in the broadest sense of the word – to the patient's condition. "The plight of the poor in a rich country, I wrote it down as I saw it," he told Edith Heal; "The times – that was the knife that was killing them" (*IWWP* 49).

The "times" means the Great Depression, which politicized the arts. Although, like Pound, Laughlin and Gorham Munson, Williams took up Social Credit as the cure for what ailed capitalism, he was on the left wing of the movement, engaged throughout the 1930s with Communist journals and left-wing writing. Michael Rozendal marks his "substantial involvement both in the decade's politically radicalized literary communities and in one of the thirties' most important genres," namely the "proletarian story" (Rozendal 137).

> From the 1926 publication of Williams's "The Five Dollar Guy" in the first issue of *The New Masses* through the headline billing of his "The Paid Nurse" in the 1939 first issue of *The New Anvil*, Williams is strikingly involved in radical publications with a left political bent. The consistency and breadth of his contributions, including translations of a miner's story from the French and republican ballads from the Spanish, mark this as much more than a phase of moonlighting. ... A recovery of the thirties little magazines forces a reconsideration of Williams as "one of the best known writers in the 'left wing' camp of American literature" ... as he was hailed by a 1934 issue of *The Magazine*. (Rozendal 138)

Williams appeared on the masthead as "advisory editor" of Fred Miller's *Blast: A Magazine of Proletarian Short Stories* that ran for five issues (September 1933–November 1934) (Rozendal 144). Each issue featured a Williams story, among them his finest: "Jean Beicke," "The Use of Force," "The Dawn of Another Day," "The Girl with a Pimply Face," and "A Night in June" (Mariani 345).

Rozendal's left-wing Williams in the "relatively marginalized decade" of the thirties, helps us read the tragic tale "Jean Beicke" as deft political allegory. When the doctors who tried to save her realized that they'd failed to detect the infant's fatal infection:

> I called up the ear man and he came down at once.
>   A clear miss, he said. I think if we'd gone in there
>   earlier, we'd have saved her.
> For what? Said I. Vote the straight Communist ticket.
> Would it make us any dumber? said the ear man.   (FD 166)

Rozendal correctly close-reads bleak "Jean Beicke" as a story of the failure of American medicine as an expression of capitalism. Properly contextualized, we understand the ending as saying – since the doctors might get smarter, why not vote the Communist ticket (Rozendal 148). Peter Halter's view that the doctors should blame themselves, not "society" for their failure – as if that is somehow irresponsible (RB 172)[7] can't work. Nor can we answer the narrator's rhetorical question, "For what?" means "It's not so bad we couldn't save her because she'd probably grow up to become a Communist." In other words, Communism is not the problem but the solution for cases like Jean's. The allegorical critique is clear: the failure of our politics to go in "earlier" – and here FDR's "New Deal" may well be meant – to diagnose and cure the total failure of American capitalism to fulfill its democratic promise.

Williams's proletarian fictions are the antithesis of *The Great American Novel* of a decade earlier. The power of these tales comes from their "reality." They seem like real-life because to a very large degree they are real-life. Their very freshness and rawness has recommended Williams's "Doctor Stories" to the curricula of medical schools who wish to remind would-be physicians that their eventual patients are human beings and that their job – keeping people alive – is ultimately impossible. Presumably the Communist political matrix is not stressed.

Although not in Gish's opinion, "fundamentally a political writer," (Gish 83), Williams actively wrote against the Depression. *The Collected Stories of William Carlos Williams* (1996) (first published by New Directions in 1950) contains fifty-two stories in all, There are many more stories, perhaps a hundred (Gish 79), most written before 1940. They reflect the remarkable resilience of those struggling in them – including the doctor narrator who is indistinguishable from Williams himself. Still, in a review of the 1961 republication, Arthur Kay noticed that aside from "dramatic monologues," Williams deployed a variety of forms, most of them verging on the artless; "vignettes, plotless slices, pieces, and hunks of life; straightforward autobiography; essays and descriptive sketches illustrated with anecdote and dialogue" (Doyle 332). "Verbal Transcription: 6 A.M." is, evidently just that. "A Difficult Man" and "The Insane" are not much more than dinner table conversations. Two of the stories were amputated from novels: "The Venus" and "The Zoo."

The realist thrust of this writing is overwhelming. "I have been watching speech in my own environment from which I continually expect to discover whatever of new is being reflected about the world" (*SL* 129), Williams wrote Kay Boyle in his 1932 "Open Letter" when he was "working with prose" (*SL* 130). "Watching speech" is a curious phrase – not listening to it. I take "watching" to mean tending, caring for, as in *minding* the language. He continues, "I have been actively at work … in the flesh, watching how words match the act, especially how they come together" (*SL* 130). This is not just about poetry; Williams notes that "art can be made of anything – provided it be seen, smelt, touched, apprehended and understood to be what it is – the flesh of a constantly repeated permanence" (*SL* 130). For Williams, words are the flesh of the world's body. Writing is a kind of palpation, the diagnostic therapeutic touch. Williams tends to language as he would care for one of his patients, alert for all kinds of new discoveries – new only in their "constantly repeated permanence" as the bodies he touches as a physician are all different – yet the same. That is how speech behaves, as the flesh of the world – the same phrases made new by each new speaker.

On occasion Williams took his mimetic impulse too far – a different kind of carelessness than that remarked on by Babette Deutsch. "The Five Dollar Guy," (which, curiously, is not among *The Collected Stories*) published in the first issue of the *New Masses* in 1926 tells the tale of "a woman friend of his who'd been … propositioned by the owner of a local oil company." In "the heat of getting the story down, he'd failed to change the names of the people involved, including the name of the oil company" Paul Mariani reports. The bourgeoisie took its revenge when Williams found himself involved in a $15,000 law suit. Williams "tried to explain that he'd heard the whole story from a woman pal of his, but she – understandably – signed a statement denying she'd ever told the doctor any such thing." He settled and wound up paying $5,000 in damages – a year's salary. "How many times" had Flossie told him "to make sure he changed names and places if he was going to publish something" (Mariani 253–55)! "The Five Dollar Guy," while "a clean piece of writing" (Mariani 254) was not a fiction.

Even Williams's experimental writing was mimetic to a fault. When Pound accepted *The Great American Novel* (1923) Williams warned him that "The mountain part – the sugar head – I copied verbatim from the Ladies Home Journal" (*P/W* 67).[8] Just because it is mimetic, plagiarism interested Williams – it is a significant theme in *Spring and All*. In Williams's mind, pasting in a piece from the *Ladies Home Journal* was no different than Duchamp appropriating a snow shovel, or even a urinal, and calling it art (see Halter 16–21). As Bryce Conrad discovered *In the American Grain* is marked by instances of plagiarism (Conrad 162–66) and there is the notorious case of Marcia Nardi's letters inserted into *Paterson*.

Could there be a connection? Could the dadaist concept of *art trouvé*, which justifies his use of "found" texts in *The Great American Novel*, underwrite Williams's transcriptive practice in his short fiction? Williams's unwillingness to reshape the materials suggests he was wary of tampering with his speakers' original expression for fear of compromising the live quality of their voices. Williams wanted to carry the living word into print and his politically motivated sincerity made it easy to "forget" to change the names of his informants. The sudden publication of *The Knife of the Times* by a small press caused a perverse flurry of anxiety in Williams. He wrote Richard Johns, editor of *Pagany*, that the release of the story collection left him "frightened lest the stories turn out to be bad. I've read them again but haven't the least idea whether there is any worth in them. Hell, sometimes I wish I had never written a word – or else nothing but incomprehensible jargon. There is too intimate a contact between one's intimate mind and an antagonistic public in all that might be worthwhile" (qtd. Mariani 324). For the first time Williams was seeing the stories as a printed book, which implied a bourgeois readership that judged "worth" by received literary standards. Reading through these eyes, Williams felt the rawness, the intimacy in the stories undisguised by the arts of fiction. He wishes instead for the "incomprehensible jargon" of his dadaist writing, where no one could draw personal inferences. From this perspective, modernist experimentation looked like an elaborate defense against intimacy – and human reality. Mariani comments on how Williams "had listened to his patients for years confess their deepest secrets to him as he examined them. He had listened with sympathy and compassion, while they spoke of broken promises and of fears never even uttered to their spouses" (Mariani 324) and Williams had refused to judge them. Now he had exposed that secret material to the judgment and condescension of the world. In the event, Williams needn't have worried. The publisher was a good printer, but no business man; nothing was done to sell the book so almost nobody was aware of it, least of all Williams's patients (Mariani 324).

If the fragmented jargon of Dada flirts with the incomprehensible, Williams's proletarian realism flirted with literary worthlessness, simply because the fate of working-class people – as people – had no value, depreciated by the middle classes as vulgar, the Communists were only interested in mobilizing "the masses," not in individual "cases."

The Stecher trilogy

Just as Williams's proletarian writing from as early as 1926 belies any simple designation of the twenties as a decade devoted to avant-garde experimentation, his associations with *Pagany*, Richard Johns's "native quarterly" review (1930–1933) and his own *Contact* (co-edited with Nathanael West, three issues in 1932), as well as the *Harvard Advocate* (edited by undergraduate James Laughlin); complicates the sense just given that in the thirties Williams was dedicated to doctrinaire social realism. The artsy, bourgeois complications amidst which *White Mule*, the story of an infant girl, was conceived and born are symptoms of a personal crisis in Williams's career as a writer.

He would be fifty in 1933, respected, but neither financially successful nor well-known. His best work, published by obscure presses in limited editions was almost impossible to find. In December 1931 Williams's *Collected Poems 1921–1931* was in limbo going the rounds of the New York publishers, "a nice book too, big and fat and willing to go to bed with anyone fer a price" he wrote Pound. "But I don't want no cheap guys," Williams added. "I wants a reglar publisher, what knows how to do it, you get me, with a limousine, flowers, a swell feed and, you know, three or four times one after the other, just like that, way up and hard" (*P/W* 113 and see Mariani 322). Underneath the tiresome ribaldry that marks the poets' letters, Williams is clearly wishing for some worldly success. His actual need for money and his psychological need for recognition as a significant writer would only become more acute as the Depression worsened.

In that same letter Williams mentioned that he was writing a serial novel, *White Mule*, for *Pagany*. The story was of Flossie's infancy, enriched by Williams's experience as a pediatrician. The project was noticed by young James Laughlin, just returned from his "semester" at Pound's "Ezuversity" in Rapallo. Laughlin had been in touch with Williams since he was an eighteen-year-old sophomore, now age 21, backed by generous relatives, he started a firm called New Directions and offered to print *White Mule* (*WCW/JL* viii–ix). Williams's elated reply is famous; "Dear God" it begins. "You mention, casually, that you are willing to publish my White Mule, that you will pay for it and that we shall then share, if any, the profits! My God!" (*WCW/JL* 5). Young Laughlin would become Williams's wished-for fancy-man. Thus, one of the most important cultural collaborations and cultural institutions in the history of 20th Century American literature was born. Williams, even more than Pound became "the cornerstone of New Directions" (*WCW/JL* 13).

Laughlin went all in. *White Mule* was printed in June 1937 (1,100 copies, although only 500 were available immediately for sale, causing problems when these rapidly sold out and no more could be had); *Life Along the Passaic River* (1938) 1,000 copies; Laughlin reprinted *In The American Grain* in 1939 and *White Mule's* sequel *In the Money* (1,500 copies) in 1940, as well as *The Complete Collected Poems of William Carlos Williams 1906–1938* (1,500 copies) (see Emily Wallace, *Bibliography* [1968] and *WCW/JL* ix).

Philip Rahv of *The Nation* was moved to something like rapture by *White Mule* (see Doyle 144); Alfred Kazin called it "a superb example" of a poet's novel at its thoughtful best: "Open Dr. Williams's book and you are in a new world of sound. Accents cling to the air. The harmony is the rough, gravely ironic rhythm of public speech. Like James Joyce ... Williams has his characters talk with such a native freshness that the sound is never obtrusive. It is a pure speech because it is so richly characteristic, and its utter realism is therefore deeper, more meaningful than the violent accuracy of naturalism" (Doyle 141).

The first two books reminded reviewers of Joyce, Dos Passos and James T. Farrell: realism 20th Century style. Williams perfectly rendered colloquial American speech and provided "objectivist" detail; "a splendidly written and completely honest book" in the words of one reviewer (qtd. in Montiero 54). The two novels are solid pieces of work, written chapter by chapter, each has its own unity. They feel like "real life"; especially the inconsequential conversations and mundane events. The terror for an infant learning to survive in the face of parental and medical ignorance and interacting with the wonderful world rings true throughout.

By the time Williams sat down to finish the saga, however, twelve years after completing *In the Money*, he couldn't sustain the original plan of tracing Flossie's life to age five. *The Build-Up* begins with Flossie age seven (BU 18) and ends tragically with the death of Paul Stecher, the promising scion of the family, in a hunting accident, and the American declaration of war on Germany in 1917. The book has become a thinly fictionalized account of Williams's own courtship and marriage. Williams himself validated this autobiographical interpretation in remarks to Edith Heal (see *IWWP* 86–87). It became clear that Flossie Stecher was in fact Flossie Herman, the woman who Williams married in December 1912, just as in the novel, while Joe Stecher, who earlier reviewers had seen as a figure for Williams himself (see Rahv in Doyle 145), reverted to an idealized portrait of Williams's father-in-law, Paul Herman – like Joe a German immigrant and printer. The belated *Build-Up* (1952) wrecks the temporal unity of the trilogy and has the unfortunate effect of showing in relief flaws in the narrative architecture of the earlier volumes too. Worse, it turns the whole business away from fiction and towards what we now call "creative non-fiction" and attendant problems of authority and fact. Too close to reality, the longer form of the trilogy results in intractable narrative contradictions – especially of chronology.

I have written elsewhere on the Stecher Trilogy and its many problems (RB 193–220). Briefly, the narrative action of the trilogy begins on April 18, 1893, with Flossie's birth (WM 11). *In the Money* picks up the narrative with Flossie "well into her second year" but as we are informed in a couple of places, the action of this novel is taking place in 1903[9] – a slippage of a decade. Yet, the final volume reverts to the earlier chronology to synchronize it with the author's own life.

Moreover, Williams blithely changed the names of many minor characters from book to book – only the Stechers and their children retain the same names. How this could happen is puzzling; *In the Money* was written not long after *White Mule* – indeed as originally conceived it was the same book,– so how could Gurlie's sister Astrid become Olga, her brother Gunnar become Einar? There can be only one explanation: Flossie and Lotte were real names and Williams did remember to call the parents Joe and Gurlie (for Paul and Nannie Herman) but the others are little more than tags to conceal real people and real events. What's truly astonishing, however, is that the glaring problem of names wasn't even noticed when the novels were in proof before the expensive and hard to alter plates had been set and cut. These rather basic issues never surface in the correspondence between Laughlin and Williams; or later at Random House where David McDowell, to whom *The Build-Up* is dedicated, was supposed to be Williams's editor.

Details are supposed to matter to Williams. A New Directions advertising circular for 1940 features a large ad for *In the Money* calling it a "new novel by one of our most distinguished literary craftsmen" (Beinecke ZaWilliams corresp. K-Lax Laughlin 1938–1957). Yet, in an "author's note" Williams concerns himself with whether he should honor the outmoded convention of using quotation marks (Beinecke, Uncat. ZA File 111) yet *White Mule* eschews quotation marks and the more recent – and presumably more *a la mode* – *In the Money* does not!

Williams liked to work quickly. He told Edith Heal that he started to write *White Mule* "without too much forethought, the way I always wrote" (*IWWP* 60). He wrote chapter by chapter, recalling that "it had the advantage of the immediate." He was composing "always just up to the publication deadline" (*IWWP* 61). In other words, he wrote the chapters much like self-contained short stories, using the infant Flossie's development as a narrative guide. When *Pagany* folded, Williams was able to place further chapters into *The Magazine*, a West Coast publication. This episodic mode may have prevented Williams from seeing the project as a whole; rather than writing his novels, they seem in many ways to have been written by events.

Paul Mariani compares the trilogy to Theodore Dreiser's *An American Tragedy* (1925) as "the ultimate failure of the American Success Story that the Hermans represented for him ... especially in *The Build-Up*" (Mariani 119–20). Indeed, there is more than a touch of Theodore Dreiser's artless but powerful realism in Williams's Stecher fictions. Both writers were determined to expose the complex hopes and disillusioning American experience of the twentieth century.

Williams's prose fiction shows him to be preoccupied with the "real" rather than the unconscious. A radical empiricist determined to tell it like it is, he uses surrealist techniques where indicated, but in the service of experience in and of the world, not the interior dream space. Williams is above all a mimetic, rather than expressive artist. His formal innovations in writing give us the world of pure experience because that's all there is, all there ever needs to be.

Works cited

Boone, April. "William Carlos Williams's *The Great American Novel*: Flamboyance and the Beginning of Art." *William Carlos Williams Review*. 26.1 Spring 2006. 1–25.

Bremen, Brian. *William Carlos Williams and the Diagnostics of Culture*. Oxford University Press. New York. 1993.

Chatlos, Jon. "A New Mimesis: Unbinding Textual Possibilities in William Carlos Williams's 'Composition.'" *William Carlos Williams Review*. 28. 1–2 Spring/Fall 2008. 1–15.

Cohen, Milton A. "Stumbling into Crossfire: William Carlos Williams, *Partisan Review*, and the Left in the 1930s." *Journal of Modern Literature*. 32.2 2009. 143–158.

Conrad, Bryce. *Refiguring America*. University of Illinois Press. Urbana. 1990.

Copestake, Ian, ed. *Rigor of Beauty: Essays in Commemoration of William Carlos Williams*. Peter Lang. Bern. 2004.

Doyle, Charles, ed. *William Carlos Williams: The Critical Heritage*. Routledge Keegan Paul. London. 1980.

Emerson, Ralph Waldo. *Essays & Lectures*. Library of America. New York. 1983.

Gish, Robert F. *William Carlos Williams: A Study of the Short Fiction*. Twayne. Boston. 1989.

von Hallberg, Robert. "The Politics of Description: W.C. Williams in the Thirties." *English Literary History*. 45.1 Spring 1978. 131–151.

Halpert, Stephen and Johns, Richard. *A Return to Pagany 1929–1932*. Beacon Press. Boston. 1969.

Halter, Peter. *The Revolution in the Visual Arts and the Poetry of William Carlos Williams*. Cambridge University Press. Cambridge. 1994.

James, William. *The Writings of William James: A Comprehensive Edition*. Edited by John J. McDermott. University of Chicago Press. Chicago. 1977.

Montiero, George. "Williams in the 1930's: Three New Reviews and a Paragraph on His Literary Income." *William Carlos Williams Review*. 23.2 Fall 1997. 53–59.

Morris, Daniel. *The Writings of William Carlos Williams: Publicity for the Self*. University of Missouri Press. Columbia. 1995.

Perloff, Marjorie. *The Poetics of Indeterminacy*. Princeton University Press. Princeton. 1981.

Peterson, Jeffrey. " 'A Laboratory … for Dissociations': Approaching Williams's Automatic Writing." *William Carlos Williams Review*. 22.1 Spring 1996. 29–43.

Poirier, Richard. *Poetry and Pragmatism*. Harvard University Press. Cambridge. 1992.

The Renewal of Literature: Emersonian Reflections. Random House. New York. 1987.

Rozendal, Michael. "Forms of Need: William Carlos Williams in the Radical Thirties Little Journals." *William Carlos Williams Review*. 27.2 Fall 2007. 137–155.

Tashjian, Dickran. "Williams and Automatic Writing: Against the Presence of Surrealism." *William Carlos Williams Review*. 22.1 Spring 1996. 5–16.

Thoreau, Henry David. *A Week, Walden, The Maine Woods, Cape Cod*. Library of America. New York. 1985.

Weaver, Mike. *William Carlos Williams: The American Background*. Cambridge University Press. Cambridge. 1971.

Whitman, Walt. *Leaves of Grass*. Dover. Mineola. 2007.

Williams, William Carlos. *The Build-Up*. Random House. New York. 1952. Correspondence. Beinecke Library. ZaWilliams 295.

In The Money. New Directions. Norfolk, CT. 1940.

"A Note by the Author." Beinecke Library. Uncat. ZA Williams, W.C. File 111.

White Mule. New Directions. Norfolk, CT. 1937.

NOTES

1. The "literal description of the rape of a dear friend (a nurse) of mine … " (*CP1* 540n).
2. See Morris, 36–62.

3. A dadaist Williams, with an emphasis on his relation to the visual arts, constitutes an entire wing of Williams scholarship. This Williams is compatible with the way of reading writing called "post-modernism" and with Louis Zukofsky (Williams's able editor) provides the basis for L=A=N=G=U=A=G=E poetry. I have heard Barrett Watten say that *Spring and All* was "the Bible" for the L=A=N=G=U=A=G=E group.

4. Poirier's two books, *The Renewal of Literature: Emersonian Reflections* (1987) and *Poetry & Pragmatism* (1992), should be crucial for Williams studies, because they revise the Emersonian tradition from that of transcendentalism to that of pragmatism. Brian Bremen has located an Emersonian tradition constructed by Kenneth Burke in his thoughtful and deep *William Carlos Williams and the Diagnostics of Culture* (1993), 133.

5. In *The Great American Novel* "Concordites" including Emerson and Thoreau are complacently "imitative" of "England" (*I* 211)!!

6. This destructive wish for violent purgation of culture is evident in *The Great American Novel* and recurs in *Paterson*, with the incineration of the Paterson Library.

7. George Monteiro, too, is strangely deaf to the politics of this story, seeing the necessary autopsy of little Jean as little more than mutilation of a corpse to serve scientific curiosity. See "The Doctor's Black Bag: William Carlos Williams' Passaic River Stories," *Modern Language Studies* 13.1 (1983): 79–84. Excerpted in Gish 169–75.

8. April Boone reports that aside from the *Ladies Home Journal* article, Williams' trove of materials included newspaper clippings, ads, catalogue copy etc.—a contemporary "post-bag" (Boone 6).

9. Even this is subject to confusion, for a time we're led to believe it is 1901. Compare *WM* 52, 116, 161).

8

ERIN E. TEMPLETON

Paterson: an epic in four or five or six parts

Despite an extensive and diverse body of work, William Carlos Williams is for many readers merely a writer of short verse. His two best-known poems, "The Red Wheelbarrow" and "This Is Just to Say," place him firmly within the imagist tradition and are the most widely read and taught of his *oeuvre*. And yet, it is his late and much longer work, *Paterson*, which consumed most of his energy and attention for what would be the last twenty years of his life. For biographer Paul Mariani, *Paterson* represents Williams's major achievement. For other critics such as Marjorie Perloff, it is a belated and uneven composition. Either way, the book-length poem is Williams's longest and most ambitious work. It may also be his most influential: it helped him win the National Book Award for Poetry in 1950 and is one of the two poems – along with *The Cantos* – that Charles Olson tried to come to terms with in his *Maximus Poems*. *Paterson* is central to any discussion of the American long poem, but it is a poem that many readers, undergraduate students in particular, usually encounter only in extracts, if they encounter it at all. This essay will examine major readings of *Paterson*, its compositional history – covering four decades – and its place within the American long poem as a genre.

Williams began to formulate *Paterson* as early as 1927, but he did not actually begin to write the poem for almost twenty years. In the interim he often grappled with a serious bout of writer's block and struggled with different ideas about the poem's form. He eventually envisioned his American epic in four parts. The poem was published volume by volume beginning in 1946; subsequent books appeared in 1948, 1949, and 1951. Although Williams planned out the structure and themes of these first four books in advance and worked on various sections of the poem simultaneously, his concept for the work changed over the compositional process. He published a fifth installment some seven years later in 1958. And still it wasn't enough. Williams began work on yet a sixth book, but the physical limitations of poor health forced him to abandon the endeavor in 1961, and it remained unfinished at the time of his death in 1963.[1]

As he considered the shape his poem would take, Williams struggled with several important artistic questions. "No ideas but in things," he famously proclaims in Book One of the poem (6), but what things? Once these things were identified, what form would they take? And what ideas would they make concrete? In his *Autobiography*, Williams claims "the first idea centering upon the poem ... [was] to find an image large enough to embody the whole knowable world about me" (391). It's an ambitious quest, but the focus on the empirical, the knowable, kept it from becoming an impossible one. In his 1951 "A Statement by William Carlos Williams About the Poem *Paterson*" the poet again emphasizes "knowability," but this time, in language: "This seemed to me to be what a poem was for, to speak to us in a language we can understand. But first before we can understand it the language must be recognizable. We must know it as our own, we must be satisfied that it speaks for us" (*P* xiii). Williams had long championed American literature and the American language, which for him was distinct from its English heritage and history. With *Paterson*, Williams felt the need to compose an American epic poem that featured American subjects and themes. Unlike Ezra Pound, T. S. Eliot, and H. D. who peppered their verses with allusions to literature centuries old and continents away, Williams was determined to keep his focus much closer to home both in time and space.

Like many of his contemporaries, Williams was deeply influenced by James Joyce's 1922 tour de force *Ulysses*. But where Eliot focused on the Homeric allusions and mythic parallels in the text, and Pound rhapsodized over the novel's polyvocal, even polyglot, nature and formal innovation, Williams was most interested in the central role that the city of Dublin played in Joyce's novel.[2] Dublin for Williams was the "hero" of the book, and he wanted to find a uniquely American analog for his own work (*IWWP* 72). He rejected out of hand what to many would be the obvious choice: New York City, because "New York was too big, too much a congeries of the entire world's facets. I wanted something nearer home, something knowable" (*P* xiii). In short, he lacked the intimate familiarity that comes from living many years of a life in a place. Williams visited New York frequently, but it was not home for him. He was born and raised in Rutherford, New Jersey. He raised his own family and also cared for patients in New Jersey. And it wasn't just the place itself that mattered, its geography and landmarks, it was also its inhabitants. In his *Autobiography*, he explained "I wanted ... to write about the people close about me, to know in detail, minutely what I was talking about – to the whites of their eyes, to their very smells ... I had no wish, nor did I have the opportunity to know New York in that way"

(*A* 391). Williams's medical career in New Jersey, its decades of house calls and patient interactions, contributed to his sense of familiarity with both the place and its people. Moreover, the city of Paterson afforded him local knowledge and a river, which for Williams was important not only because it was rich with symbolic potential but also because it was at the heart of Paterson geographically, economically, and historically.

At the outset, Williams had a fixed plan for *Paterson*, which he outlined in the 1946 "Author's Note": "[Book] One introduces the elemental character of the place. The Second Part will comprise the modern replicas. Three will seek a language to make them vocal, and Four, the river below the falls, will be reminiscent of episodes – all that any one man may achieve in a lifetime" (*P* 253). In practice, it turned out that Williams's overall conception of the poem was much more fluid than he had anticipated, and his vision for the work changed over the course of his compositional process. In his 1951 "Statement," Williams explained:

> From the beginning I decided there would be four books following the course of the river whose life seemed more and more to resemble my own life as I more and more thought of it: the river above the Falls, the catastrophe of the Falls itself, the river below the Falls and the entrance at the end into the great sea.
>
> There were a hundred modifications of this general plan as, following the theme rather than the river itself, I allowed myself to be drawn on. The noise of the Falls seemed to me to be a language which we were and are seeking and my search, as I looked about, became to struggle to interpret and use this language. This is the substance of the poem. But the poem is also the search of the poet for his language, his own language which I, quite apart from the material theme had to use to write at all. I had to write in a certain way to gain a verisimilitude with the object I had in mind. (*P* xiii)

This four-book conceit was the last of several attempts, which had also included an attempted expansion of his eighty-five line poem also titled "Paterson" (1927). While the published version of Books I–IV conforms to this overall strategy more or less, the design might suggest a far more linear path than *Paterson* would eventually take in large part thanks to the "hundred modifications" that Williams mentions. And yet, perhaps in keeping with the poem's river motif, it begins with its own literary version of tributaries, an epigraph and a preface, each offering different directions and focal points, which ultimately combine into the body of the poem itself. Not unlike the course of a river, at times this poetic body meanders; at times it gets muddied or brackish. It draws upon various source materials, some of which play a more prominent role in the poem than others, some of which were adapted to fit into verse while others were incorporated into the poem as ready-made art in prose form.

And yet, early on, it becomes clear that *Paterson* is ultimately less a poem about a river or about a city than it is a poem about language itself that uses both the river and the city as just two of several dichotomies upon which to map the poet's struggles. The diversion to which Williams alludes, the struggle for an appropriate poetic language and form, takes center stage from the beginning of *Paterson*. In the Preface to Book One, the poem's speaker cites "Rigor of beauty" as its "quest" and attempts "To make a start, / out of particulars / and make them general" (3). Over the course of the poem, Williams sets up a series of antithetical pairings: in addition to the contrast between nature and civilization, the poem highlights the tensions between male and female, past and present, poetry and prose, and more. These oppositions and the friction that they generate become a productive source of meaning throughout the work.

The dichotomies also correspond to an event in Williams's life, an evening in 1942 when he first met a woman named Marcia Nardi, whom Mariani credits with "dynamit[ing]" the "blockage Williams had been experiencing" with *Paterson* (Mariani 463). Nardi herself was a poet but had sought Williams's counsel as a doctor regarding her teenaged son. Desperate for any feedback on her writing, Nardi left a selection of her verse with Williams who agreed to read it. In the meantime, the situation with her son worked itself out without Williams's intervention, prompting Nardi to write the first of many letters to Williams informing him of the resolution and asking him, rather apologetically, to return her poems to her. So began a correspondence, by all accounts platonic, that would have important effects on both writers. Williams would help Nardi get some of her poetry published, and Nardi's letters would be transformed into the "Cress" letters of *Paterson*.[3] The Cress character becomes a central counterpoint to Dr. Paterson in the early parts of the poem. The two figures embody many of the thematic and structural binaries that drive the first two books of *Paterson*, most notably: man/woman and poetry/prose.

Originally, Williams intended to use Nardi's letters in a prologue or an interlude, but as his ideas for *Paterson* began to take on a more concrete form, they found their way into the poem itself. As he continued to work on *Paterson*, Williams tried to incorporate many of the materials he had at his disposal, which he had gathered over the better part of thirty years, into the poem. These materials included not just letters from real people (in addition to Marcia Nardi, the poem contains letters from Allen Ginsberg, Ezra Pound, Edward Dahlberg and others), but also passages from local histories, clippings from old newspapers, a geological survey, and other documents. Some of these pieces were slightly shaped or edited while others were imported wholesale into the poem. Questions of form dominated early discussions as critics wondered if there was, literally, rhyme or reason to *Paterson*. Some readers suggested that the haphazard, arbitrary form of the poem was intended to mirror the chaos of everyday experience, either intentionally or accidentally while Williams himself maintained that the poem was carefully organized and structured. Ralph Nash argues that the incorporation of prose "brings into the poem something of an air of documentation" (23).[4] Or perhaps there is a democratic impulse behind Williams's insistence on the readymade as poetry, be it metered or not.

These fragments, most of which are imported wholesale into the poem as prose paragraphs rather than reworked into poetic meter, are an essential feature of the work. As Benjamin Sankey notes:

> The most striking of Williams's innovations was doubtless the extensive use of prose, not simply in notes at the back of the poem (as in *The Waste Land*), nor blocked out as part of the verse (as in *The Cantos*), but conspicuously inserted into the text and conspicuously unpoetic in shape.[5]

While the hybrid nature of *Paterson* may have been its most striking innovation, *Paterson* was not the first of Williams's mixed-genre works. In fact, *Spring and All* (1923) also presented a hybrid form of prose and verse that, in the words of C. D. Wright, launches "a grand improvisation" and reconciles "the mash-up of affinities, free-floating associations, and spasms of anger" with "simplicity and order."[6] But where the prose interludes in *Spring and All* are just that – interludes that explore language and the role of the imagination as well as critiques of his contemporaries – in *Paterson*, the prose pieces are carefully calculated interactions that amplify and reflect or refract the themes of their poetic counterparts. They are not criticism or commentary about the text: they are as much a part of *Paterson* itself as any of its verses.

However, the incorporation of prose was not the only formal innovation that Williams achieved in *Paterson*. He also felt that he had discovered an important new poetic principle in Book II. In *I Wanted To Write a Poem*, Williams identified the "Descent beckons" passage as a personal "milestone," explaining, it was the realization of "my final conception of what my own poetry should be" (81, 82). This passage features what Williams would call "the variable foot," a prosodic technique that would allow "order in so-called free verse" (82). In the 1950s, Williams often had difficulty explaining what he meant by both the "American idiom" and "the variable foot," two concepts that were key to his late poetics and which usually went hand in hand. Hugh Kenner explains them as the way that "patterns made, though built on patterns heard, can tug against the pattern we'd normally hear."[7] For Williams, the poetry lies in the dissonance between auditory expectation and realization. In addition to the aural discrepancies created by line breaks, the poetry features an added visual dimension that Mariani refers to as the step-down line. Williams himself sometimes referred to it as the triadic stanza or the three-step line. The triadic stanza creates a visual unity that broadens our attention to the page as a unit of meaning beyond individual lines. Marjorie Perloff, a critic who prefers "the complexity and tension of Williams' earlier visual forms," has remarked that in *Paterson*, the effect seems forced: "the three step grid is an externally imposed geometric form, a kind of cookie-cutter."[8]

The tension between aural and visual language and between poetry and prose lies at the heart of *Paterson* both thematically and structurally. It also carries over into a final aspect of the poem's form: its uneasy relationship to the epic tradition. In a sense, *Paterson* might be thought of as a new kind of epic that more accurately captures modernity in the rapidly changing and growing United States of America. Or perhaps, as James Breslin has argued, *Paterson* is a "pre-epic, a rough and profuse start from which some later summative genius may extract and polish."[9] Williams had been drawn to the long poem well before he started writing *Paterson*. In part the attraction stemmed from the fact that all of his poetic contemporaries were writing long poems (or had already written them): *The Waste Land* (Eliot), "Marriage" and "An Octopus" (Marianne Moore), *The Cantos* (Pound), *The Bridge* (Hart Crane), *Trilogy* (H. D.), *Notes Toward a Supreme Fiction* (Stevens) and more.

The Waste Land, in particular, had a profound effect on Williams. In his *Autobiography*, Williams argued that Eliot's poem had almost single-handedly destroyed the indigenous art that was just beginning to emerge in the United States (146). From Williams's perspective, Eliot and his poem full of antiquity and classical allusions transformed American verse into an academic exercise rather than a living text that was generated from those who had experienced it. Moreover, Williams held that poetry should contain at least a kernel of hope not simply disillusionment and ennui.

And yet, in the years following *The Waste Land*, Williams published *Spring and All* and then did not publish another individual book of poetry for nearly a decade. Instead he turned to prose and wrote several novels, short stories and essays. Of these prose works, *In the American Grain* may have been the most directly related to *Paterson* for it is there that he tries to understand what it means to be an American and what historical forces have shaped American history, American culture, and the American language, all themes that would be prominent in the later work. Breslin cites these years as central to the poetry that would follow: "Williams spent some thirty years of living and writing in preparation for *Paterson*" (169). The epic poem is one that is civically minded. As John Beck has explained, "To write an epic is to deliberately engage in the affairs of society, to tell the tale of the tribe."[10] But Williams deliberately violates several generic hallmarks. Rather than affirming a unified cultural history and narrative, *Paterson* celebrates diversity and multiplicity. Rather than embracing a single voice, *Paterson* embraces dialogue. Rather than focusing on progress and success, *Paterson* also examines failure, destruction, and futility.

Like his poetic predecessor, Walt Whitman, Williams attempted to make *Paterson* a democratic and inclusive representation of the American experience. As such, he includes voices of men and women, young and old, and he populates the poem with members of all strata of society from both the present day and various historical moments. For a number of critics, some of these representations are problematic because of their tendency to reinforce racial or gender stereotypes. Perhaps most controversial is the presentation of a character associated with the recurring phrase "Beautiful Thing" in Book III. The character is based in part on a black patient whom Williams had treated after she had been gang-raped by two different groups of men. Sandra Gilbert and Susan Gubar argue that the use of the term "thing," particularly as a form of address, lacks sensitivity, objectifies and further victimizes the assaulted woman.[11] As Mariani points out, "Williams reenacted in his imagination the forcible rape of the woman, lashing out at what the male could not understand, and feared, and wanted therefore to destroy" (414). Gilbert and Gubar note, "[Dr. Paterson's] sympathy for this sexual victim is, curiously, accompanied by voyeuristic absorption in her mutilation" (48). Terence Diggory argues that despite the fact that Williams's poetic persona Dr. Paterson's desire "propels him toward her as a lover... the doctor channels his desire away from the body" into more appropriate outlets.[12] Louis Martz focuses his reading not so much on the real world embodied counterpart to the poetic character but rather on her symbolic meaning: "Is not the Beautiful Thing the affectionate realization of past and present in the mind of the living?" and "The Beautiful Thing then is not the girl in herself but it is the human response, the fire of the imagination, the fire of human affection."[13]

However one reads the "Beautiful Thing" passages she, like many of Williams's female characters, is intimately connected to violence and destruction. And she is just one of the many who suffer violence at male hands over the course of *Paterson*. Elsewhere in Book III, Williams refers to an "incident" involving the brutal treatment of two Native Americans "accused of killing two or three pigs." Both men, falsely accused it is later revealed, meet violent deaths while performing a ceremonial dance called the Kinte Kaye (*P* 102–03). Later in Book IV, the poem includes a story from the *New York Herald Tribune* detailing the murder of a six-month old girl by her father (194–95). *Paterson* as a whole is not lacking in brutality; brutality is an integral part of the larger theme of divorce that runs through the poem, the schism between men and women, between settlers and the land that they have appropriated as well as its indigenous inhabitants. These rifts express themselves through violence, and it is these fractures that the poem seeks to mend.

Moreover, for Williams annihilation is an essential precursor to creativity, and this binary of creation and destruction is often mapped onto the heterosexual binary: Kore and Hades, Cress and Dr. P., Beautiful Thing and her attackers. In Part III of the poem, not only do we bear witness to the "Beautiful Thing" character, whose "vulgarity of beauty surpasses all their/ perfections," but we also learn that she is "intertwined with the fire" (120) and "the flame's lover" (123). Moreover, this fire, an elemental opposite to the poem's water imagery, gives rise to another destructive and generative force. It engulfs and destroys the town library, a stifling and oppressive place that entraps language and poetry. This conflagration was based on a real fire in Paterson in 1902. The wind, which brings and fans the flames, is presented as a welcome presence that eradicates the "staleness," the "desolation," and "stagnation" of the outmoded institution and liberates culture (100, 101). For Williams:

> The province of the poem is the world.
> When the sun rises, it rises in the poem
> and when it sets darkness comes down
> and the poem is dark. (100)

Poetry, and by extension art, belongs in the world rather than imprisoned in books or libraries. It should be born of experience rather than limited to stale and musty bookshelves. At first glance, this passage of *Paterson III* seems almost Emersonian in its rejection of the library and all of its books in favor of lived experience. The blaze literally burns to the ground history and institutionalized knowledge. But for Williams the binary is never so simple. Albert Gelpi reminds us of "the imagination's participation in the destructive/re-creative force of nature" that this scene epitomizes.[14] The creative process, both artistic and scholastic, depends upon devastation and demolition; for Williams the two are intertwined and inseparable.

Reinforcing the important role that destruction plays in the creative process for Williams, Book IV revisits several of the important themes of *Paterson* as a whole: language, creativity, and the importance of the local.

It also challenges assumptions about the value of purity and whiteness particularly through the vehicle of the pastoral tradition. According to Williams's original schema, *Paterson IV* (1951) was to be the final part of the poem, "the river below the falls ... reminiscent of episodes – all that any one man may achieve in a lifetime" (*P* 253). It features, as Ann Mikkelsen notes, "a series of idylls depicting amorous, often disturbing, and sometimes comic encounters between a middle-aged, gay, wealthy woman; her younger employee, a nurse, and Dr. Paterson himself."[15] Corydon and Phyllis are two stock pastoral figures who are based on real women: one a prominent New York socialite and the other a nurse whom Williams had once known in Paterson (288). Mikkelsen points out that the pastoral is not unique to *Paterson IV*. In fact, *Paterson I* opens with a pastoral scene, albeit one of a very different tone: Dr. Paterson surrounded by the wonders of the Passaic Falls and natural world. In the opening book of the poem, the pastoral and the epic poetic traditions seem to complement each other as Williams marries the mythic elements of both Dr. P and his female counterpart, whether we call her Cress or Kore, with local history and the local landscape.

Williams's return to the pastoral in Book IV considers not just the sometimes comic sometimes lewd love triangle between the three characters of Corydon, Phyllis, and Dr. P., but it also raises questions about the industrialized landscape of the river and its surrounding environs. The sordidness of these relationships might mirror the contaminated landscape and suggest that progress does not always conform to expectations of tradition, particularly a tradition as outdated as the pastoral in industrial New Jersey with its factories and manufacturing plants. Book IV also explores the idea of infection and pollution as productive sites of creativity by introducing Marie Curie and her "radiant gist." Curie is presented "with ponderous belly, full / of thought!" and "knowledge, the contaminant" (176, 177). Earlier in this part of the poem, Williams claims – not once but twice – "dissonance ... leads to discovery" (175). Friction is again the site of productivity. By the end of the book, the river has reached the sea, which may or may not be "our home" and may or may not be safe to inhabit. The sea is variously described as "a sea of blood," as inhabited by a shark "that snaps / at his own trailing guts," and as otherwise inhospitable (199). It closes with a public execution in prose and a final crash of the waves:

> This is the blast
> the eternal close
> the spiral
> the final somersault
>   the end.   (202)

The word "final" and the last line of the book, "the end," might suggest resolution. But the circular motions of the spiral and the somersault also imply a return to the beginning, a cycle, a circle, and ultimately a more ambiguous ending than one might expect for the final lines of what was supposed to be the final book of *Paterson*. Ultimately, Williams himself found the poem's conclusion less than satisfactory, writing to his publisher, New Directions, "I have been forced to recognize that there can be no end to such a story I have envisioned with the terms which I had laid down for myself" (*P* xiv).

As previously noted, Williams's original plan for *Paterson* did not include Book V, and Williams's own explanation is vague and offers little guiding imagery or theme. It took him the better part of a decade to publish Book V (1958). Williams "got side-tracked" when his original concept became the long poem "Asphodel, That Greeny Flower" (*P* xii, 295). When Book V was finally published, on Williams's seventy-fifth birthday, it was structurally different from its predecessors: Book V did not have a title of its own, and it is much shorter in length – just two-thirds the length of each of the other books. But despite formal modifications, it returns to many of the themes of the rest of the poem. The book opens with a defiant acknowledgement of Williams's aging mind and body, which had begun to fail in the intervening years:

> In old age
> the mind
> casts off
> rebelliously
> an eagle
> from its crag   (*P* 205)

Not only does he answer those critics who suggest that his poetic prowess has declined with his health, but he also returns to the formal experimentation that has marked the whole of *Paterson*, specifically the variable foot and the descending triad. The central figures of the poem are a unicorn and a woman embodying the "virgin/whore" dichotomy (Williams's description). The latter two, arguably, are not new to *Paterson* V: most recently, the pastoral section of Book IV portrayed Phyllis as both the innocent virgin and the teasing whore, and previously, one might argue that Beautiful Thing shares some of the same character traits as do Cress and Kore from Books I and II. Purity, pollution, and sexuality more generally have propelled the poem forward from its beginning. The unicorn refers to a tapestry collection housed in the Cloisters branch of the Metropolitan Museum of Modern Art. Further, Book V changes its referential scope from local figures and histories to Williams's contemporaries and artistic influences. Jackson Pollock, Juan

Gris, Peter Brueghel and many others make appearances. This broadening of perspective places Williams and his verse more directly in conversation with his artistic peers and makes explicit the lines of influence between them.

Finally, while the previous books of *Paterson* have all indirectly addressed questions about the nature of poetry and its role in American culture, Book V confronts the question directly in one of its prose sections, an excerpt from an interview with journalist Mike Wallace. Wallace asks Williams about an E. E. Cummings poem, also included in *Paterson*, "is it poetry?" and then points to one of Williams's own poems and asks whether it is a poem or "a fashionable grocery list." Williams's response is telling: "Anything is good material for poetry. Anything" (222). But while anything can be good material for poetry, a poem is more than its ingredients. Equally important is the treatment of the material. For Williams, poetry is not defined by its subject but rather by its metric arrangement. Elsewhere in the interview, he explained, "poetry is language charged with emotion. It's words, rhythmically organized" (221). Thus Book Five concludes with a reflection on measure:

> The measure intervenes, to measure is all we know,
> a choice among the measures   .   .
> the measured dance
>
> . . . .
> We know nothing and can know nothing   .
> but
> the dance, to dance to a measure
> contrapuntally,
> Satyrically, the tragic foot.   (*P* 235–236)

Ultimately, Williams uses music, art, tapestries, paintings, poetry, and dance, to draw together all of the themes of the poem into a final coda, but as in Book IV, there is no resolution. In fact, Williams acknowledges at the end of Book V that there can be no resolution after all: "We know nothing and can know nothing / but / the dance." The knowledge and meaning of art reside in its lived experience, which can be joyous, raucous, and tragic – sometimes all at once. To try to formulate a more fixed definition is futile.

And yet even after the publication of Book V Williams still did not feel that he was done with *Paterson*, and he was at work on a sixth book at the time of his death, but increasing difficulties brought on by his declining health prevented much progress. Only four preliminary pages of the typescript Book VI remain (*P* 237–40). These fragments revisit a number of familiar figures and motifs from the earlier books of the poem. The pages return to the beginnings of American history with George

Washington, Alexander Hamilton, John Jay and others. But they also reach back further to Montezuma, Socrates, and Li Po. They revisit the Falls and the fire, destroyer of libraries (this time in ancient Alexandria). They reconsider questions of language and form, maintaining the hybrid verse and prose structure that characterizes the rest of the work. Finally, they bear witness to the struggle that Williams faced in writing at the end of his life when a series of strokes had compromised both his vision and his dexterity.

Paterson's critical reception was decidedly mixed. Writing about *Paterson I* and *II*, Robert Lowell proclaims, "*Paterson* is Whitman's America, grown pathetic and tragic, brutalized by inequality, disorganized by industrial chaos, and faced with annihilation. No poet has written of it with such a combination of brilliance, sympathy, and experience, with such alertness and energy."[16] Randall Jarrell, who had selected and introduced Williams's *Selected Poems*, praised the first book but found the later installments inconsistent and ultimately disappointing: "*Paterson (Book I)* seems to me the best thing William Carlos Williams has ever written," but "[n]ow that Book IV has been printed, one can come to some conclusions about 'Paterson' as a whole. My first conclusion is this: it doesn't seem to *be* a whole; my second: 'Paterson' has been getting rather steadily worse" and "Book IV is so disappointing that I do not want to write about it at any length."[17] Not everyone shared Jarrell's opinion – after all, *Paterson III* earned Williams the prestigious National Book Award (along with his *Selected Poems* published in 1949) demonstrating that critical reception for *Paterson* was uneven and polarized. *Paterson's* relationship with the epic was also addressed in the scholarly criticism: Breslin argues that Williams's dedication is to openness "as the primary literary and human value" while the epic is a closed and totalizing form.[18] Marjorie Perloff does not share Breslin's perspective, contending "the poem that finally made [Williams] famous ... for all its seeming openness ... manifested a symbolic superstructure."[19] In other words, the poem isn't all that open after all. Michael André Bernstein argues the contrary, that *Paterson* offers so many different versions of closure that they cancel each other out, and as a result, the poem remains open.[20] Perloff also takes issue with Mariani's claim that the poem is "a *process* of unfolding, of discovery" and with Breslin's pre-epic reading: "successive readings have convinced me that it is, in fact, a much more 'closed' poem than either Williams or his best critics care to admit."[21] Linda Wagner-Martin argues that Williams's "differing techniques used within the first four books are proof of his search for new, more effective expression" and links this search to Williams's "physical breakdown" which she claims "brought a noticeable modification in his methods of writing."

Forced to slow the composition process because of embodied limitations (a stroke cost the use of his right hand), Williams, in Wagner-Martin's reading, gained an "aura of contentment, of joy".[22]

Despite the mixed reception, *Paterson* is a substantial achievement for one of the United States' most influential poets. Even those readers, like Jarrell, who were disappointed, or Charles Olson, who found it rather sentimental, claiming that the "blueberry America" that Williams depicts in *Paterson* has little relation to the modern industrial city, had to come to terms with it.[23] Most significantly this poem demonstrates his full range of poetic accomplishment, a range that extends far beyond "This Is Just to Say" and "The Red Wheelbarrow" in vitally important ways. It stands in sharp contrast to *The Waste Land* and *The Cantos*, both global examples of the modernist long poem, and stakes a claim for the local and the everyday as a worthy subject of epic verse. It consumed much of Williams's time and attention in the final years of his life and however one finally evaluates it, stands as an important contribution to American poetry in the mid-twentieth century.

NOTES

1. As the result of a series of strokes, Williams had lost some of his eyesight and the use of his right arm in the mid-1950s. But by 1961, not only had his dexterity deteriorated even further making typing more challenging, he was also experiencing difficulty concentrating, which made writing coherent sentences hard and reading impossible.

2. See T.S. Eliot, "'Ulysses,' Order and Myth," in *Selected Prose of T. S. Eliot*, ed. Frank Kermode (New York: Harcourt, Brace, 1975) 175-78 and Ezra Pound, "Joyce" in *Literary Essays of Ezra Pound*, ed. T.S. Eliot (New York: New Directions, 1968) 410-17.

3. The surviving correspondence between Nardi and Williams is reproduced in Elizabeth Murrie O'Neil ed., *The Last Word: Letters Between Marcia Nardi and William Carlos Williams* (Iowa City: University of Iowa Press, 1994).

4. Ralph Nash, "The Use of Prose in 'Paterson'," in *Merrill Studies in Paterson*, ed. John Engels (Columbus, OH: Charles E. Merrill, 1971) 23.

5. Benjamin Sankey, *A Companion to William Carlos Williams's Paterson* (Berkeley, CA: University of California Press, 1971) 16.

6. C.D. Wright ed., William Carlos Williams, *Spring and All* (New York: New Directions, 2011) x–xi.

7. Hugh Kenner, "William Carlos Williams's Rhythm of Ideas," *New York Times Book Review*, September 18, 1983: p. 15.

8. Marjorie Perloff, "To Give a Design: Williams and the Visualization of Poetry," in *William Carlos Williams: Man and Poet* (National Poetry Foundation, University of Maine at Orono, 1983) 159–186, 181.

9. James E. B. Breslin, *William Carlos Williams, An American Artist* (Chicago: University of Chicago Press, 1985) 172.

10. John Beck, *Writing the Radical Center: William Carlos Williams, John Dewey, and American Cultural Politics* (Albany, NY: SUNY Press, 2001) 136.

11. Sandra M. Gilbert and Susan Gubar, *No Man's Land: The Place of the Woman Writer in the Twentieth Century. Vol. 1, The War of the Words* (New Haven: Yale UP, 1988) 48.

12. Terence Diggory, *William Carlos Williams and the Ethics of Painting* (Princeton, NJ: Princeton UP, 1991) 51.

13. Louis L. Martz, *Many Gods and Many Voices: The Role of the Prophet in English and American Modernism* (Columbia, MO: U Missouri Press, 1998) 65, 67.

14. Albert Gelpi, *A Coherent Splendor: The American Poetic Renaissance, 1910–1950* (New York: Cambridge UP, 1987) 357.

15. Ann Marie Mikkelsen, *Pastoral, Pragmatism, and Twentieth-Century American Poetry* (New York: Palgrave MacMillan, 2011) 70.

16. Robert Lowell, "*[Paterson I and II]*" in *Profile of William Carlos Williams*, ed. Jerome Mazzaro (Columbus OH: Charles E. Merrill Publishing, 1971) 77.

17. Randall Jarrell, "Dr. Williams' *Paterson*" in *Profile of William Carlos Williams*, 62, 68.

18. Breslin, 170.

19. Perloff, *The Poetics of Indeterminacy: Rimbaud to Cage* (Princeton: Princeton UP, 1981) 148.

20. Michael André Bernstein, *The Tale of the Tribe: Ezra Pound and the Modern Verse Epic* (Princeton: Princeton UP, 1980).

21. Perloff, *Poetics*, 151.

22. Linda Wagner, "A Bunch of Marigolds" in *Merrill Studies in Paterson*, 75.

23. Charles Olson, *Selected Writings of Charles Olson* (New York: New Directions, 1966) 84.

9

CRISTINA GIORCELLI

Pictures from Brueghel: looking backward, pointing forward

William Carlos Williams's early experimental works of the so-called cubist and dadaist periods – especially, *Kora in Hell: Improvisations* (1920) and *Spring and All* (1923) – have been considered his most significant and innovative by many illustrious critics. In form as well as content, however, his final collection, *Pictures from Brueghel and Other Poems* (1962),[1] not only sums up a lifetime devoted to perfecting his sensitive craft, but, with effective concision, also experiments with new modalities and manifests new, or at least, different views of, and attitudes toward, reality: more inclusive, sensory, and compassionate. As Hugh Kenner claimed, this final work was his "most poignant, simplest and loveliest," because it was born of "an effortless artless eloquence, as tender or as vigorous as he could want it to be."[2] Commenting on some compositions in this collection, Williams's publisher and fellow-poet, James Laughlin, held that "These/ Small descriptive poems are/ Among his finest, glimpses/ Into a past which he made/ Contemporary in his vision."[3] And Denise Levertov, Williams's devoted pupil and affectionate friend, in 1962, on receiving a copy of the book, wrote him a letter in which she stated that "in your 'small' poems, by which I mean simply short poems that apparently focus on some single detail, there is always the reverberation of the total . . . of your vision of the world, or of what it is to be living; so that every poem is at once a complete thing, as a carved stone is, and at the same time relates to all your other poems" (*DL/ WCW* 116).

While Levertov compares Williams's last poems to carved stones, Paul Mariani defines him as an "untiring sculptor of the word" (Mariani 724). Indeed, it is on Williams's three-dimensional capacities – thanks to a language which is more precise and more dexterous than the finest chisel – that this essay intends to linger. Eschewing sentimentality, especially in *Pictures from Brueghel*, but also in several poems in his two previous collections, he stirs our emotions by presenting the "thing" designated by the word in what James Breslin calls its "literal specificity" (52) (freed, as much as

115

possible, of its connotative values) and, because of spatial organization, also in a vivid visual dimension and a precisely ordered rhythm. By rendering "the thing" tangibly (visibly and audibly), for and by itself, what is static becomes dynamic, the literal glides into the figurative, and the ordinary turns into the extraordinary. Present in our mind's eye and in our ear, it reverberates in our mind/memory creating infinite ripples in the imagination.[4] This attention to things through words inevitably entails also an attention to language, to language as "thing" and to the poem itself as a "thing." At the same time, however, in the collections under scrutiny, Williams often introduces a lyric subject that points to a mode of lyricism that verges on the confessional.[5]

Aged seventy-one, after a heart attack (1948) and two strokes (1951 and 1952), followed by a long period of severe depression (1953), Williams published *The Desert Music and Other Poems* in 1954 and *Journey to Love* the following year. Both collections are characterized by his use of the prosodic measure which, found after decades of striving to accommodate order and disorder, freedom and discipline, fixity and flux, he believed would suit the tempo of the American idiom, the beat and the cadence of its words and locutions:[6] the staggered, stepped-down, triadic stanza with the "variable" foot.[7] This measure – so oxymoronic, or, at least, so vague, in its formulation – has been amply and controversially debated,[8] even though, as Stephen Cushman rightly observes, since it recalls Dante's *terza rima*, its rhythm is well suited to conveying the largely meditative content of the poems in these two collections.[9]

The Desert Music is permeated by Williams's dejection after his illnesses and, above all, after years of public neglect and, consequently, of doubts about himself. The composition that gives the collection its title (*CP2* 273–84) was written after a 1950 lecture-tour of several west coast universities and a memorable visit with Robert McAlmon[10] to El Paso and Juárez, cities of transition on the border between the USA and Mexico. In June 1951 (a couple of months after his first stroke) Williams read it at Harvard's Alpha Chapter of the Phi Beta Kappa society that had commissioned a fifteen-minute poem from him. It is a polyphonic work,[11] which, while giving a bird's eye view of various scenes, registers in a fragmented and intrusive way the sounds, words, and noises, emitted by ticking rails, musical instruments, various adults' voices, pleading children, "screaming" sparrows, and the picturesque, albeit menacing, crowds of the market district in Juárez. In a situation in which movement, time, and space seem to converge,[12] the speaker's anguish about his identity as a poet – "I am that he whose brains/ are scattered/aimlessly" – surfaces with extraordinary poignancy: in "an agony of self-realization." But the derelict figure of an old Mexican Indian on the bridge over the Rio Grande (an "inhuman shapelessness,/knees hugged tight up into the belly/Egg-shaped!")[13] and "an old whore . . ., her bare/can waggling crazily" in a strip-tease joint – both functioning as the poet's alter egos – make him realize that, by imitating nature's ways, that is, by inventing, by *creating*, disintegration can be turned into form. In effect, the shapeless form reminds the poet of an embryo and, with a nod to Greek mythology evoked in the midst of such vulgarity ("This place is rank"), the striptease dancer (a "worn-out trouper") becomes Andromeda, redeemed by the poet/Perseus ("The bright-colored candy/of her nakedness lifts her unexpectedly/to partake of its tune"). Indeed, both presences bring forth tunes that can trigger a dance, that can trigger a poem (each of these literally based on "feet": the former a figure of the latter).[14] This "music of survival"[15] (associated with Casals's "deep cello tone") spurs him to cry out, even if with a stutter – the typography with its spaces signals the slowed down tempo, that is, the hesitancy caused by fear, insecurity, and bashfulness –"I *am* a poet! I/ am.   I am.   I am a poet, I reaffirmed, ashamed."   On the verge of a profound crisis, in a cultural, social, and geographic area marked by in-betweenness, where various ethnicities had been strenuously interacting for centuries, Williams, who belonged to two of them (the Anglo-Saxon and the Spanish) and had forcefully deplored the white man's exploitation of the third (the Native American),[16] succeeds in liberating his inner, creative, strength – although, he concedes, this only happens intermittently ("sometimes").[17] This composition is a powerful statement of what it is to be a poet nowadays and from what kind of degraded circumstances and cacophony poetry and the liberating as well as erotic dance it enacts can *still* arise. As, by way of a pun, but also by pointing forward to later postmodernist, self-reflexive writings, Sherman Paul summarizes, "In this poem the poet has certified that he is a poet by making a poem about the making of poems."[18]

In another composition, "The Descent" (*CP2* 245–46) (taken from *Paterson* II), Williams refers once again to the myth of Kore/Persephone and the often deployed movement of descent/ascent (also signified by the shape of the triadic stanza) with its related themes of sterility/fertility, death/rebirth, silence/song. In spite of a pervasive tentativeness, he wishfully and encouragingly affirms, "No defeat is made up entirely of defeat–since/the world it opens is always a place/formerly/unsuspected" and also "The descent/made up of despairs/and without accomplishment/realizes a new awakening:/which is a reversal/of despair." In "To a Dog Injured in the Street" (*CP2* 255–57), the unfaltering faith in the power of poetry to heal and to comfort is again manifest: "With invention and courage/we shall surpass/the pitiful dumb beasts,/ let all men believe it." The same conviction animates the delightful "The Artist" (*CP2* 267–68), where Williams draws a charming domestic scene, peopled by a sympathetic audience, to extol the levity and grace of a "perfectly achieved" *entrechat*: the pirouette, that, besides imitating nature's cyclical processes, is the very epitome of dancing.[19] Despite being disheveled and "in a soiled undershirt," the dancer (as the poet's alter ego) "whirled about/ bounded/into the air and ... completed the figure" and thus deserves to be praised (and remembered through time, as the past tense indicates). But, notwithstanding his singularity (he is mentioned in the first line), that is, notwithstanding his individual expression of motion and form, the dancer remains almost anonymous ("Mr. T.") – a way of signifying that what counts is, ultimately, the artistic result rather than the performer. Some of the lines and stanzas in this poem are end-stopped as they correspond with syntactical units, yet we do not miss the "spontaneity, surprise, or shock of the unfolding action"[20] that we find elsewhere because their perfect balance, their self-sufficiency, together with the accompanying rhyming devices of alliteration and assonance, match the poise that is being celebrated.

The mood of reflection, under the aegis of both memory and the imagination ("We/ should be lost/without its wings to/fly off upon," Williams declares in "To Daphne and Virginia" [*CP2* 246–50]), that characterizes this collection does, however, occasionally bring with it a tendency to fall into generalized symbolization and abstraction (in "The Yellow Flower" or "The Orchestra," for instance. [*CP2* 257–59, *CP2* 250–52]) – a mode of thinking and writing that he had spent a lifetime trying to avoid and openly chastising.

Similarly, some of the poems in *Journey to Love* share the same (disconcerting) trait. The opening composition, "A Negro Woman" (*CP2* 287), is emblematic. In the first half, its protagonist is presented – in all her simplicity – as a physically solid ("bareheaded,/the bulk/of her thighs/causing her to waddle") and emotionally endearing presence ("carrying a bunch of marigolds/ wrapped/ in an old newspaper"). In the second half, on the contrary, she turns into "an ambassador/ from another world" (Kore? Hermes? Orpheus?), holding her flowers as if they were a torch, as if she were the Statue of Liberty. This dual level of reference enfeebles, not only ideologically (as she is said to be "not knowing what she does"),[21] a presentation that, having started with precise and clear-cut contours, ends up with de-personalizing and incongruous ones ("holding the flowers upright/as a torch/so early in the morning"). This same symbolizing tendency can also be found in "View by Color Photography on a Commercial Calendar" (*CP2* 290–91), for instance.

The most celebrated poem in this collection, "Asphodel, That Greeny Flower" (*CP2* 310–37) (in three Books and a Coda), is dedicated to

Williams's wife, Flossie. Here, while declaring his enduring – even if at times difficult[22] – love for her, Williams asks forgiveness for his trespasses.[23] Robert Lowell defined it, "a triumph of simple confession ... something that [is] both poetry and beyond poetry."[24] That this praise is as high as it is generic may also be due to what Bob Perelman has singled out in the poem: "it can be prolix, words are repeated carelessly, the rhetoric is clumsy in places ... when Williams addresses his wife Flossie [it] can be strained and mawkish."[25] Yet, taking a lesson from the simple asphodel – "wooden," "colorless," with "no odor," but resilient (because deeply rooted), it is the flower of Hades – Williams insists on the power of the past (be it personal or of humanity in general), when remembered with love and revisited with imagination,[26] to restore and enliven the present (as T. S. Eliot, long contested by him, had maintained). And this notwithstanding the fact that the present is marked by bewildering events, like the dropping of the atomic bomb. Williams, who mentions the bomb several times in his late poetry, refers to it in a contradictory way as both destroyer and flower, catastrophe and blessing (similar to the moments of great conflict, followed by reconciliation, in a married life?). Its intrusion in the poem (twisting its mood from personal to political), its *raison d'être*, may be due to science's new discoveries as "Einsteinian physics offered a new vision of matter, terrifyingly alive ... spinning with Dionysian splendor."[27] While bringing a sense of urgency ("There is something/something urgent/I have to say to you" and "Listen while I talk on/against time") and a sense of energy and movement to a world where relativity has changed traditional values, but where "Light, the imagination/and love/ ... maintain/ all of a piece/ their dominance," the bomb's tremendous physical and emotional impact and radiance can paradoxically kindle the poet's inventiveness and even ward off death.[28] According to Marilyn Kallet, it is the triadic stanza with its rhythm paced and measured that contributes to this effect since "[t]he longer line length holds off terror, holds off death for a time."[29] In this collection too Williams's anguish about his significance as a poet returns, together with his stubborn insistence on and relentless dedication to his art (in "The Pink Locust" [*CP2* 299–301] he writes, "A rose *is* a rose/and the poem equals it/if it be well made" and also "I am not,/I know,/in the galaxy of poets/a rose/but *who*, among the rest,/will deny me/my place"). One may agree with Jerome Mazzaro that if some of these poems "represent a loss of vividness, the order implicit in the threeness of their triadic lines can permit Williams to enter the more overtly moral poetry of his final years."[30]

Characterizing many of the poems in these two collections, as in several previous ones, is what Williams calls in one of them ("For Eleanor and Bill Monahan" [*CP2* 252–55] from *The Desert Music*) "[t]he female principle of the world," that is, woman, idealistically seen as the epitome of tenderness, humility, and love.[31] And this not only because, as he had declared, "Somehow poetry and the female sex were allied in my mind. The beauty of girls seemed the same to me as the beauty of a poem"(*IWWP* 14), but because he conceived of woman as the fecundating Other "at the bottom of all art" (*A* 373). Williams presents himself in this same poem as the androgynous Tiresias[32] ("I confess/to being/half man and half/woman"), since, as an artist, he believes he incorporates both principles. Williams sees woman as both virgin and whore ("an identity:/– through its disguises" [*P* 208]), as both the Mother of God and Venus (like Andromeda and the strip-tease dancer in "The Desert Music"). To illustrate his point, in another poem from *Journey to Love*, "The King!" (*CP2* 295–96), he celebrates Nell Gwyn, the English actress and publicly acknowledged "whore," because she "served" her King in many ways. In return, "the King's bountiful/water ... magically,/ with the grit, took away/all her sins." Through her, Williams sings of any woman, "whose husband makes her/the 'King's whore'" – where the repeated capital letter, together with the exclamation mark of the title, triumphantly and ecstatically assert who, institutionally and privately, is in a position of dominance. Thus, as has been argued (see Driscoll and Leibowitz), Williams's view of woman is often patriarchal, essentialist, and conflictual (if not frankly sexist): she is both the powerful life-giver but, at times, also a human being to be belittled as passive and unreflective. And she may even be the terrible Gorgon, Medusa, as in "Classic Picture"[33] (from *Journey to Love* [*CP2* 301–02]): "Under/ their [women's] ornate coiffures/ lurks a specter,/coiling snakes/ doubling for tresses," where the alliteration recalls the hissing of the serpents. To show, however, how the poet's vision of woman is multifaceted, the protagonist of "The Lady Speaks"[34] (*CP2* 303) is specifically a "lady": in its formality, the term indicates the respect and, perhaps, even the (untranscendental) awe she commands. The poem registers the consequences of a storm watched by her and her husband from inside their house. As the house, the trees, and the moss are "whipped" by the strong winds but remain "upright," she wishes that "it be so/ ... in the final/ fury." As "the steady, step-by-step progression of Williams' triadic line honors the spiritual willpower of the married couple,"[35] the poem's possible metaphorical meaning does not detract from its "scrupulously" (*SE* 128) chosen words (like those he praised in Marianne Moore) to designate all-expressive details (emphasized by alliteration), and the woman's subsumed dignity and courage.

By the time Williams started to write several of the poems which, one year before his death, would appear in *Pictures from Brueghel*, he stated that the triadic stanza was "overdone, artificial, archaic – smacking of Spencer [*sic*] and his final Alexandrine" (Mariani 689). Looking for a renewal and new inspiration he translated poetry from other languages: Spanish, French, and Greek.[36] But, above all, he turned to Chinese, a more distant language with its more minimalistic kind of poetry and emphasis on spatial design, recalling his experimentation of the 1920's. Zhaoming Qian has persuasively argued[37] that the prosody of this last book may have also been influenced by Williams's collaborative translations/"recreations" of classic Chinese lyrics, desultorily carried out between, approximately, 1958 and 1960 (*CP2* 500–02). As "Chinese poetry is distinguished by its reliance on simply naming things after things after things to stir up the imagination,"[38] these adaptations into English, often in quatrains[39] that reproduce the rectangular form of their succinct originals, are striking in their "economy, understatement, and power."[40] In addition, since in these Chinese poems syntactical connections are tenuous, meanings have to be inferred through a sharp and learned attention to their contexts. This elusiveness may have appealed to Williams, who devised their oddly divided lines so as to bring forth, thanks to a dramatically "sensual" (*SE* 206) structure and an implicit confidence in the reader's inventiveness, the poems' complex meanings together with the concreteness and compression of their painterly qualities (to which he, at times, was even willing to sacrifice the naturalness of his idiom).[41] As Williams was "the best/ Line-breaker of his time; i.e./ He had the most sensitive ear/ For judging which word should/ End a line and how the syntax/ Should turn against the flow/ Of lines,"[42] he succeeded in his intent to give his work "such intensity of perception that it lives with an intrinsic movement of its own" (*CP2* 54). Certainly, in *Pictures from Brueghel* he was able to make visual objects – the sensuous, tactile material world – "stand out, one by one, as in a series of film shots,"[43] as Marjorie Perloff claimed when analyzing Williams's poems of the 1920's: except that now the influence, rather than just from cubism and dadaism, may have come *also* from China. His typical subjects are to be found in this collection: art, flowers, birds, women, the imagination. In addition, we can find in them also a sense of impending death that may have induced him to look more attentively and more sympathetically at human beings and "things" – among them, poems themselves, whose meaning for and in today's world is not only often questioned, but whose content may self-reflexively be the very act of making them (as in "Erica," for instance [*CP2* 397–98]).

Ten poems (one is subdivided into three sections) stand out at the beginning of the collection; they are devoted to ten paintings by Brueghel,[44] an artist who, like Botticelli, Dürer, and Juan Gris, was one of Williams's favorites.[45] The poet shared several characteristics with Brueghel, such as: an attention to the reality of his country, independence from foreign models, a focus on the "local," a concern for the structure and rhythm of the represented scene, and (occasionally) a caustic sense of humor. Being, like his mother, a lover of painting, Williams once declared, "as I've grown older, I've attempted to fuse the poetry and painting to make it the same thing . . . to give a design. A design in the poem and a design in the picture should make them more or less the same thing."[46] Significantly in "Song" (CP2 395) he writes, "the ear and the eye lie/down together in the same bed," pointing toward a form of synesthesia. Usually ekphrases are not only (verbal) representations of (visual) representations, but they may also be interpretations of (or speculations, reflections on) such representations. In these poems – besides praising Brueghel, who "saw it all/and with his grim/humor faithfully/recorded/it" (CP2 394) – Williams seems to be motivated by a (didactic) project: he directs our eyes sequentially from one chosen detail to the other in any given painting[47] so as to disclose what he considers relevant to its structure, to its organization, to the dynamic tensions that hold it together, and to the spatial relations between and among its various features.[48] Not only, but in so doing, Williams makes us relive the process of creating the painting step by step, while "[a]loof, detached, [he] acts as an observer of the events in the painting, adopting the same distance Brueghel assumes through the aerial perspective of his composition."[49] Most definitely, his details "illuminate rather than decorate."[50] At the same time, however, in order to enact such a revelation, he implicitly urges us to look at and hear how he handles the language (and its silences) so as to impinge on its very structure (through unconventional syntax, unusual grammatical forms, enjambments, emphases on articles, conjunctions, prepositions, lack of punctuation, idiosyncratic lineation, and an abundance of spaces indicating pauses, for instance).[51] In so doing, that is, in defamiliarizing the language, he makes us realize the compositions' status as not mere descriptions, but as re-creations (Sayre 135) – as, indeed, *poetry*.[52]

In this collection several poems are devoted to paintings or works of art[53]: among them, "The Fruit" (CP2 416). Referring to Picasso's "Old Blind Beggar with a Boy" (1903) – from the artist's "Blue Period" – this slender and dense poem, with its sparse punctuation, leaves the speaker of the first and eleventh lines, "Waking," ambiguous. This matter is important because, if the person who says "Waking" is "I" – a (highly probable) man – he is in complete control of the situation in which the female voice – who twice says "I was eating pears!"[54] – by uttering a perplexity, would, perhaps, signal a subterranean request for help and/or an implicit desire for a real encounter. In this case, the "I," physically present, but emotionally distant, is so turned in on himself and on his thoughts that rather than seeing the woman with her actual (however gaunt) body, he sees her *through* that of the emaciated young boy in Picasso's painting. If, on the contrary, it is the female voice who also says "Waking," then "she," aware of the physical-psychical moments of her existence, of her coming to consciousness/awareness, is pointing out her request more vividly (even if indirectly). That she may indeed be the one who says "Waking" may be suggested by the iconic position of the second "she said" (line 13). After the hiatus of the previous stanza break and at the beginning of the final stanza, rather than being "gathered//into himself" like Picasso's boy and the "I," her twice-repeated utterance would make her the one who opens up the possibility of a more than perfunctory communication – even if difficult, as signaled by the oxymoronic "separate jointly." And "jointly," at the end of the penultimate line, looks and tends to "we embraced" in the final line since, as in many other cases, the poem "lives in its trajectory, not in its statements."[55] Thanks, probably, to her insistence/persistence, at the very end "I" and "she" finally become "we." At this stage in his artistic maturity, Williams does not need a cubist painting to inspire him: as juxtaposition, fragmentation and intersection come from the language, a painting from Picasso's "Blue Period" is sufficient to evoke a disjointed (but ultimately conjoined) state of being.

In another composition, "The Gift" (*CP2* 430–31), dedicated once again to the adoration of the Magi[56] – and, like the two previous poems on the same subject, employing (even if not exclusively) the staggered tercet – Williams covertly refers to Botticelli's "Mystical Nativity" in the National Gallery in London. This is an extremely strange painting in which the Magi (extraneous to the scene of the nativity proper) and the devils (unconnected to both the nativity and the epiphany) are present.[57] While merging two distinct events (Jesus's birth and his being shown to the world), the painting also hints at a third one: Jesus's Second Coming at the end of times.[58] What is even stranger is that Botticelli's Magi carry no gifts, although Williams – not moved by religious faith, but by emotional fervor – seems to expand on them from the first line ("the wise men of old brought gifts"). But "of old" may indicate a tradition disregarded by Botticelli with whom, however, the poet agrees as he points out the futility of such presents ("What could a baby know/of gold ornaments/or frankincense and myrrh" and "The rich gifts/so unsuitable for a child"). Williams, in fact, hails what the Magi (like the shepherds in a traditional "Nativity") did before "the god of love": they "bowed down/ to worship/this perfection." They brought Jesus the *real* "hard gold," the true "Gift" (in the singular): love. Prosodically connected, in part, to the poems in the two previous volumes,[59] "The Gift" again emphasizes the role of the imagination that "knows all stories/before they are told/and knows the truth of this one." And thus the poet can conclude his artistic and personal life ("old" is repeated three times) by stating what he had never dared write so clearly before: "What is death,/beside this?// Nothing." A lyric poet, a singer of love, in the very last poem of this collection ("The Rewaking," *CP2* 437) he can reiterate a final reference to it as indispensable even to our planet's source of energy and light: "by/your love the very sun/itself is revived."

NOTES

1. For this volume Williams received, posthumously, the Pulitzer Prize.
2. Hugh Kenner, "William Carlos Williams: In Memoriam," in Jerome Mazzaro, ed., *Profile of William Carlos Williams* (Columbus, OH: Charles E. Merrill, 1971), 116.
3. James Laughlin, *Remembering William Carlos Williams* (New York: New Directions, 1995), 37.
4. James E.B. Breslin, *William Carlos Williams, An American Artist* (Chicago: University of Chicago Press, 1985); as Peter Halter claims, in "Williams's successful poems, words are ... also things, word sounds to be heard and word bodies to be seen on the page, audible and visible presences which can be arranged into sound patterns or visual designs." Peter Halter, *The Revolution in the Visual Arts and the Poetry of William Carlos Williams* (Cambridge: Cambridge University Press, 1994), 213.
5. See also Zachariah Pickard, "William Carlos Williams, Description, and the Avant-Garde," *American Literary History* 22.1 (2010): 85–108.
6. In a 1955 letter to John C. Thirlwall, Williams called the variable foot a "solution of the problem of modern verse" (*SL* 334).
7. Williams would also use it in *Paterson* V (1958). He had first used it at some length in *Paterson* II, although traces of it may also be found elsewhere: for instance, in "To Ford Madox Ford in Heaven" (1940) and in "Choral: The Pink Church" (1949).
8. On this subject, comments by Denise Levertov are particularly enlightening: "Each segment of a triadic cluster is a foot, and each has the same *duration* ... the reader must give full value to the spaces between the words ... duration in time, not number of syllables nor of stresses (or accents), is the simple, open secret of the variable foot" and also "An effect of the triadic line seems to me to be a certain stateliness of pace, even though individual line-segments may move swiftly. Thus they seem peculiarly appropriate to his late years and to express formally a hard-earned wisdom." (Denise Levertov, "On Williams' Triadic Line: or How to Dance on Variable Feet," in James McCorkle, ed., *Conversant Essays: Contemporary Poets on Poetry* [Detroit: Wayne State University Press, 1990], 143, 147). Cureton has underlined the importance of the interaction of visual prosody with the text's phonological, syntactic, and narrative systems (Richard D. Cureton, *Rhythmic Phrasing in English Verse* [London: Longman, 1992]).
9. Stephen Cushman, *William Carlos Williams and the Meanings of Measure* (New Haven, CT: Yale University Press, 1985), 92, "the triadic stanza replaces the elegiac couplet ... It is the modern elegiac format ... The poems of the middle fifties constitute an elegiac meditation on death, time, and change. In the

inscriptional format of the triadic stanza, Williams finds a visual design that is symmetrically elegant and dignified ... the triadic stanza has many uses, ranging from the celebration of erotic love to the lament for mortality and the search for consolation." According to some scholars, the triadic stanza was prompted by physical necessities after his stroke. Jerome Mazzaro, for instance, hypothesizes that it was due to his being unable to "return his gaze quickly to the left margin of a page" (Jerome Mazzaro, *William Carlos Williams. The Later Poems* [Ithaca: Cornell University Press, 1973], 79).

10. On the occasion of Williams's visit, McAlmon, very sick, forgotten, and bankrupt, represented what the poet feared most: failure.

11. Mariani calls it a "crazy quilt of forms" (Mariani 633).

12. Hillis Miller has described its general effect thus: "many actions are going on at once in a perpetual present, the poetic space, and though the images are necessarily sequential they form a chord which exists in a single moment" (J. Hillis Miller, *Poets of Reality* [Cambridge: Harvard University Press, 1965], 301).

13. This incident is recalled in his *Autobiography* together with the somewhat related French song "Sur le pont d'Avignon" (*A* 388–89). It is highly symbolic that this medieval bridge in Avignon has been broken since the seventeenth century: only four of its original twenty-two arches remain, and yet in the song "once dances, one dances" upon it.

14. In a 1955 letter to Thirlwall Williams wrote, "Poetry began ... with the dance, whose divisions ... are still known as measures ... and we still speak of their minuter elements as feet" (*SL* 331). Williams admired Isadora Duncan and knew Martha Graham personally (*A* 236–37).

15. See Sherman Paul, *The Music of Survival: A Biography of a Poem by William Carlos Williams* (Urbana: University of Illinois Press, 1968).

16. Especially in *IAG* (1925), but also in *Paterson* III and in the three Nahuatl poems in *Pictures from Brueghel* (see Christopher MacGowan, "'The Indian Emerging': Native American History in Later Williams," in *Rigor of Beauty: Essays in Commemoration of William Carlos Williams* [Bern: Peter Lang, 2004], 327–38).

17. These are the poem's final lines: "And I could not help thinking/of the wonders of the brain that/hears that music and of our/skill sometimes to record it."

18. Paul, *The Music of Survival*, 97.

19. Williams wrote that the imagination is best understood when words are considered "as a dance" so that "the author and reader are liberated *to pirouette* with the words" and create poetry (*CP1* 234; emphasis mine).

20. Natalie Gerber, "Tracing the Trajectory of a Williams Poem: From the Variable Foot to Triadic-Line Verse," *Paideuma* 38 (2011): 157–96; 181.

21. As Mariani observes, Williams did not "always escape the popular racial myths of his time" (Mariani 412).

22. From this same collection, "The Ivy Crown" is also a meditation on the meaning of love ("the jeweled prize") for an old couple: "The business of love is/cruelty *which,*/by our wills,/we transform/to live together" and "At our age the imagination/across the sorry facts/lifts us/to make roses/stand before thorns"(*CP2* 287–90).

23. About his interest in women on which he expanded in his *Autobiography*, he elsewhere said, "I had never been a roué and women remained an enigma; no two

had the same interest for me; they were all different. I was consequently interested in too many of them; and trying to find out about them all" (*IWWP* 64).
Such a statement makes his interest in women seem more cerebral than carnal.
As for Flossie, he once told Thirlwall, "I was always repulsed by her. She was
never passionately loving. I was completely devoted to her"(*CP1* 479).

24. Robert Lowell, "William Carlos Williams," *Hudson Review* 14.4 (1961–62):
530–36, 536.

25. Bob Perelman, "Doctor Williams's Position, Updated," in Louis Armand, ed.,
Contemporary Poetics (Evanston, IL: Northwestern University Press, 2007), 73.

26. In "Shadows," from this same collection, he writes, "things the imagination feeds
upon,/the scent of the rose,/startle us anew" (*CP2* 308–10).

27. Joan Burbick, "Grimaces of a New Age: The Postwar Poetry and Painting of
William Carlos Williams and Jackson Pollock," *Boundary 2* 10.3 (1982):
109–23, 111.

28. In "To a Dog Injured in the Street" from *The Desert Music* he writes of the bomb,
"I can do nothing/but sing about it/and so I am assuaged/from my pain"
(*CP2* 255).

29. Marilyn Kallet, *Honest Simplicity in William Carlos Williams's "Asphodel, That
Greeny Flower"* (Baton Rouge: Louisiana State University Press, 1985), 84.

30. Mazzaro, *William Carlos Williams: The Later Poems*, 89.

31. As early as 1914, in "Transitional," he had stated, "It is the woman in us/That
makes us write" (*CP1* 40). Diggory points out that in Williams's opinion, "the
woman's experience will be simply unimaginable ... She will remain Other
despite the artist's desire to possess her, and even, more mysteriously, despite
her own apparent willingness to be possessed." (Terence Diggory, *William
Carlos Williams and the Ethics of Painting* [Princeton, NJ: Princeton
University Press, 1991], 89).

32. Tiresias was also blind as Williams almost was in his last years.

33. The qualifier, "classic," may refer both to the indirectly evoked ancient mythology and to traditional, sexist thinking, and, therefore, take on an ironic edge,
since here he also writes, "A woman's brains/ which can be keen/are condemned,/
like a poet's."

34. Admittedly this is one of the few poems in which the speaker is a woman. His wife
pronounces a few words in "The Desert Music" and his mother's aphorisms are
recorded in his book-length memoir, *Yes, Mrs. Williams.*

35. Peter Schmidt, *William Carlos Williams, The Arts, and Literary Tradition* (Baton
Rouge: LSU Press, 1988), 208.

36. Something that his friends Pound and Moore had often done. Williams beautifully translates one of the most famous fragments by Sappho, whose prosodic
inventions, direct style, capacity to render physical and emotional desire, love's
despair and ecstasy, he could not but be consonant with.

37. Zhaoming Qian, "William Carlos Williams, David Raphael Wang, and the
Dynamic of East/West Collaboration," *Modern Philology*, 108.2 (2010):
304–21. In 1966, three years after Williams's death, *The Cassia Tree* – his
translations or, rather, his "recreations" of thirty-seven Chinese poems, written
in collaboration with David Raphael Wang – was published by New Directions.
See also, Zhaoming Qian, *Orientalism and Modernism. The Legacy of China
in Pound and Williams* (Durham, NC: Duke University Press, 1995), 113–65,

where Qian posits that Williams's interest in Chinese lyrics dated back to around 1916 when he was attracted by the brevity of the lines and the number of syllables they contain (usually 12) as well as by their elusiveness due to the dearth of syntactical connections.

38. Qian, *Orientalism and Modernism. The Legacy of China in Pound and Williams*, 163.

39. "... the trinity always seemed unstable. It lacked a fourth member, the devil. I found myself always conceiving my abstract designs as possessing four sides. That was natural enough with spring, summer, autumn and winter always before me." (*SL* 333[1955]).

40. Qian, "William Carlos Williams, David Raphael Wang, and the Dynamic of East/West Collaboration," 321.

41. Ibid., 317.

42. Laughlin, Remembering William Carlos Williams, 46. Cushman does not share Laughlin's opinion (*William Carlos Williams and the Meanings of Measure*, 15–50) nor does Donald Davie, in "A Demurral," *The New Republic* (April 20, 1987): 34–39.

43. Marjorie Perloff, "'To Give a Design': Williams and the Visualization of Poetry," in *The Dance of the Intellect: Studies in the Poetry of the Poundian Tradition* (Cambridge: Cambridge University Press, 1985), 104.

44. The first one, "Self-Portrait," is no longer believed to be by the Flemish master or a portrait of him (*CP2* 504–05).

45. There are many scholarly works devoted to the study of these paintings. To mention just a few: Grant F. Scott, "Ekphrasis and the Picture Gallery," in Thomas A. Sebeok and others, eds., *Advances in Visual Semiotics: The Semiotic Web 1992–1993* (Berlin: Mouton de Gruyter, 1995), 403–21; Wendy Steiner, *The Colors of Rhetoric* (Chicago: University of Chicago Press, 1982), 71–92; Mary Ann Caws, "A Double Reading by Design: Brueghel, Auden, and Williams," *The Journal of Aesthetics and Art Criticism* 41 (1983): 323–30; Irene R. Fairley, "On Reading Poems: Visual & Verbal Icons in William Carlos Williams' 'Landscape with the Fall of Icarus,'" *Studies in 20th Century Literature* 6 (1981): 67–97. For excellent analyses of some poems from this collection, see: for "Poem," Peter Halter, "Iconic Rendering of Motion and Process in the Poetry of William Carlos Williams," in Max Nanny and Olga Fisher, eds., *Form Miming Meaning: Iconicity in Language and Literature* (Amsterdam: Benjamins, 1999), 246–47; for "Iris," Schmidt 244–45; for "He Has Beaten about the Bush Long Enough" and "Poem (on getting a card)," Terence Diggory, "Image and Statement in the Late Poetics of William Carlos Williams," *WCWR* 19 (1993): 6–14.

46. "Interviews with William Carlos Williams." *Speaking Straight Ahead,* ed. Linda Welshimer Wagner (New York: New Directions, 1976), 53. When in a 1929 interview Williams was asked what his most salient characteristic was, he answered, "My sight" ("Questionnaire," *The Little Review,* XII.2 (1929): 87). In 1922 Burke had called him, "the master of the glimpse." Kenneth Burke, "Heaven's First Law," *The Dial* 72 (1922): 197–200, 197.

47. "An ekphrasis ... typically presents a reconfiguration and reordering of the artwork: some elements are given prominence and importance, others are down-played or ignored. Ekphrasis tiers the visual artwork in ways that subtly alter its

presence and shape its meaning" (Scott, "Ekphrasis and the Picture Gallery," 404).

48. Altieri maintains that for Williams poetry "consists less in what is said than in the compositional energies that give the saying a distinctive presence" (Charles Altieri, *Painterly Abstraction in Modernist American Poetry* [Cambridge: Cambridge University Press, 1989], 13). For instance, to highlight the diagonal slant that characterizes "Peasant Wedding," in following the poet's directions our eyes trace several diagonal lines across the canvas; in "The Corn Harvest," our eyes trace a triangle/cone (from the reaper to the women to the tree's foliage – that provides the shade – and back to the reaper) to underline the many triangular/conic shapes in the painting (sheaves, hats, steeples, the fork leant on the tree); in "The Adoration of the Kings," the movement of our eyes from the child to the Magi to Joseph and the soldiery traces a left-spiral like those to be found on shells to which "the downcast eyes of the Virgin" may resemble; in "The Parable of the Blind," where the title is part of the text and where the word "composition" is repeated three times, in a sort of self-reflexivity, the poem says that the "beggars" lead each other "diagonally downward//across the canvas." This process is not metaphorical, or not meant to be metaphorical: it is figurative, but also very concrete. Not in all the poems, by following the poet's indications, one can single out the predominant structural arrangement, but, perhaps, one can say that, if Williams creates "a dozen cubist portraits, fracturing Brueghel's surfaces to create new ones," he does so *not only* because he sees them with a cubist eye (Mariani 747).

49. Scott, "Ekphrasis and the Picture Gallery," 415.

50. Alice Entwistle, "'For W.C.W.', 'Yet Complexly': Creeley and Williams," *English: The Journal of the English Association* 50, 197 (2001): 127–48, 130.

51. In "An Approach to the Poem" (1947), he wrote, that "the poem … is a thing made up of words and punctuation, that is, words and the spaces between them" (*English Institute Essays, 1947* [New York: AMS Press, 1965] 52).

52. According to Sayre the reasons for these recreations are due to the fact that, "[i]n the heterogeneous modern world – a world marked by difference and divorce – no connection except an *aesthetic* one seems to exist between subject and object" (Sayre 132). In his 1936 book, *Bilder aus Bruegels Bildern*, the renowned art historian Gustav Glück focused on several details in some of the Flemish artist's paintings, maintaining that "in order to appreciate the whole one must be able to understand and enjoy the part" (Gustav Glück, *Brueghel. Details from His Pictures*, trans. Elizabeth Byam Shaw [London: Williams and Norgate, 1936], 9). Glück's 1952 *Peter Brueghel the Elder* was a major source for Williams's sequence (*CP2* 504).

53. Some of them refer back to others published in other collections: for instance, "The Wedding Dance in the Open Air" (*CP2* 390–91) recalls "The Dance" (*CP2* 58–59) and "A Formal Design" (*CP2* 414) recalls the unicorn tapestries in *Paterson* V.

54. Symbolically, pears stand for eroticism and sensuality (Jean Chevalier and Alain Gheerbrant, *Dictionary of Symbols* [London: Penguin Books, 1996], 742). Their shape may recall a woman's torso (as Man Ray showed in his photograph, "Le violon d'Ingres" [1924]).

55. Hugh Kenner, "The Drama of Utterance," *The Massachusetts Review* 3.2 (1962): 328–30, 329.
56. Williams had already celebrated the Epiphany in *Paterson* V and in this same volume in "The Adoration of the Kings." In both poems he refers to the painting as a Nativity. For a detailed analysis of the three poems see Diggory, *William Carlos Williams and the Ethics of Painting.*
57. Traditionally, neither Joseph, nor the ass and the ox should be part of the scene of the Epiphany. This painting, the only one signed and dated (1501) by its author, shows the influence of Girolamo Savonarola's sermons on Botticelli.
58. It is the presence of the fleeing or dying devils that suggests the Universal Judgment (from *The Book of Revelation* 12:13).
59. MacGowan has shown how two compositions from *Pictures from Brueghel* ("The High Bridge Above the Tagus River at Toledo" and "Tapiola") may function as transition poems between this collection and the two previous ones since they focus on memory and survival, even if they make use of a looser line than the triadic one. (Christopher MacGowan, "Williams' Last Decade: Bridging the Impasse," *Twentieth Century Literature* 35 [1989]:389–405).

10

IAN COPESTAKE

Williams in the American grain

Williams's place in a lineage informed by nineteenth-century American Romanticism is rendered ambiguous by his own selective acknowledgement of its importance to his development as a poet. In the main this was a pragmatic decision on his part, informed by the pressures he felt, particularly in the 1920s, in eking out a path for an American literature and culture that, if it was to truly thrive, needed to be released from the accrued cultural authority of Europe's artistic achievements. The answer to questions of lineage was thus, as Williams cited in his prose works of the first half of that decade, one of violence against the past, of cutting oneself free of ascriptions to tradition and established convention in order to "make it new."

Williams's sense of the key to initiating a modern American renaissance in the arts was stated by the narrator of his work, *The Great American Novel* (1923), who declared it time for American culture to stand on its own two feet:

> We are only children when we acknowledge ourselves to be children. Weight of culture, weight of learning, weight of everything such as abandon in any sense has nothing to do with it. We must first isolate ourselves. Free ourselves even more than we have. Let us learn the essentials of the American situation. (*I* 211)

Williams was soon to set himself the task of scrutinizing those essentials by rewriting a history of America itself, through the eighteen impressionistic essays of *In the American Grain* published in 1925. Here Williams beat a chronological trail through the lives of men such as "Eric the Red," Cotton Mather and Père Sebastian Rasles to outline his sense of the consequences of a wrong turn that he perceived America had taken in its historical development. Plumbing the depths of those essentials also led the way to a commitment to symbolic violence, which he expressed in the prose sections of his 1923 sequence *Spring and All*, a trope used to convey a need to tap the repressed energies and creative impulses that he saw as key to reviving culture in an American grain. What needed to be broken through, in Williams's rather reductive thesis, were the Puritanical restrictions he traced in his history of America and the subsequent forms of prohibition that the country now literally found itself in in the 1920s. Thus the fierce iconoclasm of his writing in this period was driven by a commitment to the imagination, and the possibility for cultural renewal that Williams felt it could inspire, a dedication expressed in *Spring and All* by the following call to arms: "The imagination, intoxicated by prohibitions, rises to drunken heights to destroy the world. Let it rage, let it kill. The imagination is supreme" (*CP1* 179).

One by-product of the violent need to separate American art from the weight of European culture and its past was in the choice of lineage Williams, like other modernist voices in America at this time, felt comfortable claiming. Whitman, for instance, was part of a usable past for establishing modern writing on an independent footing in the United States due to his nativist associations, but Emerson was not. This established a contradiction, for Williams writes very much out of an Emersonian tradition, and Whitman saw himself as an answer to Emerson's similar mid-nineteenth-century call for a national literature. Yet in the context of American modernism's struggle for cultural independence and validation, only one of these precursors was deemed claimable. One of Williams's rare explicit references to Emerson is in *The Great American Novel*, and it shows Williams making use of the influential terms established by George Santayana's 1911 address "The Genteel Tradition in American Philosophy." In his talk, Santayana argued that Emerson, along with Poe and Hawthorne, had not been rigorous enough in their thought and art to free America from being, as he put it, "a young country with an old mentality," one of reverence to the thought and traditions of the past. Furthermore, it had become a country with "two mentalities," in which, Santayana claimed, "one-half of the American mind, that not occupied intensely in practical affairs, has remained, I will not say high-and-dry, but slightly becalmed; it has floated gently in the back-water, while, alongside, in invention and industry and social organisation the other half of the mind was leaping down a sort of Niagara Rapids." His speech contained an assessment of Whitman as "[t]he one American writer who has left the genteel tradition entirely behind," though he underlined the limitations of Whitman's example as would Williams.[1]

This utilizing of the terms of Santayana's polarizing argument reflected Williams's own desperation during the interwar years in the face of threats to the renewed sense of possibility for American letters which he had fought to stimulate. While part of that process was to pragmatically condemn Emerson as "imitative" (*I* 211) and point to the nativist example of Whitman as a starting point for American creativity in the arts, this approach obscured the fact that Williams's attitude to Emerson constituted an Emersonian attitude, as the end towards which he employed Emerson and Whitman in opposition to each other emulated the former's desire to see "new thoughts" preserved from the dangers of heavy reliance on "the dead forms of our forefathers."[2]

It was also an attitude that showed Williams's deep understanding of Emerson, as the latter argued that the authority invested in revered conveyors of truth and knowledge must be questioned. Yet it is the manner of Williams's pursuit of this end that obscures the Emersonian nature of his intent. For Williams, like Emerson, man's relationship to creeds and written versions of American history, or, in Emerson's case, the authority of biblical scripture, needed to heed the Concordite's observation that "the truest state of mind, rested in, becomes false. Thought is the manna which cannot be stored. It will sour if kept, & tomorrow must be gathered anew."[3] Williams's own approach to the writing of history reflects this questioning of authorized narratives and sees him take personal responsibility for gathering anew and understanding the information contained within established versions of history. In such historical writings as *In the American Grain* (1925) and his essay "The American Background" (1934) Williams presents himself as a student of the American past, seeking evidence of the roots of a "culture devoid of the undue influence of European values."[4] Writing reflectively to Horace Gregory in 1939, Williams indicated that his construction of such historical studies of America allowed him to take sole responsibility for the terms of his own relationship to his country's past:

> I felt from earliest childhood that America was the only home I could ever possibly call my own. I felt that it was expressly founded for me, personally, and that it must be my first business in life to possess it; that only by making it my own from the beginning to my own day, in detail, should I ever have a basis for knowing where I stood. I must have a basis for orienting myself formally in the beliefs which activated me from day to day. Nothing in the school histories interested me, so I decided as far as possible to go to whatever source material I could get at and start my own valuations there: to establish myself from my own reading, in my own way, in the locality which by birthright had become my own. (*SL* 185)

Significantly, it is Emerson's thought and example that, as Bryce Conrad has argued, underlies Williams's perception of history:

> More than any of his contemporaries, Williams shared Emerson's profound engagement with the process of creating historical knowledge. Like Emerson, whose essays again and again assert the primacy of self-education, Williams felt

the need to investigate the epistemological basis of the act of knowing itself. And in locating the presence of history in the locus of the perceiver, Williams uses much the same formulation that Emerson had in his essay 'History:' "We are always coming up with the emphatic facts of history in our private experience and verifying them here. All history becomes subjective; in other words there is properly no history, only biography. Every mind must know the whole lesson for itself – must go over the whole ground. What it does not see, what it does not live, it will not know."[5]

Williams's sense of frustration at America's continued cultural dependence on a European past was at its most acute in the 1920s, for by this time America had shown itself to be capable of invention in all other aspects of modern existence, in terms of its politics and economy especially, while the endeavours of its innovative artists and writers remained confined to small circulation publications and far from public recognition. He thus often took a strident tone, sometimes close to one of despair, in imploring contemporary America to recognize its own vital relationship to the language and ideas embodied in tradition, and to attack the perception that such traditions rendered futile and worthless America's own thought and art. For Williams the modern imagination, particularly in his country, was seen to lack confidence in the belief that it could produce works of art and ideas capable of standing alongside the established traditions of the world.

Williams addressed this lack of confidence in his essay "Yours, O Youth" (1921). In it he bemoaned his country's consistent inability to recognize the value of its contemporary experience as a basis for invention in the arts:

> It has been by paying naked attention first to the thing itself that American plumbing, American shoes, American bridges, indexing systems, locomotives, printing presses, city buildings, farm implements, and a thousand other things have become notable in the world. Yet we are timid in believing that in the arts discovery and invention will take the same course. And there is no reason why they should unless our writers have the inventive intelligence of our engineers and cobblers. (*SE* 35)

There is a clear but unacknowledged repetition of Emerson here, this time from a famous passage in "The Poet" (1844):

> Our logrolling, our stumps and their politics, our fisheries, our Negroes, and Indians, our boasts, and our repudiations, the wrath of rogues, and the pusillanimity of honest men, the northern trade, the southern planting, the western clearing, Oregon, and Texas, are yet unsung. Yet America is a poem in our eyes; its ample geography dazzles the imagination, and it will not wait long for metres.[6]

Consistent with his pragmatic use of Santayana's polarizing terms, the title Williams gave to his essay, "Yours, O Youth," echoes and adapts the inference contained in the title and sense of Whitman's poem "Pioneers! O Pioneers" (1865, 1881), and so he demonstrates his preference for Whitman's example over Emerson's, and does not acknowledge his text's shadowing of the latter's famous clarion call. Williams, in Whitmanesque pose, thus implored his fellow American artists to follow the example set by the modern pioneers who had established his country's worldwide fame in his own age, by reiterating Whitman's call to a previous American epoch.

An additional reason for Williams's heightened desperation in this decade was the 1922 publication and success of T. S. Eliot's poem *The Waste Land*, which Williams, in his autobiography, called "the great catastrophe to our letters" (*A* 146). Eliot's unwillingness in that poem to see beyond what he condemned as the barrenness and sterility of modern existence left no room for the optimism inherent in Williams's view of the possibility inherent in local conditions for the growth of culture:

> I felt [Eliot] had rejected America and I refused to be rejected and so my reaction was violent. I realized the responsibility I must accept. I knew he would influence all subsequent American poets and take them out of my sphere. I had envisaged a new form of poetic composition, a form for the future. It was a shock to me that he was so tremendously successful; my contemporaries flocked to him – away from what I wanted. It forced me to be successful. (*IWWP* 30)

Eliot's success was aided by the editing and promotional skills of Williams's close friend Ezra Pound, who had established himself in Europe and so set himself against Williams's stubborn, nativist dedication to nurturing a culture of writing on home soil. Faced with modernism's perceived movement away from his own sense of its potential, Williams adopted a polarizing rhetoric in which he set his own nativist agenda against those who fled to Europe and thus promoted the "nativist" example of Whitman as a starting point to be built on. A year after the appearance of Eliot's poem, Williams's narrator in *The Great American Novel* mocked the habitual dismissiveness associated with any attempt to establish America's cultural independence from Europe:

> "do you mean that you are attempting to set down the American background? You will go mad. Why? Because you are trying to do nothing at all. The American background? It is Europe. It can be nothing else. (*I* 196)

In his 1934 essay "The American Background," Williams's nativist argument for American culture continued to support Emerson's recognition that

"America is a poem in our eyes; its ample geography dazzles the imagination, and it will not wait long for metres" ("The Poet" 1844).

Echoing the two-mentalities thesis that Santayana had earlier proffered, Williams's study of America's history drew out a further sense of a split in America's attitude to experience, one which he felt was instrumental in cutting it off from self-reliance in exploring and valuing its own creative responses to its environment. The blame for this lack of willingness to embrace reality wholeheartedly, and instead place reason before a sensual engagement with the world, was the persistence of old-world religious influences such as Puritanism on the American psyche. The element of "contact" which he found the English settlers in particular to be averse to, whether it be in the nature of their engagement with the natives they encountered or their aesthetic response, or lack of it, to the American landscape itself, determined Williams's own establishment of a small press journal of that name in 1920, with Robert McAlmon, which sought to advance the nativist argument as a definition of culture, and to showcase what could be achieved in the arts in America.

An example of the "contact" that Williams's felt defined the success of other modern writers, and which Americans could aspire to, was embodied in the writing of James Joyce. In his editorial comment to the 1921 issue of *Contact*, he outlined a relationship to traditions of the past that, unlike Eliot's longing for a return to lost values, could establish a healthy burgeoning of creative expression reflective of modern conditions. Williams saw the startling modernity of Joyce's writing as, paradoxically, a reflection of "a classical method," in which the modern world is witnessed "emerging among the living ancients by paying attention to the immediacy of its own contact" (*SE* 28). As a living reflection of the past such writing embodied contact with one's contemporary moment, and gave it a distinctive and appropriate form. As Paul Mariani points out, "Joyce's *Ulysses*, [appeared] in instalments in *The Little Review* at the same time that Williams was publishing [parts of *Kora in Hell*] in the same magazine" (Mariani 149). Joyce's example thus represented for Williams the successful development of a modern aesthetic situating the present moment in a healthy relationship to the spirit of foreign traditions. The warning that Americans "are still too prone to admire and to copy... the thing which is French or Irish alone," prompted Williams in his editorial to urge American artists to focus on "the local phase of the game of writing," and so "give all our energy to the setting up of new vigors of artistic perception, invention and expression in the United States" (*SE* 29). His concern with locality is here a concern not with place but with the local terms of one's struggle with the "staid incumbrances" (*SE* 28) of language, a challenge he was to fully address through his long poem *Paterson*.

Furthermore, he insists that America can, by following this path, legitimately take its place among the living traditions of the past by echoing the distinctive responses of other times and places to their own day.

Williams's own sense of the need for "contact" with American realities, and of the need to find adequate, modern poetic forms and styles to express them in, included his demand for poetry to reflect modern American patterns of speech. Such innovations, however, emerged through his historical engagement with his country's relationship to Europe. It is for this reason that Louis Martz called *In the American Grain* Williams's "prose-preparation" for *Paterson*, and more specifically in this regard underlined the importance of the chapter entitled "Père Sebastian Rasles."[7] In this chapter, following on as it does from Williams's overview of Cotton Mather, Williams switches attention away from his focus on important figures in American history and begins with an autobiographical account of his arrival in Paris in January 1923 for a sojourn that saw him engage with a host of the emergent greats of modernist art and writing. An imposing list of names immediately greets the reader and Williams soon begins to chart his own sudden awakening to parallels between these contemporary experimenters and his subsequent portrait of Rasles:

> Picasso (turning to look back, with a smile), Braque (brown cotton), Gertrude Stein (opening the doors of a cabinet of MSS), Tzara (grinning), André Germain (blocking the door), Van der Pyl (speaking of St. Cloud), Bob Chandler (prodding Marcel), Marcel (shouting), Salmon (in a corner) and my good friends Philippe and Madam Soupault; the Prince of Dahomi, Clive Bell (dressed), Nancy, Sylvia, Clotilde, Sally, Kitty, Mina and her two lovely daughters; James and Norah Joyce (in a taxi at the Place de l'Étoile), McAlmon, Antheil, Bryher, H.D. and dear Ezra who took me to talk with Léger; and finally Adrienne Monnier – these were my six weeks in Paris. (*IAG* 105)

Williams explains that in meeting these people he was at first confronted by "that resistant core of nature upon which I had so long been driven for support" (105). In berating himself he clarifies his aim in writing his history of America, and in doing so engages directly with the issue of morality:

> we have no conception at all of what is meant by moral, since we recognize no ground our own – and that this rudeness rests all upon the unstudied character of our beginnings. (109)

Williams attempts to drive out into the open the resistance to experience that he feels within himself, and that he sees as intrinsically immoral, and in tracing this resistance historically he points to the enduring influence of what he terms "Puritanism":

There is a "puritanism" – of which you hear, of course, but you have never felt
it stinking all about you – that has survived to us from the past.   (115)

For Williams the American modernist project finds an idealized precursor in
the figure of Rasles, whom he describes as

a spirit, rich, blossoming, generous, able to give and to receive, full of taste,
a nose, a tongue, a laugh, enduring, self-forgetful in beneficence – a new spirit in
the New World.
All that will be new in America will be anti-Puritan. It will be of another root.
It will be more from the heart of Rasles, in the north.   (120)

For Williams the rejection of a Puritanical resistance to experience is
a rejection of the stern dogmatic insistence upon a moral code that deter-
mines the manner in which meaning is given to experience. The manner of
Williams's embrace of Rasles thus sees him revive the moral question by
associating it with openness to the world, rather than the imposition of
a collective will upon that world:

He was a great MAN. Reading his letters, it is a river that brings sweet water
to us. THIS is a moral source not reckoned with, peculiarly sensitive and
daring in its close embrace of native things. His sensitive mind. For everything
his fine sense, blossoming, thriving, opening, reviving – not shutting out – was
tuned.   (121)

Williams insists on the moral nature of this openness. The contact that Rasles
is seen to embody through his enactment of a "close embrace of native
things" allows Williams to underline a tradition of which he sees himself
part, and which he engages with directly through his struggle with his
personal European heritage (Williams's father was English). As such he
experiences the effort that he deems necessary to establish a ground for the
burgeoning of creative expression on American soil. Williams's own poetic
exploration of that local soil through the project that came to form his
subsequent life-work, the writing of Paterson, saw him reflect on, and dig
into, a single 'unpoetic' American location, the "vilest swillhole in christen-
dom," of Paterson, New Jersey (IAG 195). However, before he could set his
mind to mining that locality for his poem, the 1920s saw him grappling with
America's, and his own, European past in order to identify how best to avoid
the mistakes of those early arrivals to the new world. Williams's In the
American Grain, his manuscript Rome, unpublished until 1978, and his
first novel A Voyage to Pagany (1928) all emerged from his year-long
sabbatical in 1923–1924, including six months in Europe, in which he left
behind Rutherford and his medical practice for almost a year in order to
write.

Part of what Williams saw as the madness of the American background that he investigated in the writing that emerged from this journey was that of desire, of the need for creativity to feed off the imagination by breaking through to instincts that had, in America, been culturally repressed. This imaginative erotic journey is re-enacted in Williams's fictionalized account of his year abroad in *A Voyage to Pagany*, through the person of Dev Evans and his arrival in Rome and the "Ancient Springs of Purity and of Plenty" (*VP*83) he experiences there. Evans's experience of a "resurgent paganism" (*VP* 105) in that city was carried forth by Williams into his exploration of the trope of sexual desire, both in that work and through the far more unencumbered expression of erotic desire which rendered his subsequent manuscript *Rome* unpublishable. In these works Williams established a means of reconnecting the split mentalities and division he had identified in his own Puritan-influenced culture by re-engaging with the regenerative processes of the imagination through the agency of the female body, and symbolized by the fecundity of the earth.

What Williams's poetry at its most forceful confronts is not only an appeal to the imagination, which becomes his life-work to advance, but also an articulation of the deleterious effects on the culture of the United States of its historical failure to attach value to the realities of the American environment. Instead, by continuing to view the country as a blank canvas, just as the colonial settlers did, it is made receptive to notions of progress based on greed, acquisitiveness and the imposition of human will. One of Williams's most powerful expressions of the consequences of the historical wrong turn taken by his country is poem "XVIII" of *Spring and All* (1923), more commonly known as "To Elsie."

In the poem Williams again plays on the association of madness with the American background, but here it is the effect of the country's materialistic, superficial culture on one lost individual, "some Elsie," who is presented as "expressing with broken // brain the truth about us" (*CP1* 218). Williams writes specifically here of his family's mentally ill maid, whose dire background saw her

> rescued by an
> agent—
> reared by the state and
>
> sent out at fifteen to work in
> some hard-pressed
> house in the suburbs—
>
> some doctor's family   (218)

The alliteration of "s" sounds in this passage emphasizes the repeated epithet "some," and thus underlines the quality of vagueness and detachment that pervades the poem. Such repetitions were traditionally used in lyric poetry to evoke sensuousness, but Williams parodies this association by showing that desire in the poem is despoiled and disassociated from feeling. Instead, vulnerable women such as Elsie are

> tricked out that night
> with gauds
> from imaginations which have no
>
> peasant traditions to give them
> character
> but flutter and flaunt
>
> sheer rags—succumbing without
> emotion
> save numbed terror
>
> under some hedge of choke-cherry
> or viburnum—   (217)

The lack of "peasant traditions" alludes to forms of grounding or contact which have become unhinged and replaced by material aspiration and, for the religious, otherworldly reward, which further undermines the value seen in the reality we inhabit. Desire is instead "addressed to cheap / jewelry / and rich young men with fine eyes // as if the earth under our feet / were / an excrement of some sky" (218). The role of the imagination as a means of re-engaging with "the earth under our feet" is left vulnerable to this onslaught, as "it is only in isolate flecks that / something / is given off" (219). For Williams the poem acts as both a warning and an affirmation of the fact that it is the poet, writer and artist who can act as witnesses to such moments and so preserve hope. Without this, as the poem concludes, there is "No one / to witness / and adjust, no one to drive the car" (219).

Williams's long poem *Paterson* constitutes his continuing dramatization of the conflict between America's cultural inheritance and the plight of the imagination, the only means to renew engagement with the world. Though it was originally intended to be published as four books, which came out between 1946 and 1951, a fifth appeared in 1958, while fragments of a sixth remained in his papers after his death. In that draft he returned to his earlier focus on formative American historical figures, and these extensions of his project confirmed his development of an open-ended quest to affirm a poet's role in a world riven by disconnection from language, experience, knowledge and history. His focus on the city of Paterson served to exemplify the plight of

America – as its history, dominated by the plans realized there for economic expansion established by Alexander Hamilton, and based on utilizing the power of the Passaic river, revealed the commercial and political forces which raped the landscape, leaving it poisoned and crippled. The optimistic fervour with which Williams had engaged with American history in the early 1920s had also, by the 1940s, been confronted by the economic realities of the plight of the artist. The paucity of sales of *In the American Grain* confirmed the huge hurdles facing Williams in his efforts to advance his arguments and break through to a wider audience. But despite these struggles to be heard, the roots of *Paterson* had been laid.

Among the challenges facing Williams in writing *Paterson* was to find an appropriate form for a poem which set out to expose myths about American power and progress, a power which, as James Guimond stated, quoting Robert Lowell's laudatory review of Book II, "is almost entirely evil, the destructive producer of an 'America grown pathetic and tragic, brutalized by inequality, disorganized by industrial chaos, and faced with annihilation.' "[8] Thus he sought to find a language and structure for the poem that did not join forces with such powers by similarly imposing its meaning on the reader through force of will and discursive logic, but instead allowed for the discovery of meaning among the details – including letter fragments and newspaper cuttings, all of which constituted the river of language captured by the poem. Similarly, Williams's growing need to make sense of the path he had chosen, and to assess the merits or otherwise of the artistic faith he had maintained in his own work, also became a central autobiographical issue of *Paterson*. Increasingly apparent to the poet-protagonist is the fact that the world he inhabits is one in which "Divorce is / the sign of knowledge in our time" (*P* 17). The wanderings of Paterson take in his frustrated efforts to attain, or see reflected elsewhere in his environment, his own desire for contact with the world. Through the figure of the doctor-poet Paterson, Williams also reflects on the example of his own lifelong struggle to affirm faith in a type of knowledge distinct from the materialistic values which predominate. The form of the poem thus affords readers a comparable experience of the struggle to attain contact with forms of grounding, through the homologous nature of the need to assimilate and order their responses to the details and fragments of the poem.

Williams's aversion to a more reader-friendly and logical approach established his determination to make the form of *Paterson* actively reflect the quest for knowledge he had experienced in his own life. As he stated to Kenneth Burke in 1947, in his poem he was trying "to work out the problems of a new prosody – but I am doing it by writing rather than 'logic' which might castrate me" (*SL* 257–58). Williams's efforts to dramatize the struggles inherent in his life as a poet through the persona of Paterson thus constitute the means by which he continues to be a "witness" (*P* 31, 207), and to report honestly. As such the issue of contact also constituted a form of education, a means of learning and teaching how to re-establish a connection between human consciousness and the world, ideas which Williams had engaged in through his reading of, among others, John Dewey, and the findings of which he committed to notes, published in 1974, eleven years after his death, as *The Embodiment of Knowledge*. These notes further establish his place within a pragmatic tradition running from Emerson, a tradition that was committed, as Dewey perceived it, "to the use of freed intelligence as the method of directing change."[9] Furthermore, in finding an appropriate form for his long poem, Williams called on his non-discursive conception of the poem as a "machine made of words," in which it isn't what the poet says "that counts as a work of art" but "what he makes, with such intensity of perception that it lives with an intrinsic movement of its own to verify its authenticity" (*SE* 256–57). The object made by the poet can thus reflect the authenticity of his response to the reality before him, and to the materials at hand, through his efforts to find an appropriate form. For the form of the poem to continue to be authentic, it also needed to reflect the struggle inherent in Williams's efforts to realize his sense of self and his wider aims as an artist. Williams's desire for contact with reality through authentic means thus progressed from his scrutiny of the details and events of the world around him to the language commonly ignored as the means by which that world is brought into view.

Williams's career beyond the 1940s again responded to the deepening of the poet's response to the need to bear witness, especially in the face of his near annihilation through the strokes that began to incapacitate him after 1951. However, he continued to reaffirm his intention, as he expressed it in 1955 in "To Asphodel, That Greeny Flower," to demonstrate that

> It is difficult
> to get the news from poems
>   yet men die miserably every day
>   for lack
> of what is found there.   (*CP*2 318)

This was true especially of his self-reflective analysis of the values his life had been lived to fulfil. *Paterson* represents the apotheosis of this process of self-scrutiny, and stands as a poetic dramatization of Williams's concern for contact with the American grain. That the process was unending showed in his return to American history in the four pages of typescripts of his projected Book VI of *Paterson*, in which Washington and Alexander Hamilton resurface. Throughout his engagement with American history, Williams foregrounded his fears for the efficacy of his quest to understand it and give it expression, but never reneged on his commitment to confront it, or his sense of the wider social importance of making that effort.

NOTES

1. George Santayana, *The Genteel Tradition: Nine Essays by George Santayana*, ed. Douglas L. Wilson (Cambridge, MA: Harvard University Press, 1967), 39–40, 52.
2. Ralph Waldo Emerson. journal entry. 2 June 1835. *Emerson in His Journals*, ed. Joel Porte (Cambridge, MA: Harvard University Press, 1984), 83.
3. Ralph Waldo Emerson. journal entry. 13 May 1835. *Emerson in His Journals*. 138.
4. Ron Callan. *William Carlos Williams and Transcendentalism: Fitting the Crab in a Box* (New York: St. Martin's Press, 1992), 10.
5. Bryce Conrad. *Refiguring America: A Study of William Carlos Williams'* In the American Grain (Urbana: University of Illinois Press, 1990), 20–21.
6. Ralph Waldo Emerson. *The Journals and Miscellaneous Notebooks of Ralph Waldo Emerson*, Vol. 3, ed. Joseph Slater (Cambridge, MA: Belknap Press, 1965), 21–22.
7. Louis Martz, *The Poem of the Mind* (New York: OUP, 1966), 134.
8. James K. Guimond, *The Art of William Carlos Williams: A Discovery and Possession of America* (Chicago: University of Illinois Press, 1968), 169.
9. *John Dewey: The Later Works, 1925–53*, Vol. 11, ed. Jo Ann Boydston (Carbondale: Southern Illinois University Press, 2008), 41.

11

KERRY DRISCOLL

Williams and women

I "their skirted galleons of sex"

Even the most casual reader of William Carlos Williams's poetry cannot help but notice the frequency and imaginative fervor with which he writes about women, ranging from members of his immediate family – most notably, his mother, grandmother, and wife – to casual acquaintances and passing strangers. Women are everywhere in his work, an abiding source of fascination and inspiration. As Doc, the poet's persona in his 1942 play *Many Loves*, exclaims: "Women! With their small heads and big lustrous eyes. All my life I have never been able to escape them" (*ML* 84). Williams attributed this attraction largely to the circumstances of his upbringing, explaining in his 1951 *Autobiography*: "I never had a sister, no aunts and no female cousins, at least within striking distance. So that aside from Mother and Grandma [Emily Wellcome, his father's mother] I never knew a female intimately for my entire young life. That was very important. It generated in me enough curiosity to burn up fifty growing boys" (*A* 4–5).

In some respects, Williams's curiosity about the otherness of women was self-reflexive, stemming from a desire to understand the sources of his own creativity. His early views on the subject were influenced by Otto Weininger's 1903 *Sex and Character*,[1] which divided the field of psychology into male and female halves and proposed that "woman was essentially substance, subject to man's genial capacity for forming her ... Woman was passive, man active; woman wholly sexual in her nature, man only partly so."[2] These polarities, Weininger alleged, could be resolved by the idea of a third, intermediate gender in which male and female characteristics converged. Williams's reading of *Sex and Character* fostered a recognition of "his own sexual admixture";[3] as he told Viola Baxter Jordan in 1911: "You are quite right ... men are not strong enough to 'bat air' with women. That forever proves to me I am not a man; they, men, disgust me and if I must say it fill me with awe and admiration. I am too much a woman."[4]

Williams addresses the issue of artistic androgyny in his 1914 poem "Transitional," which is structured as a dialogue between two male voices –

writers respectively identified only as "He" and "I" – who "undergo a blurring of gender identities."[5] "He" initiates the conversation by announcing: "It is the woman in us/ That makes us write –/ Let us acknowledge it –/ Men would be silent" (*CP1* 40). When "I" inquires whether his companion dares make this credo his "propaganda," "he" coyly responds, "Am I not I – here?" suggesting that identity itself is indeterminate.

Three years later, Williams used Weininger's theory of male and female psychology to frame his critique of "Lingual Psychology," a series of essays on language and creativity by the feminist philosopher Dora Marsden published in *The Egoist*. In "The Great Sex Spiral" – as the poet entitled his expansive two-part letter to the magazine's editor Harriet Shaw Weaver – he argues that "reality ... is very different for the male and female" due to the "completely opposed sense-experience" of their bodies:

> Man's only positive connexion with the earth is in the fleeting sex function. When not in pursuit of the female man has absolutely no necessity to exist ... Thus the male pursuit leads only to further pursuit, that is, not toward the earth, but away from it – not to concreteness, but to further hunting, to stargazing, to idleness. On this fundamental basis rests male psychology ... Female psychology, on the other hand, is characterized by a trend not away from, but toward the earth, toward concreteness, since by her experience the reality of fact is firmly established for her.[6]

For Williams, the factual "reality" of women's experience was grounded in their biological capacity to bear children – a phenomenon with which he was well acquainted as an obstetrician. The "physical results" of gestation and maternity, he believed, connected women "indisputably and firmly with the earth ... by an unalterable chain."[7] According to Linda A. Kinnahan, this "inscription of the feminine as a combination of the sexual and the maternal provides [Williams] with the basis of his poetics and helps shape a theory of the imagination and its operations."[8]

The strong sympathies Williams expresses for women in his poetry are complicated – and to some extent compromised – by the erotic lens through which he tended to view them. This sensibility is exemplified in the 1916 lyric "The Young Housewife," which describes an anonymous woman in nightclothes who emerges from the privacy of her home to secure provisions from a street vendor. The speaker, passing in his car, immediately notes the vulnerability of this "shy, uncorseted" figure and likens her to "a fallen leaf," concluding:

> The noiseless wheels of my car
> rush with a crackling sound over
> dried leaves as I bow and pass smiling   (*CP1* 57).

As Williams informed John Thirlwall in the 1950s, he regarded this poem as an unequivocal tribute to its anonymous subject: "Whenever a man sees a beautiful woman it's an occasion for poetry – compensating beauty with beauty" (*CP1* 479). Some three decades later, however, Marjorie Perloff offered a starkly different interpretation, arguing that the poet's comparison of the young housewife to a "fallen leaf," when read in conjunction with the closing image of his car wheels "rush[ing] with a crackling sound over/dried leaves," not only objectifies her but also represents a violent "fantasy of sexual possession."[9] Like so many of Williams's poems about women, "The Young Housewife" celebrates the privilege and power of the male gaze.[10] Although the speaker describes himself as a benign, courtly presence, bowing and smiling as he drives past, the very fact of his mobility counterpoints the woman's confinement within the "wooden walls of her husband's house" – a metonym for the domestic limits of her existence. His power is further aggrandized by a god-like penetrating vision which allows him to imaginatively see her moving in dishabille behind closed doors before she literally appears at the curb. But most importantly, the speaker possesses the advantage of effacement – able to keenly observe the woman's vulnerability while himself remaining invisible. He surveys and passes judgment, deeming her "fallen," whereas she remains locked in the passivity of her unwitting subject position.

The chauvinistic sight lines of Williams's gaze are more apparent in a 1939 poem called "The Return to Work" in which the speaker ogles two secretaries "Promenading their/ skirted galleons of sex" as they "rock unevenly" down a staircase en route to their office after lunch. The poet transforms this quotidian scene by means of a playful extended metaphor wherein the land becomes sea, the stairs waves, and the tipsy secretaries boats, blown to their destination by the invisible "trade wind" of his approving gaze. As in the "The Red Wheelbarrow," "so much depends" here upon the romantic connotations of the archaic word "galleons" – large European sailing vessels commonly used from the sixteenth to eighteenth centuries. Often referred to as "treasure fleets," these ships – powered solely by wind – transported precious cargo like silver and gold from the New World to the Old. In this context, Williams's allusion suggests that the women's sexuality is the "treasure" concealed within the 'hold' of their garments.

In contrast to "The Young Housewife," the poem's unseen speaker observes his subjects not from the detached vantage point of a car, but trailing several steps behind on foot. Absorbed in the pleasure of one another's company, the women are unaware of being watched; nonetheless, they are acted upon, imaginatively propelled forward – in the "trade wind" of his admiration. With characteristic economy, Williams captures the identity of his female subjects in both poems by means of a single telling gesture – the housewife self-consciously "tucking in/stray ends of hair" and the gleeful secretary "gently/ slapping her thighs." These actions, respectively signifying diffidence and self-possession, suggest an awareness of women's disparate responses in negotiating the challenges of a male-dominated society.

The seductive allure of women's bodies, however, ultimately transcends Eros. As Linda A. Kinnahan has argued, Williams's work "develops complex interactions between fixed ideas of the feminine and socially constructed ideas of gender,"[11] while simultaneously appearing to reinforce them. In the foreword to his 1951 *Autobiography*, Williams hinted at the source of his fascination with women, stating: "I am extremely sexual in my desires: I carry them everywhere and at all times. I think that from that arises the drive which empowers us all. Given that drive, a man does with it what his mind directs." This allusion to "drive" – something beyond and larger than lust, though often expressed in those terms – suggests that more than three decades after writing "Transitional," the poet still associated women with a mysterious generative essence of creativity – the "radiant gist" (*P* 185) of life itself. Brendan Gill, who once accompanied the doctor on a round of housecalls, humorously recalls being baffled by his exuberant response to a "slatternly" female patient "wearing a soiled rayon dressing gown and with her dyed hair done up in a dozen or so pink plastic curlers" and suffering from "a severe case of post-nasal drip" "Williams wouldn't be daunted. He would examine [her] baby, write out a prescription, and then spend five or ten minutes in happy banter with the dull, distracted, and wholly undesirable mother. Back in the car, he would be breathing hard and radiant. 'What a girl!'"[12] The ardor of Williams's response prompted Gill to wonder if they had actually seen the same woman or even inhabited the same world. According to the poet's biographer Paul Mariani, the answer was simple: of course not. When it came to women, the poet's angle of vision was unique (Mariani 695).

Two essays written in the late 1940s reflect both the lingering influence of Weininger's gender theories as well as Williams's growing divergence from them. His discussion of the so-called "supplying female" in "Letter to an Australian Editor" (1946) echoes the philosopher's thesis that men are active and women passive by implying that women provide "the material, the raw life, to be shaped into works of art by predominantly male geniuses."[13] And yet, as Bryce Conrad and Peter Schmidt have argued, Williams's use of the term "female" is not a literal, biological referent, but rather a "metaphor (or personification, giving voice) of all that has been excluded by the dominant culture. Therefore, his definition of the "supplying female," of what is excluded and silenced, may be seen as a cultural construction subject to contestation and revision."[14]

Similarly, in "Woman as Operator," a 1948 essay written to accompany an exhibit of contemporary paintings at Manhattan's Kootz Gallery,[15] Williams upholds Weininger's belief in the existence of distinct male and female psychologies, but rejects his representation of women as passive, instead granting them agency as "operators." In his estimation, the elusive essence of women is "something unassailable" and "remote"; even in the "voluptuous enjoyment" of sexual union, she remains "below the possibility of [a man's] deepest masculine approaches" and therefore cannot be accurately represented in art. Confronted with this conundrum, he asks:

> What is he to do? Impregnate her? Kill her? Avoid her? You see, it all amounts to the same thing: do what he will she remains in spite of his greatest doing or not doing the same thing, woman, woman in the abstract, something without a face, something beyond his power – something that (according to his nature) he can abstract, generalize upon, devise means for elucidating but ... (*ARI* 180–81)

Although Bram Dijkstra considers Williams's essentialist references to "Woman" throughout this essay sexist, its overarching thesis is in fact progressive.[16] In acknowledging the limits of his male perspective, the poet posits a need for change: "With woman there's something under the surface which we've been blind to, something profound, basic. We need, perhaps more than anything else today, to discover woman; we need badly to discover woman in her intimate (unmasculine) nature – maybe when we do we'll have no more wars" (*ARI* 182–83).

Given the ubiquity of women in Williams's prose and poetry, no single scholarly study can comprehensively address this topic. Critics have instead chosen to focus on key tropes, relationships, or in-depth analysis of individual works: Marilyn Kallet's *Honest Simplicity in William Carlos Williams' 'Asphodel, That Greeny Flower'* (1985), for example, examines the poet's tortured, late-life confession to Flossie about his infidelities; Audrey Rodgers's *Virgin and Whore: The Image of Women in the Poetry of William Carlos Williams* (1987) addresses the tensions underlying those mythic dichotomies; and my own *William Carlos Williams and the Maternal Muse* (1987) explores the poet's often conflicted representations of his mother, Raquel Elena Hoheb. Bryce Conrad's *Refiguring America* (1990) and Linda A. Kinnahan's *Poetics of the Feminine* (1994) offer groundbreaking analyses of gender in *In the American Grain*. Williams's appropriation of letters from Marcia Nardi in *Paterson* has been discussed in important essays by Sandra Gilbert, Rachel Blau DuPlessis, and Theodora Rapp Graham; the history of that contentious relationship has also been documented in *The Last Word* (1994), an edition of their correspondence edited by Elizabeth Murrie O'Neil.[17] More recent work on the subject of women includes a 2006 reprinting of Williams's 1924 improvisation "Rome" alongside Peter Schmidt's insightful essay, "*Chora* in Hell, The Sewer Venus, Sexual Politics, and Williams' Improvisation 'Rome,'" and my essay, "Inversions, Evasions, Strange Machinations of Desire: William Carlos Williams and the Baroness Revisited,"[18] in *William Carlos Williams and the Language of Poetry* (2002). Further discoveries doubtlessly await as new archival resources become available.

II "[A] sense of lift, the opening of a door"

Williams's perceptions of women underwent a noticeable shift in the late 1940s as the result of the serendipitous intersection of two figures – Harriet Saltonstall Gratwick (1907–1999) and the pioneering musicologist Sophie Drinker (1888–1967), whose book *Music and Women* he credited with "opening up a new chapter" in both his "gratitude toward women" and understanding of the "dimensions" of his lifelong relationships with them. The poet met Gratwick through her brother-in-law Charles Abbott, the curator of the University of Buffalo's Poetry Collection; she, her husband William, and their three daughters lived with the librarian and his wife on a sprawling upstate farm known as both Linwood and Gratwick Highlands. According to Emily Mitchell Wallace, the Williamses stayed at the Highlands on at least ten different occasions between 1940 and 1958, and regarded it as an edenic respite from the world's cares.[19] "Never in my life," the poet wrote in his *Autobiography*, have "I ... experienced such a luxury of sound and rustic profusion" (*A* 325) as at the farm. The tonic of "good country air" and the "kindness of dear friends" not only restored his sense of wellbeing "physically, mentally, and morally" but also inspired him to write.[20]

Much of the estate's charm stemmed from the creativity of its cosmopolitan residents – William Gratwick was a sculptor and a hybridizer of rare Chinese tree peonies; his sister Theresa (Abbott's spouse) was a painter; and Harriet was a gifted musician as well as the founder of the Linwood Music School, established on the property in 1947. Writers and artists such as Wyndham Lewis and Nassos Daphnis were frequent guests. With each visit, Williams grew increasingly interested in – and then actively involved with – Harriet's musical activities. In March 1947, she invited him to compose a poem for the Livingston County Pomona Grange's annual celebration of the spring planting season at the Avon Methodist Church. Their correspondence concerning this piece, eventually published as "Rogation Sunday" (*CP2* 110–11), indicates that its creation was a uniquely collaborative effort.

On March 4, Williams dashed off a first draft on prescription blanks "while driving around" and sent it to Harriet, indicating: "Make any suggestions you please, I'll do my best to please you."[21] A week later, he again encouraged her to "chop into it," treating the poem as "something to work with rather than as a finished thing."[22]

Conductor Theodore Hollenbach and composer Thomas Canning discuss the music for "Rogation Sunday" with WCW and Harriet Gratwick prior to its premier performance by the Linwood Music School at Gratwick Highlands on 13 August 1950.
Photo reproduced with the permission of Lee Gratwick.

The favorable reception the poem received when it was first recited on May 18, 1947 led Harriet to envision it set to music in the form of a hymn. She immediately began seeking a composer, enjoining Williams to join in the search. Their letters from the winter of 1948 discuss a series of possible choices – Virgil Thomson, Aaron Copeland, and an unnamed "young man at the Juilliard School" – but more importantly, reveal the instrumentality of Harriet's role in determining the final form of the poem's closing lines. On February 25th, Williams wrote: "I agree; something more should be done with the Coda, it is not quite right as it stands: too material & too one-sided. I'll do what I can to remedy this but, if possible, without increasing the length of the whole. I'll do this at once ... and enclose the result in this letter."[23] Several days later, Harriet returned the poet's revision with her own handwritten version of the Coda on the back, changing his line "No man – but all men together" to the more inclusive, egalitarian

"No man – but men & women together," thereby introducing the theme of gender and female agency. She also questioned his elimination of the definite article "the" in one of the poem's earlier lines – "Let the seeds & the tubers be planted," stating: "Why not leave "the" in here? I like it." In a note jotted at the bottom of the page, she indicated "Please return to me. H.," which Williams promptly did, along with an enthusiastic endorsement of her proposed changes: "Dear Harriet: Yes, by all means, make the final reading of the Coda the one which you have selected . . . [and] get the revised edition to the composer at once."[24]

The breezy confidence with which Harriet addresses Williams in this exchange bespeaks the intimacy of their friendship; notwithstanding an age difference of almost twenty-five years, he treats her as a respected peer rather than protégé. Moreover, the poet's acceptance of Gratwick's proposed changes stands in marked contrast to his defensive response to H. D.'s editorial recommendations regarding the "flippancies" and "derivative" touches she identified in his 1916 lyric "March." Although Williams "eventually accepted the validity of H. D.'s criticisms" (CP1 493–94) and incorporated her suggestions in subsequent printings of the text, he bristled at her interference, including both her letter and his testy response – "I'll write whatever I damn please, whenever I damn please and as I damn please" – in the "Prologue" to Kora in Hell (I 13).[25]

In the midst of this collaborative venture, Harriet sent Williams a gift – Sophie Drinker's recent book Music and Women. Gratwick and Drinker were personal friends and colleagues, linked by a strong interest in the history of women's choral music.[26] Beginning in the late 1920s, Drinker hosted regular performances of the "Academia dei Dilettanti di Musica" – a group of amateur singers and instrumentalists she had founded – in her Merion, Pennsylvania home.[27] Harriet occasionally attended and participated in these "singing parties," during which she also served as a sounding board for the older woman's questions about her forthcoming book. Indeed, Drinker names Gratwick first in the work's acknowledgements, citing her – along with a handful of other women – for "challenging the validity of my interpretations and helping me to verify them from the authority of their own experience and knowledge."[28]

The product of nearly two decades of research, Music and Women was an ambitious undertaking, and was described in The Saturday Review as "one of the most devastating challenges to our culture, our religion, our social justice, our psychological perspicacity that has come from an American woman."[29] Analyzing the primacy of female voices and creative power in the ancient civilizations of Egypt, Sumer, and Greece as well as contemporary primitive cultures around the globe, Drinker claims that "women are the chief repositories for racial musical expression"[30] due to their ability to bring forth new life. Music, she argues, is rooted in female incantation – the wail of childbirth, crooning of lullabies, and keening of grief. Over time, this rich matriarchal tradition dwindled, consigning women to marginalization and silence. Drinker thus asks:

> What has happened to the woman of our civilization? Why are we not matching in creative output the simple women of cultures much less developed...? Are we less women than these singers and musicians? We love, work, play, bear children, seek reassurance in a sense of oneness with the life force. We inherit a magnificent art of music. Why, then, do not women as composers make, on the level of our highly developed culture, symphonies, requiems, songs, dances equivalent to those that are created by women everywhere in other cultures? Why are we so inhibited?[31]

These observations about the inhibition and stifling of female creativity in modern industrialized society resonated deeply with Williams, as attested in his enthusiastic letter of thanks to Harriet on 18 March. He praised the bold originality of her book's premise – "address[ing] itself to a field which looks to me to have been signally neglected heretofore – in this man's world," adding:

> This book already, just to hold it in my hand, supplies me with a sense of lift, the opening of a door. Music may be the key, but it goes deeper than music. We are all half starved in our lives today – this book at least envisages something of the reason for our undernourishment ...
>
> The first impression I get of the book is one of discovery of a lost tribe. I don't know what in God's name has become of woman but here in America at least she is certainly a curio in the full magic sense which this book depicts. I suppose the primary cause of this is that she had been immobilized too long in the home and that outside the home she is lost, can't really find any really womanly thing to do ... To me as a privileged man, a physician before whom a woman is conventionally permitted to strip herself of her clothes and her restraints of whatever sort at will, she is a marvelous source of primitive wit and energy – that has been conserved by events in a more elemental manner than the male can ever supply – except as artist.[32]

The poet's allusion to a "lost tribe" refers to one of the volume's illustrations – an ethnographic photo of a small group of African women clad in traditional ceremonial garb kneeling on a mat in front of several thatched-roof structures. Their heads are adorned with silver crescent-shaped ornaments symbolizing, as Drinker asserts, the link between the moon and "rhythmic drama of a woman's bodily life, of which childbirth is the great climax."[33] As the caption notes, "these singers of the Dahomey tribe ...

represent the army of 10,000 women warriors, famous in former times."[34] Williams was at once intrigued and troubled by this image, which reified Drinker's argument about the erosion of female power in western culture. "It gave me the creeps," he confided to Harriet, "when I saw those kneeling remnants of the Amazon army of twenty thousand or so who once waged war in Southern Africa. They looked as though all they need today is numbers and the will for it to be still effective."[35]

The fervor of the poet's initial impression deepened as he perused *Music and Women*. Three months later – on June 22, 1948 – he wrote Harriet again, asking her to forward a "heartfelt" if somewhat "thickly expressed" letter to Drinker on his behalf since he did not know her address. Williams's original is apparently lost; what survives is Gratwick's transcription – four pages of neat, cramped handwriting on lined notebook filler paper – in the Poetry Collection of the University at Buffalo. While Harriet's reasons for copying the letter – a task involving a substantial commitment of time given its length – are unclear, the mere fact of the document's existence bespeaks the importance she ascribed to the ideas contained therein.[36] Indeed, whatever the motive, her instinct was astute since the letter represents a shift in the poet's thinking about gender and women's place in society. His salutation, "My dear Sophie Drinker," establishes a tone of intimate familiarity presaging the disclosures that follow:

Reading your book, *Women and Music* [sic], I realize clearly the dimensions, for the first time in my life, of my relationship with women. Always up to this point, I have felt dissatisfied with the understanding, the sensual, intellectual quantities involved. I have plunged ahead with the several women I have loved, always ill at ease in one way & always certain of myself in others – practically knowing that what I enjoyed was the thing that I knew was there but always bought at a cost which seemed to me stupid & the product of an official suppression.

Everything in this world worth possessing involves danger, but it need not involve cowardice. Also it need not countenance deceit, a pretense of freedom, either, to cover license. In any case it was up to woman to lift the cloud which has always been very real for me – & which I have not been able to raise myself in the role I have to play & have had to play as a man. Damn it, if she didn't know how to assert herself who was going to assert for her? And not the usual masculine side of an assertion but the woman's side – subtle, insistent, virginal – in your sense. I salute you with gratitude.

It is a curious book in that it is often, too often, repetitious – a sort of catalogue of historical events that doesn't pick one up & carry one forward. But at moments it flares in such a way that I know nothing like it. I caught myself, last night looking at some Mary Wallace roses that Mrs. Williams had put in a vase on top of the radio. I was listening to some music, I've forgot what.

But as I looked at the roses in the lamplight I noticed a brilliance about them – and their leaves astonished me. And I said to myself I've never seen roses with that peculiar brilliance about them. Why? The answer was instantaneous: It's because of that book about women & their actual worth so long submerged. It was a feeling as of the first roses in the world – borrowed from the intellectual quality you had given your pages. This is no invention of mine but an accurate reporting of what happened – with no emotional adornment on my part.

Your book was sent to me by Harriet Gratwick – a woman I greatly admire (I notice her name in the introduction.) It's opened a new chapter for me – at this late date – in my gratitude toward women generally. But what I've been trying to say is that it has <u>confirmed</u> in me the accuracy & the truth of my experience with women – a complex commingling of reactions which have been very important to me in my life – that seems to find its basis in what you have lucidly said & which I have not found expressed anywhere else – not surely in anything any male has written ... By the way, I haven't yet finished reading the book – have only got to the old Abbesses. I'm a painfully slow reader, sad to relate. I'll finish it in the next couple of weeks.[37]

In this document, Williams makes a series of claims, chief among them that Drinker's book has "opened a new chapter" in his understanding of women and lifelong relationship to them. He describes his epiphany – the lifting of a cloud "which has always been very real for me" – as an experience of vivid illumination, clarity, and corrective realignment of vision. His anecdote about the Mary Wallace roses – a common pink rambler still widely sold in American garden centers today – underscores the profundity of his reaction. Set atop the radio in the familiar domestic space of 9 Ridge Road, these mundane flowers suddenly acquire a preternatural brilliance that elicits "a feeling as of the first roses in the world." Williams thus sees – and for the first time truly appreciates – the essential beauty of their form, attributing his shift in perspective to the 'flare' of Drinker's argument about the "actual worth [of women] so long submerged" in patriarchal western society.

Williams's effusive expression of gratitude is, however, tempered by both the paradoxical quality of his pronouncements and opacity of his references to "license," "official suppression," "danger" and the "pretense of free-dom" – terms rife with sexual innuendo. Four times within the letter's opening paragraph, he repeats the adverb "always" to describe the absolut-ism that had characterized his prior perceptions of women. He admits, for example, to *always* feeling "dissatisfied" with his tendency to dichotomize "the sensual [and] intellectual quantities involved" in these relationships, explaining that this "understanding" left him "*always* ill at ease in one way & *always* certain of myself in others" [emphasis added]. The poet specifically credits *Music and Women* with helping him to recognize the constraints of "the usual masculine side of an assertion" – socially-prescribed gender traits such as agency, strength, volition, and domination – by exploring "the woman's side," which he describes as "subtle, insistent, virginal – in your sense."

This caveat regarding Drinker's use of the term "virginal" proves integral to comprehending both the work's thesis and the ways in which it influenced Williams's thinking. The tripartite structure of *Music and Women* is organized around two major tropes – the moon and the Greek goddess Artemis – that unify her sweeping analysis of female disempowerment. As Elizabeth Wood notes in her preface to the 1995 reissue of the text,

> Drinker spurned conventional modes of a linear, developmental history of music in Western Civilization for an alternative, radically feminine prototype. Devoting more than half of her narrative to pre-Christian and non-Western cultures, Drinker conjured a cyclical narrative of female history modeled on the waxing, full, and waning movements of the moon-mother-musician-Goddess and her dancing attendants.[38]

Part 1 is thus anchored by an entire chapter on Artemis, a figure she identifies with "integrity, the self; the part of the individual soul that must preserve its independence or perish."[39] Although the goddess has neither mate nor children, Drinker contends that her status as a virgin refers not to chastity but is rather a metaphor for a female ideal of free selfhood and independent spiritual power: "She represents at once the creative individual who meets life with a proud, positive attitude and the creative freedom of collective womanhood."[40] For Williams, this quasi-mystical notion of a generative female essence powerfully "confirmed ... the accuracy & the truth of my experience with women," clarifying the irresistible allure of the amorphous "thing that I knew was there but always bought at a cost." For the gift of this insight, he informed Drinker, "I salute you with gratitude."

Parts 2 and 3 of *Music and Women* correspondingly contain chapters on "Artemis Bound," discussing how the Christian insistence on the Virgin Mary's sexually inviolate status represents a loss of female creative power, and "Artemis Stirring" in which Drinker argues that present-day women are reclaiming their collective autonomy through music, particularly the formation of female choral groups. She traces the origin of this phenomenon to the establishment of religious orders by noblewomen in the Middle Ages, "often on lands they themselves owned and flatly refused to transfer to a husband." By embarking on celibate lives as nuns, figures like Abbess Hildegard of Bingen – whom Drinker singles out for special attention – "reassert[ed] the ancient power and independence that women had held ... from time immemorial."[41]

Drinker's innovative historiography also cast Harriet Gratwick herself in a new light for Williams, much in the same way as the luminous Mary Wallace roses mentioned in his 1948 letter. Discussing the importance of present-day women's choruses in the book's conclusion, Drinker specifically cites the Grange – "one of the most remarkable institutions of American folk life" – as an ideal venue for the reclamation of this lost matriarchal power, a place where "an opportunity for creative work awaits a woman of talent and initiative."[42] Harriet had a long-standing professional association with the Livingston County Pomona Grange, the organization for which "Rogation Sunday" had been composed a year earlier. Indeed, the program for the "Rural Life Sunday" service on May 18, 1947, where the piece was first recited indicates that it was "written especially for the Linwood Grange Agricultural Chorus."[43] The poet thus came to imaginatively align Harriet with the mythic power of the ancient female singers Drinker so vividly described; not only was she "strong, wise, [and] creative by right of her womanhood"[44] but also a metaphorical wellspring of life. "Dear Fountain," he playfully addressed her in a 1951 letter, explaining: "You do keep the world, your world and that about you, from drying up. Or don't you think so? Perhaps you think the whole landscape is full of springs. It isn't."[45]

Williams's late-life epiphany concerning women – fostered in part through his association with Harriet Gratwick and Sophie Drinker – is illustrated in "To Daphne and Virginia," a 1952 poem addressed to his two daughters-in-law. This meditation on sexuality, gender, and old age is not only set on the Gratwick farm, but to some extent made possible by its unique intellectual atmosphere. For example, the poet's allusion to a lost "woman's world,/ of crossed sticks" to which the mind "flies off" effectively "stopping/ thought," evokes the ancient matriarchal rituals that Drinker discusses in the opening chapters of *Music and Women*. Moreover, in pondering the ways that male desire objectifies women, 'binding' and 'snaring' them in a position of powerlessness, Williams acknowledges the existence of a "counter stress,/ born of the sexual shock,/ which survives it/ consonant with the moon,/ to keep its own mind" through which female autonomy is preserved. "Counter stress" is a double-entendre, conjoining denotations of emotional strain and prosodic emphasis linked explicitly with the rhythmic cycles of the moon. This imagery echoes Drinker's mythic representation of women as "Daughters of the Moon"[46] whose ability to create life is correlated with the waxing and waning of that celestial body. While Williams's expression of sympathy for the plight of women "facing men" is – as he admits – inevitably limited by the alterity of his androcentric perspective, this awareness simultaneously serves as a source of creative inspiration: "At least/ while this healing odor is abroad," he declares, "one can write a poem" (CP2 246–250).

The later books of *Paterson* also bear the unmistakable imprint of Drinker's influence. In Book 3 (1949), for example, Williams incorporates a lengthy quotation from *Music and Women* concerning a fertility rite practiced by the Ibibio people of Africa that suggests the ways in which the text changed his perception of women (P 143–44).[47] This passage, which recapitulates Drinker's thesis, upends conventional western gender roles by foregrounding female agency and spiritual authority. The collective actions of these married women – rescuing the corpse of the fallen tribal leader, bearing him aloft to the glade, cutting and waving boughs over his genitals while singing incantations to transfer the "spirit of virility" into the leaves – counterpoint the passivity of "the 9 women/ of some African chief semi-naked" (P 13) seated astraddle a phallic log in the *National Geographic* photo described in *Paterson 1*. Williams's incorporation of this material intimates a newfound awareness of, and respect for, female power. In performing this ritual and preserving its secrecy, the Ibibio women mediate between life and death, channeling supernatural energy that will ensure the tribe's future.

More subtle allusions to *Music and Women* surface in Williams's discussion of Marie Curie and the discovery of radium in *Paterson 4* (1951). In section 2, he introduces the opprobrium faced by the unnamed female photographer who returns from the West with her child "openly/taking it to her girls' parties" with the simile, "As Carrie Nation/ to Artemis/ so is our life today," then links her brazen behavior with that of the Abbess Hildegard, who enjoined her followers – "all/ women" – to perform a choral piece she had composed for the occasion of her own funeral in 1179, "and it was done" (P 179). Through this multi-layered analogy, Williams critiques the diminution and circumscription of women in modern life – as embodied in the hatchet-wielding temperance advocate Carrie Nation – by likening the single mother's flouting of moralistic social norms to two of Drinker's prime exemplars of female autonomy and creative power.

It is, however, in *Paterson 5* (1958) that Drinker's radical revisioning of female power in *Music and Women* most fully coalesces – in Williams's assertion that the dichotomous labels of "virgin" and "whore" represent a single "identity" cloaked in multifarious "disguises" (P 208); in his evocation of the legacy of Sappho, the ancient Greek poet whose verses – sung in a "clear gentle tinkling voice" (P 215) to the accompaniment of a flute and lyre – Drinker described as "the last perfect flowering of thousands of years of women's song";[48] and in the image of the enigmatic androgynous woman he encounters on the city's streets. Clad in "worn slacks" and a "shapeless hat," she possesses the telltale "Grey eyes" of the goddess Athena and strides purposefully through the crowd, transfixing the poet. In contrast to the seductive allure of the skirted secretaries described in "The Return to Work," physical desire plays no role in the poet's attraction to this figure: "Neither short/ nor tall, nor old nor young/ her/ face would attract no// adolescent" (P 217). Indeed, it is precisely the indeterminacy of her appearance that intrigues him – the way in which a single detail, an inconspicuous flower "made of sombre cloth" pinned to the coat of her otherwise masculine attire, blurs the conventional binaries of gender identity. Her defiant rejection of femininity – "as much as to say to// hell with you" (P 217) – proves, on closer inspection, to be a more nuanced, complex assertion – at once a proclamation of her womanhood and a warning of "her mood." The poet, possessed by "a/ thousand questions," seeks to re-inscribe her within the traditional parameters of female selfhood wondering, "Are you married?/ Have you any// children?" But the woman vanishes before they can speak, ultimately remaining a cipher. Seeking her "daily without success," the poet wishes most urgently to know "have you read anything that I have written?" declaring "It is all for you" (P 218).

Williams's fascination with women persisted throughout the last decade of his life, as reflected in poems featuring those closest to him – his wife Flossie ("Asphodel, That Greeny Flower," "To Be Recited to Flossie on Her Birthday") and granddaughters ("3 Stances," "Suzy"), as well as evocative strangers such as the Tijuana stripper in "The Desert Music" and "A Negro Woman" carrying a "torch" of marigolds on the early morning streets, and representations of diverse female figures in art ranging from a pre-Columbian Inca sculpture ("Portrait of a Woman at Her Bath") to the serene visage of the "lady with the tail of her dress/ on her arm" depicted in the medieval Unicorn tapestries (P 212). As he explained to interviewer Edith Heal in 1956,

> I'll die before I've said my fill about women. I feel I am saying flattering things about them but they won't take it. After all there are only two kinds of us, men and women, the he and the she of it, yet some antagonism, some self-defense seems to rise out of a woman when a man tries to understand her. I am so terribly conscious of woman as woman that it is hard for me to write about a woman – I become self-conscious – too aware that she is there ready to tell me I've got her all wrong. (IWWP 63–64)

The rich legacy of Williams's work attests that his awareness of this elusive – if not altogether futile – goal never deterred him from its pursuit.

NOTES

1. Weininger's influence on Williams's work, first discussed in Mike Weaver's *William Carlos Williams: The American Background* (Cambridge: Cambridge University Press, 1971), has been debated by numerous scholars including Bram Dijkstra in his introduction to *A Recognizable Image: William Carlos Williams on Art and Artists* (New York: New Directions, 1978), John Palattella in "In the Midst of Living Hell: The Great War, Masculinity, and Maternity in Williams' *Kora in Hell* and 'Three Professional Studies'" (*WCWR* 17.2, Fall 1991), Linda A. Kinnahan, *Poetics of the Feminine: Authority and Literary Tradition in William Carlos Williams, Mina Loy, Denise Levertov, and Kathleen Fraser* (Cambridge: Cambridge University Press, 1994), and Bruce Clarke, *Dora Marsden and Early Modernism: Gender, Individualism, Science* (Ann Arbor: University of Michigan Press, 1996).
2. Otto Weininger, *Sex and Character*, Trans. William Heinemann (New York: G.P. Putnam's Sons, 1906), 183 as quoted in Weaver, *William Carlos Williams*, 18.
3. Clarke, *Dora Marsden and Early Modernism*, 181.
4. Quoted in Weaver, *William Carlos Williams*, 22.
5. Kinnahan, *Poetics of the Feminine*, 30.
6. William Carlos Williams, "The Great Sex Spiral (Part 2)," *Egoist* 4.7 (1917): 111; reprinted in *WCWR* 30.1–2 (Spring/Fall 2013), 23.
7. Ibid., 23.
8. Kinnahan, *Poetics of the Feminine*, 40.
9. Marjorie Perloff, "The Man Who Loved Women: The Medical Fictions of William Carlos Williams," *Georgia Review* 34.4 (Winter 1980): 847.
10. For more on this, see Carl Eby, 'The Ogre' and The 'Beautiful Thing': Voyeurism, Exhibitionism, and the Image of 'Woman' in the Poetry of William Carlos Williams," *WCWR* 22.2 (Fall 1996): 29–45.
11. Kinnahan, *Poetics of the Feminine*, 8.
12. Brendan Gill, *Here at the New Yorker* (New York, Random House, 1975), 332–33.
13. Peter Schmidt, "Introduction to Williams' 'Letter to an Australian Editor' (1946): Williams' Manifesto for Multiculturalism," *WCWR* 17.2 (Fall 1991): 6.
14. Ibid.
15. The exhibit took place in 1947; according to Bram Dijkstra, *Women: A Collaboration of Artists and Writers*, the 1948 catalog in which Williams's essay appeared, was conceived as an "afterthought" by gallery owner Samuel Kootz who "requested "a number of writers, ranging from Jean-Paul Sartre and Benjamin Péret to Paul Goodman and Williams, to note down their impressions of one or another of the works included in the show." See "Introduction," *ARI* 36–37.
16. See Dijkstra's "Introduction" to *ARI* 36–38. Dijsktra similarly overstates Weininger's influence on the essay, arguing: "the connections between … 'Woman as Operator' and *Sex and Character* are so immediate that it would not be surprising to discover that Williams had reread Weininger in order to write this article."
17. See Theodora Rapp Graham, "Her Heigh Compleynte: The Cress Letters of William Carlos Williams' *Paterson*," in Daniel Hoffman, ed., *Ezra Pound and*

William Carlos Williams: The University of Pennsylvania Conference Papers (Philadelphia, PA: University of Pennsylvania Press, 1983); Sandra Gilbert, "Purloined Letters: William Carlos Williams and 'Cress,'" *WCWR* 11.2 (Fall 1985); Rachel Blau DuPlessis, "Pater-Daughter," in *The Pink Guitar* (New York: Routledge, 1990).

18. "Rome" appears in *WCWR* 26.2 (Fall 2006) and the Baroness essay in *William Carlos Williams and the Language of Poetry*, ed. Burton Hatlen and Demtres Tryphonopoulos (Orono: National Poetry Foundation, 2002).

19. Emily Mitchell Wallace, "A Musing in the Highlands and Valleys: The Poetry of Gratwick Farm," *WCWR* 8.1 (Spring 1982): 8–41.

20. WCW to Harriet Gratwick, August 11, 1949. Quoted with the permission of the Poetry Collection of the University Libraries, University at Buffalo (cited hereafter as Buffalo).

21. WCW to Harriet Gratwick, March 4, 1947 (Buffalo).

22. WCW to Harriet Gratwick, March 12, 1947 (Buffalo).

23. WCW to Harriet Gratwick, February 25, 1948 (Buffalo).

24. Harriet Gratwick to WCW, with his response on verso, March 4, 1948 (Buffalo).

25. As Bruce Clarke observes in *Dora Marsden and Early Modernism*, "there is a long-standing urge in Williams to establish creative agons with strong (if often struggling) females … beginning with his mother, Elena, and falling into line with his literary relations to H.D., Gertrude Stein, Marianne Moore, and perhaps most significantly, Marcia Nardi" (179). Although it is beyond the scope of my essay to fully address this topic, Williams's correspondence with Denise Levertov offers important insights into the evolution of this gendered dynamic. In 1959, for example, Levertov criticized Williams's characterization of Agnes Breen's lesbianism in *Many Loves* as too heavy-handed, prompting the poet to revise the dialogue in this scene when the play was published in 1961 in order to convey her sexual preferences subtly (*DL/WCW* 83–85).

26. The women were also related by marriage since Harriet's younger brother Henry was the spouse of Drinker's daughter Cecilia.

27. Sophie Drinker, *Music and Women: The Story of Women in Their Relation to Music* (New York: The Feminist Press of the City University of New York, 1995), 286. This edition reprints the original published by Coward-McCann in 1948.

28. Ibid., xviii.

29. Sydney Greenbie, "Melody from the Distaff," *The Saturday Review*, April 24, 1948, 30.

30. Drinker, *Music and Women*, 15.

31. Ibid., 54.

32. WCW to Harriet Gratwick, March 18, 1948 (Buffalo).

33. Drinker, *Music and Women*, 4.

34. Figure 5, located between pages 24–25 of *Music and Women*.

35. WCW to Harriet Gratwick, March 18, 1948 (Buffalo).

36. At the top of the first page of the transcription, Gratwick wrote: "Letter to Sophie Drinker from W.C.W. June 22 1948" (Buffalo). Lee Gratwick, Harriet's only surviving child, confirms that "my mother was deeply inspired by [Drinker's] book" (personal correspondence, December 14, 2014).

37. WCW to Sophie Drinker, June 22, 1948 (Buffalo).

38. Drinker, *Music and Women*, viii.

39. Ibid., 122.
40. Ibid., 121.
41. Ibid., 186.
42. Ibid., 290.
43. In a letter dated May 25, 1947, Williams acknowledged receipt of Gratwick's gift: "Thank you for the Rogation Sunday program, could you please send me another, or two or three more? I appreciate having them" (Buffalo).
44. Drinker, *Music and Women*, 19.
45. WCW to Harriet Gratwick, June 13, 1951 (Buffalo).
46. Drinker, *Music and Women*, 3.
47. The transcription in *Paterson* contains several significant changes from Drinker's original text, although it is impossible to ascertain whether these are errors inadvertently introduced by Williams's typist Kitty Hoagland or intentional changes made by the poet. For example, Drinker uses the possessive pronoun "his" to describe the "spirit of fertility" extracted from the genitals of the deceased warrior, whereas the passage in *Paterson* alludes more abstractly to "the spirit of fertility." Similarly, Drinker's phrase concerning "married women who have felt the virility of men in their bodies" is rendered more literally as "the fertility of men" in the poem.
48. Drinker, *Music and Women*, 107.

12

J. A. MARZÁN

Reading Carlos: baroque as straight ahead

My study *The Spanish American Roots of William Carlos Williams* (1994) did not pretend to remake Williams into a poet seeking to recover an American ethnic identity that did not exist in his day. My Williams was the same poet whose wide ideational range is read in the scholarship. My claim was that his opening the American imagination to modernity included challenging American culture historically misguided by mythic tradition, in order to wall out his Hispanic heritage as foundational tributary. I did not have to unearth new evidence; my project consisted of picking up footage from the scholarship's cutting room floor, episodes of his work deemed inconsistent with traditional canonical ethnocentric parameters.

Williams's being the son of immigrants provided a rhetorical reprieve from his problematic biography, allowing the invoking of immigrants who arrived to shed their Old World past, a model inapplicable to any Spanish-speaking immigrant from the Americas – whose Old World is America itself – and least of all to Williams's parents. In his classic apologia of poorer Latin America, the essay *La Raza Cósmica (The Cosmic Race, 1925)*, the Mexican José Vasconcelos celebrated its blended cultures and its being wealthier in humanistic values over divisive, materialistic, and gracelessly Teutonic Anglo-America. That emergent middle-class Latin American perception of Anglo culture was shared by both Williams's parents, who to Williams's dismay, declined to become citizens.[1]

Williams's English-born father also served to give Williams a respectable Anglo pedigree except that William George left England at the age of five and grew up in the Dominican Republic, never to return to England, which held no memories for him. A fluent Spanish speaker, it was William George and not the Puerto Rican Elena, a painter and more a Francophile, who imparted a love for Spanish-language and literature. William George's being English certainly diluted in Williams's imagination Anglo/Hispanic differences that his American cultural consciousness mystified.

His mother Elena's Francophilia equally served the criticism to raise Williams's biography above a less prestigious American ethnic template. But French language, art and literature bespoke of the family's sophistication, not determining its cultural identity. Spanish, which William George preferred, was the language whose literature brought Williams closer to his otherwise distant father and that filled the house when relatives visited. Williams firmly identified with America but conflicted in not hearing Spanish as toxic as his American consciousness expected of him. One can deduce that his non-compliance with the expectation that he disconnect with the Hispanic culture that bonded his family prompted Williams to more sharply delineate his American identity.

Paul Mariani describes Williams as growing up living up to his parents' expectations that he be perfect as a son, notably in not lying, presumably even to himself, a high standard suggested in the importance he gave to choosing his writer's name. "I had a great time making up my mind what my literary signature should be – something of profound importance, obviously" (*A* 108). His social world knew him as Bill, and at home he was Willie. Carlos, his second given name after his mother's adored brother, had not been a public persona and was potentially a liability. But, suggestive that his Carlos consciousness was already informing his earliest poems, Williams realized that Carlos was ineluctable: "To me the full name seemed most revealing and therefore better" (*A* 108). "Most revealing" encompassed a semantic range.

Carlos evoked his physical appearance, darkly Mediterranean; the 1906 University of Pennsylvania Medical School yearbook described him as a "dark Spanish beauty." In *The Autobiography*, in which his Carlos consciousness is conspicuously subdued, he suggests that his official name at the French Hospital, founded by his father's close friend Dr. José Julio Henna, did not include Carlos. So we must conclude from his speculating about the reaction of Gaskin, an intern competing for a residency:

> When he saw me for the first time, having from my name expected a rough, sandy-haired Welshman, he let out a wild howl.
> "There it is, there it is. Didn't I tell you?" He blamed Henna and family connections and whatnot for my success in getting on the staff.   (*A* 84)

Carlos as "dark Spanish beauty" was also a sensual metonymy that, as will be demonstrated, would become the subject of introspective poems on his sexual desires, the sensuality that both sought out and drew women. Underlying the Baroness Elsa's review of *Kora in Hell* was her feeling of being deceived by his transition from tempter to a "wobbly-legged business satchel-carrying little louse!" of the poet she called "Carlos Williams" (Leibowitz 145).

Carlos also descended from Elena's "'line,'" as yet an overwhelming ball of entwined threads to disentangle in future writings. Elena's being a frustrated artist unable to complete her studies in Paris would also mold him in a way he had yet to comprehend. His being her surrogate as Carlos would also be the source both of his male passion for women and his female creative fecundity. Through her he received the legacy of great Spanish writings. And also yet to loom was the irony that Elena would provide the confidence of his seeing himself as a truly American poet.

For it was as Carlos that Williams reread history and concluded that the true American spirit did not begin with the Puritans, who came to suppress it. They arrived a century after that defining spirit had been sown by the Spanish, who came to "touch" and "marry" the native (*IAG* 121), producing its quintessential mingling spirit "greater than the metal they killed the natives for" (*YMW* 136), which he would receive through his mother: "In the West Indies ... the races of the world mingled and intermarried ... . It is in the best spirit of the New World" (*YMW* 30). In contrast, the Puritans arrived to keep away from demonized American fecundity in nature and in the native, whom they touched "with malice" (*IAG* 80). Not despite but because of Elena he was a "pure product of America"; Carlos's Hispanic heritage, then, was his American pedigree, his riposte to being excluded from the circle of Anglo Saxon prestige enjoyed by Pound and H. D.

But Williams's honesty in his literary conviction struggled with his also wanting to be acknowledged as Bill, so his advancing what was a precursor to today's multiculturalism did not resolve his original conflict between being American and the expectation of his disconnecting from his foreignizing culture, from his being socially Bill and personally also Carlos. In one of his translations, from the Spanish of "Three Nahuatl Poems," the speaker asks where he can find "the road to Two-Gods," (*CP2* 429), a felicitous metaphor of the inner drama at the core of his work.

Williams's last interview, published in *The Paris Review* in 1964 contains this exchange:

INTERVIEWER
What I was getting at is that you have kept the name "Carlos."
WILLIAMS
I had no choice but to keep the "Carlos."
INTERVIEWER
I understand Solomon Hoheb, your mother's father, was Dutch.
WILLIAMS
Maybe. The Spanish came from the Sephardic Jews. Though the English was strong indeed, through my grandfather.

You've been more conscious of the Spanish, then, than of the other.
Yes! I've insisted on breaking with my brother's memory of the Williamses as English . . . [2]

In Jorge Luis Borges' essay "Borges and I," the first-person narrator deline-ates the attributes of Borges the writer from the attributes of Borges the man but concludes he cannot say which of the two has been writing. Williams could say the same of his responses in that interview.

In *The Autobiography* Bill had played up the Dutch and English lines; here Williams brushes that aside although briefly assuming his Bill voice when he refers to an English grandfather who was actually a secret that died with Grandma Wellcome. Then he immediately corrects by underscoring that he broke with the memory of the Williamses as English. Until late in his life, Bill was the default, with Carlos an insistent moral obligation: "I had no choice but to keep the 'Carlos.' Williams had no choice but reveal the other source of the two dynamics that had always competed in his imagination.

Anne W. Fisher-Worth notes that in *The Autobiography* that other Williams is kept incognito, presenting "a one-sided self-portrait" written to "strengthen the theme of innocence, as becomes clear once one perceives that the things suppressed are *eros* and *thanatos*" (*William Carlos Williams and Autobiography: The Woods of His Own Nature*, 39). In other words, to create the antithesis of what one can interpret as the sensuality that English associates with Latins.

Rod Townley writes "between the two bland William's of his name there lurks a Carlos, a 'dark Spanish beauty,'" the same tension and balance is in the protagonist's name in *Voyage to Pagany*, Evan Dionysus Evans (*The Early Poetry of William Carlos Williams*, 64). In between Evan-ness fertility.

Charles Demuth's painting *I Saw the Figure 5 in Gold*, based on Williams's poem "The Great Figure," provides a metaphor of his friend's inner conflict. "Bill" and "Carlo" appear widely separated in a circular cubist maelstrom of a fire-engine's red, an image that captures the symbiosis that Williams expressed in that poem and numerous others: Carlos the fire and Bill, the red-colored engine that races to douse fires.

Williams's Bill persona as his more virtuous and intellectual conscious-ness, in contrast to the visceral, sensual Carlos, expresses the conflicting sexual attitudes characteristic of an Anglo-Latin/Mediterranean cultural difference that goes back centuries. The English saw their superiority against Iberian "savagery" not just because of the conquistadors' cruelty but because they copulated with New World natives, which the English propagandized as the Spanish's practice of bestiality, implicitly promising a colonization of superior sexual restraint. Intimations of moral superiority survive in caricatures of the Don Juan, the Latin lover and "hot señoritas," against which the Spanish mocks the relative frigidity of the Anglo Saxon. Contrasting Latin and Anglo sexual attitudes has become a recurring theme of an emergent writing.

Richard Rodriguez's unreliable narrative in *Hunger of Memory: The Education of Richard Rodriguez* (1982), written when he was still a closeted gay, offers as motive for assimilating and leaving behind his humble Mexican parents his being different, a "scholarship boy," when – as a subsequent, "coming out" book confirmed – he had been escaping the peculiarly Mexican exhibition of masculinity for a sexually-subtler American identity. In my *The Bonjour Gene* (2005) a Puerto Rican young man is engaged to an Italo-American woman from New England whose parents have adopted Yankee values and constantly refer to their sensually vain relatives as "real" Italian, tacitly placing his unrepentant Latin identity in their same cheaper league. In Junot Díaz's, *This Is How You Lose Her* (2012) Dominican hyperbolic sexuality becomes a flint of tragicomic incongruity in its new American cultural setting. In his conflicted Bill stereotyping of Carlos's sinful sensuality, Williams is an antecedent to this writing.

Williams made this troubling discovery of his conflicting sexual attitudes when he wrote his early psychodramatic epic "Philip and Oradie." Set in Spain, it is narrated by a young Bill-like prince morally offended by his stone-hearted father, appropriately named Don Pedro, who "grated up his front" from forty years of "wasting war" (Marzán, *Spanish American Roots* 33) too crude to relate in detail: "Nor fit a tongue's report" (34). The prince rejects descending from his father's immoral line, the phallic "Altamont," writing as if born of his mother's loneliness.

Her name Beatrix descends – not just from Dante – etymologically from Viatrix, signifying voyager, traveler and later merging with the Latin *beatus*, saint. Like Elena, the traveler whom fate cast adrift in New Jersey, Beatrix filled the boy's mind with stories of "foreign kingdoms o'er the sea" (35). But in the prince's identifying with Beatrix, implicitly he was suddenly Carlos, that chip off the old Don Pedro block, a hazard that gave him at least one reason why to leave the poem unfinished.

Years later, Williams told Edith Heal, using private Carlos/baroque humor, that he threw the poem "in a furnace" (*IWWP* 26) in other words, into the heat where it belonged (actually, the handwritten poem is in Yale's Beinecke collection), quickly adding that "The Wanderer: A Rococo Study" took its place. Unironically and consciously, the subtitle moves the poem north of Spain, lightening from the baroque to produce a "Rococo" poem written in the voice of a sexually undistracted Bill, wandering in New Jersey, seeking to mirror his modernity and guided by a figuration of his English Grandmother.

Carlos's sexual sinfulness judged by Bill is the subject of "The Ordeal" (*CP1* 8), in which a salamander who can survive both heat and cold is beseeched to rescue "our fellow" from a sexual and creative flame "Predestined to disman." He urges the salamander: "Gnaw out and drown/ The fire roots that circle him/ Until the Hell-flower dies down/And he comes home again." As repeated in Williams's lexicon, the woman is a flower if a "Hell-flower," which attracts "our fellow," surely not just the character of the poem but a pun on the Spanish *falo*, phallus.

The salvation sought is not just from the fire or sexual sin; the heat is also a metaphor of the creativity that distracts from Bill's normal life, that *dismanning*. A parallel *dismanning* is referred to in the appropriately titled "Transitional" *(CP1* 40), a dialogue between poet and self: "First he said:/ It is the woman in us/That makes us write . . .. " Sensuality, synonymous with creativity, silences normal men, makes them fecund and female, *dismans*, even as the process involves another erection, "Unbent by the sensual/As befits accuracy." Sensuality, of course, is also a euphemism for the 'disman-ning' effect of Carlos on Williams, making him no longer the man Bill in control but the passion or *duende* Carlos.

Bill kept Williams home; Carlos fired him up to wander, sexually and to explore his poetic drive. Williams as artist cheated on Flossie in merely separating himself to write poetry and identifying with Carlos's sexual freedom – which he did if only he could bring "our fellow" back to his flameless home again. To have stayed in the flame and be permanently consumed meant being only Carlos, no more also Grandma Wellcome's Bill, mortally tilting his necessarily balanced American identity. On the other hand, this was his "Ordeal": shamed Bill's interfering with Carlos's baser desires that produce art.

Bill's love was agape. "Asphodel, That Greeny Flower" was an honest love poem by Bill, who married Flossie's Anglo propriety. Between his two selves, Bill could be happy with the best Flossie had to give: "a grateful love,/ a love of nature, of people,/animals,/ a love engendering/gentleness and goodness/ that moved me/and *that* I saw in you" (*CP2* 317), lines of agape that reiterate what he had written to Flossie in letters.

In "To Be Recited to Flossie on Her Birthday" Bill expresses more agape, tortured agape: "Let him who may/ among the continuing lines/seek out// that tortured constancy affirms/where I persist//let me say/across cross pur-poses/that the flower bloomed// struggling to assert itself/simply under/the conflicting lights" (*CP2* 410).

Carlos's love was, of course, "eros" but, being sinful, necessarily turned into art; all women a particular becoming a metaphor of a mystery, elevating his contemplation of her sexuality from the mundane to Bill's universal – another way of Williams's achieving stasis. This erotic contemplation of women included his mother Elena and Grandma Wellcome.

Grandma Wellcome figures in his imagination both for her English origins (Bill) and for her darker side (Carlos), having given birth to William George under unspeakable circumstances. In "The Wanderer" her surrogate is described as an "old harlot of greatest lusting" (CP1 30). In *The Autobiography* she is portrayed as competing with an almost sexual obsession for control of Willie against his mother Elena, whose defining drama is her sexually mismatched marriage to William George, which Williams painfully reduced to "The Marriage of Souls": "That heat!/ That terrible heat/ That coldness!/ That terrible coldness" (CP2 233).

At home from his sales trips through Latin America William George was cold. Mariani observes that "What Williams remembered most was the silence .... Neither in his letters nor in his *Autobiography* has Williams recorded more than a few short conversations he had with his father" (Mariani 13). Meanwhile, William George also betrayed a hot inner secret, giving Williams justification to imagine his adopting a Latin alter ego as he traveled through Latin America to be a Don Pedro or a naked Adam steeped in temptation – having sexual adventures with the dark woman with whom Carlos fantasized.

To the "black eyed/ susan" – flower and woman – in "XXVII" from *Spring and All* (1923), he wrote: "the white daisy/is not/enough," not like the black-haired gypsy girl he remembered from Granada. The poem concludes: "But you/are rich/in savagery – //Arab/Indian/dark woman" (CP1 236). "Savagery" echoes the English characterization of the Spanish for having sex with the natives, and Pound used 'savage' to describe Spanish culture,[3] why he gave Williams his anthology of Spanish poems (IWWP 16). The "savagery" cited in "XXVII" was the hyperbole implied in Williams's description of the sexual freedom he saw in "The Colored Girls of Passenack – Old and New" – "Old and New" applying not just to old and young but to those women as timeless archetypes: "I've seen tremendous furnaces of emotional power in certain colored women, unmatched in any white –" (FD 55).

That absolute statement is balanced with this interjection on white women: "outside, perhaps, the devotional females who make up 'society,' and whose decadent fervors are so little understood. There, in the heat of 'entertainments,' of pleasure perhaps, the Negress can be matched." Perhaps, he wonders, the black woman enjoys the freedom of society women because like them "the colored race" is spared the moral standards of the "socially restricted areas," what he experienced as Bill. But in the end the white woman still falls short of Carlos's ideal: "But I do know that I have had my breath taken away by sights of colored women that no white woman has equalled for me" (55).

In "Fertile" (*CP2* 19) Carlos criticizes the "American woman," implicitly the white woman, encompassing Flossie, for only desiring an idea, not the body: "You want love, only love! rarest/ of male fruit!" He advises the American woman to take the "male fruit" and "Break it open," where she will find "in the white of the crisp flesh" Carlos, the male counterpart to the dark woman: "the symmetrical brown seeds." Symmetrical to each seed or the balance to the white crisp flesh? White women offered a sexually-tinged but ultimately intellectual excitement closer to the sexually subdued creative intercourse with the women poets he admired.

In the 1943 version of "The Gentle Negress" (*CP2* 47), Lillian reiterates what Williams had written about the "furnace" found nowhere else but in the black woman: "No other such luxuriance: ...," evoking a jungle primitiveness: "the/ elephant among bending trees,/ the grass parting .... " In this poem, one of several tributes to and imitations of poet Luis Palés Matos, including his translation "Prelude in Boricua" (*CP2* 45–46) Williams exploited the imaginary translation opportunities of transliterating Palés's word *lujuria*, Spanish for "lust," used to describe a black goddesses' jungle setting. Williams's repeated "luxuriance" echoes the controlling tonal ambiguity that braids the sexual and moralistic, a brilliance and a moral excess.

The 1944 version of "The Gentle Negress" (*CP2* 94) modernizes and reclaims the poem away from imitating Palés Matos, portraying the pair as implied cats on a roof: "Wandering among the chimneys/ my love and I would meet/I with a pale skin," the phrasing suggesting that he wore the skin for the occasion to be the paler Bill, who comes along as moral conscience, providing the sexual ambiguity as he contemplates "a longing hard to fathom." Are we to understand that her mysterious longing was difficult to understand or that she was "longing hard" to understand him or the relationship? He gives "comfort," ambiguously, possibly sitting on the bed on which she is physically lying, or sitting to comfort with his untrue words, and sitting on the bed to comfort the woman as either he or she is being untruthful in bed: "as I sat to comfort her/lying in bed."

Palés Matos was another baroque poet that Williams as Carlos added to his personal pantheon, along with Neruda and Lorca, in the lineage that he imagined as figuratively descending to him from Elena, the maternal role that he asks of her in "Tribute to Neruda the Poet Collector of Seashells" (*CP2*

357–58), that baroque tradition having informed Williams's Carlos consciousness from diverse sources in his formation, from the banal to the literate.

As Williams noted in *Yes, Mrs. Williams*, Elena was wont to cite Quevedo, about whose word trickery jokes abound in Spanish humor. Actually, the two masters of the Spanish baroque poetry, Quevedo and Góngora, represent extremes of Spanish natural wordplay, staple of its popular jokes. Williams's imitating Spanish wordplay in his English indicates that even if he never became a proficient speaker – a common second-generation reluctance pattern – he as poet had evidently engraved a proclivity toward its wordplay, of which more evidence appears in his incorrigibly making private semantic connections in his prose. This incorrigibility is doubtless what convinced Williams of his descending from the baroque "line"[4] and having no choice but to keep the Carlos.

In his essay "Federico García Lorca," Williams more specifically traced his Carlos "line" to Góngora, praised as "the man" (*SE* 225) his diction suggesting that Góngora is also "El Hombre" who is rendered homage in that poem, which Wallace Stevens cited for its surface, metaphysical evocations:

> It's a strange courage
> you give me ancient star:
>
> Shine alone in the sunrise
> toward which you lend no part!

The Spanish title invites us to find Carlos in that poem, in which he is present in a second semantic layer, in the Latin etymology of *strange* and *courage* and *ancient* and the Greek etymology of Helen (Helene), and thus star, along with the pun on "son" in *sunrise*: "It is a foreign heart/ you give me old Helen// shine alone in the son's rise/toward which you lend no part." Elena inspired but didn't care for her son's work.

The baroque was also the Hispanic artistic and literary aesthetic sown with the conquest in the Americas history that he recovered to define his American identity, and the style to which Latin American literature has cyclically returned – most recently in the Nobel laureates Miguel Ángel Asturias, Pablo Neruda and Gabriel García Márquez. His baroque "line," then, was Carlos's literary pedigree, his Hispanic heritage as the parallel foundational pedigree in response to the classic American story from which he felt excluded.

The baroque also provided a scheme for encoding himself more fully as a stasis of Bill and Carlos. The previously cited "Transitional" contained the inner debate of both voices, its title indicating his transit from one persona to the other. He also referred to the process as translation. The punning title "Hymn to Love Ended" has the subtitle "Imaginary translation from the Spanish" (*CP1* 391) while exhibiting no evident connection to the Spanish. The poem, "Translation" (*CP2* 198–99) also shows no external sign of its being one but by its title signals a connecting source calling the reader's attention, as did the title "El Hombre," to a more complex semantic bridging. In sum, the baroque implicitly signified an aesthetic translation, the function of the poem, from the mundane to the general: Carlos's mundane sexuality redeemed by Bill's/Williams's play with semantics, phonological form, etymology, and pun, affording Williams the opportunity to fully reveal himself, a stasis of his duplicity as Bill and Carlos.

In the essay "Against the Weather: A Study of the Artist" Williams universalized his need to translate his particulars as the mission of the artist. His argument compared the Archpriest of Hita's freedom to celebrate sexual love in *Libro de Buen Amor* and Dante's "passion ... restricted by the narrow corset of the times," referring to the Church. Unlike the Archpriest who could celebrate love freely, Dante had to condemn Paolo and Francesca as sinners but seemed to pity them "by the grace with which he has portrayed them," an illustration that in "the structure the artist speaks as an artist purely." Tacitly equating Carlos's sensuality as his creative force, he argued that "Pan is the artist's patron." But how "have morality and the Church compromised to bring him in and be saved?" (*SE* 204-05). Through the structure of the work, and Dante achieved what Williams described as every artist's objective: to "wrestle his content out of the narrow into the greater meaning" (*SE* 205)

> Dante was the agent of art facing a time and place and enforcement which were his "weather." Taking this weather as his starting point, as an artist, he had to deal with it to affirm that which to him was greater than it. By his structure he shows this struggle   (*SE* 205).

In *Paterson* Williams describes himself as "creature of the weather" (*P* 29). Like Dante, his objective was to translate Carlos's struggle to the general, into art, having to deal with his weather "to affirm that which to him was greater than it."

Williams's artist "weather" was the threatening inclemency of being trapped in an inferior conversation not suitable for serious writing, his consciousness of the "prevailing American attitude toward 'furriners' and immigrant people with even slightly dark skin like himself, whether from Spain or Latin America" that behooved his need "to cover the Spanish part of his ethnic identity in certain public situations – to fit in to succeed."[5] This fitting in with artist friends he had to do despite the alienation he experienced "At Kenneth Burke's Place":

> And "the earth under our feet,"
> we say glibly, hating
> the "Esoteric" which is not
> to be included in our anthologies, the
> unthinkable: the younger generation
> the colored (unless marketable)
> and – Plato was no different – the
> "private language."   (CP2 106–07)

The gathered had expressed "hating / the 'Esoteric' which is not/ to be included in our anthologies." These are defined with ambiguous wordplay, their being also intellectually inferior as the "unthinkable": "the younger generation/ the colored." He too had a private baroque language and Elena's family was vaguely "colored" in the past.

His riposte in this poem translates the local to the universal, starting with the allusion to Plato, then proceeding to invoke superior nature over the prejudice of small minds: "The earth/ is the esoteric to our dullness,/it opens caves, it distils dews: ... Catalogues are not its business./ ... its business is/ external to anthologies, outside the/ orthodoxy of plotted murders." The earth, lived reality outside insulated minds, is also "the green apple smudged with/ a sooty life that clings, ..." (107). He points to a basket of them:

> There is a basketful
> of them half rotted on the half rotten
> bench. Take up one
> and bite into it. It is still good
> even unusual compared with the usual,
> as if a taste long lost and regretted
> had in the end, finally,
> been brought to life again.   (107–08)

Art was Williams's ennobling shield from being limited by the narrow-mindedness at Kenneth Burke's; baroquely duplicitous art offered the strength of his "line."

Yes, Mrs. Williams: A Personal Record of My Mother (1959) was Carlos's corrective to Bill's mainstream-ingratiating portrayal of her in *The Autobiography*. He had long promised Elena that book about her, but his finally keeping his promise in 1959, ten years after her death, must be contextualized in the American fifties, reversing its intent to universalize by recovering its particulars. For, notwithstanding Williams's finessing his connection to an ethnic background with which both he and Elena did not identify, his book was as much a consequence of and response to it.

The background in question is the post-WWII Puerto Rican migration that most Americans know of through *West Side Story* but that was the larger and continuing chapter of a demographic shift whose origins date back to before the island's becoming a territory in 1898. Along with Williams's parents Dr. José Julio Henna also predated 1898, and later arrived the critic and translator Angel Flores. Williams devoting a chapter to both men acknowledged an important balance to his Bill-pose toward that background in *The Autobiography*, which also omits any impact on the family of the Spanish-American War and the subsequent extending of citizenship to Puerto Ricans.

Nevertheless, both Henna and Flores represented the pre-war skilled and cultured community described in *Las Memorias de Bernardo Vega* as distinct from the later migration of rural and urban poor. Henna, who as founder of The French Hospital hired Williams as an intern, came to the United States exiled for plotting against Spain to liberate one of its last two American colonies. His continuing social involvement led to his having a private audience with Theodore Roosevelt, recommending as a solution to bigotry making Puerto Ricans citizens. Either owing to conversations with Henna or to Henna's taking Williams to a Hispanic social club would explain why Williams's ideas sound much like those of José Martí in the essay *Our America*. [6]

Meanwhile, Williams leaves the connection that leads him to Angel Flores unclear. Flores's Dragon Press published Williams's book of stories *The Knife of the Times and Other Stories* (1932) and could have been the publisher of *Al Que Quiere!* [7] Consistent with downplaying Carlos, in *The Autobiography* Bill treated with irony Henna's efforts to involve him with things Hispanic and titled the unflattering chapter on Flores "White Mule."

The same back-handed treatment is given his having accepted two invitations to Puerto Rico, remembered as fortunate gigs providing other opportunities, superceding the obvious but implicitly delusional idea of his host's associating him with Puerto Rico. [8,9] The first invitation, in 1941, was to attend an Inter-American Writers Conference, where he met Luis Palés Matos, who although white had written a book of "Afro-Antillean" poetry that began a Spanish-language movement counterpart to the French *negritud* movement, *Tuntún de Pasa y Grifería: Poemas Afro-Antillanos* (Drumbeat of Kinky Hair and Black Things: Afro-Caribbean Poems) (1937). Palés Matos's use of popular idiom, notably black diction, in formalist, non-folk poetry, had made it a landmark in Latin American poetry.

Carlos obviously saw himself reflected in Palés's baroque style as well as his larger vision, epitomized in "Mulata-Antilla," which sang to the Caribbean islands as the naked body of Palés Matos's African Kore: "In you now, mulata, . . . /I cling to the lukewarm sea of the Antilles/ . . . in your womb, both my races conjugate/ their essential, affable juices." Williams's informing Edith Heal that "by 1941" he had come upon what he called the "artistic form" (*IWWP* 72) for *Paterson* strongly suggests where he found the scheme for his poem on a man defined by the tributaries of a region. Book One contains an imitation of Palés (Marzán 218–21).

At the highpoint of the Puerto Rican migration, in 1956, and seven years after Elena's death, Williams accepted an invitation to read at the university campus in her island home city, Mayagüez, this time providing as reason for accepting the chance to get more biographical information for his book on her. He had already amassed material, having written down conversations, anecdotes, and her sayings, and if he had postponed writing that book, it was doubtless until he came upon an aesthetic scheme. Her out-loud thoughts, her linguistic interferences, and her narratives of island childhood build her as a metaphor of poetry's spontaneity. Only scheming art would justify the bold coming out of Carlos, Williams's finishing in prose his incomplete "Philip and Oradie," the prince devoting himself without guilt to Beatrix.

According to Mariani, Williams scanned "every newspaper, every journal, every letter, for hints as to what is going on in the world of events" (Mariani 732). But Bill doesn't represent himself as putting himself in Carlos's social context – "esoteric" subjects inferior for true art. Nevertheless, aside from the obvious impetus of old age catching up to him, in preparing *Yes, Mrs. Williams*, Williams took on the same subjects of two hallmarks of that decade: the 1957 Broadway premier of *West Side Story* and the national introspection on race that began in 1955, prompted by Martin Luther King, Jr.'s boycott of the public buses in Montgomery, Alabama.

In *Yes, Mrs. Williams*, Williams wrote of Elena's Caribbean as the matrix where the American 'mingling' spirit was born, so that its expression in the civil rights cause would certainly not have escaped Carlos, who couldn't remain silent at the dismissal of the "colored" in "At Kenneth Burke's Place." Nor could Carlos have covered his ears to the nation's singing about "María"–who wanted to marry, as did Elena, a man not of her "own kind"–in a brilliantly-scored musical about the Americanization of the people from Elena's idealized island. Inconceivable that Williams could insulate himself from the profound impact on New York of a migration whose metaphors moved Leonard Bernstein and Arthur Laurents to change their original plan to produce a musical about tensions between the Irish and the Jews and make Puerto Ricans symbols of America's unforgiven groups.

Williams's silence on that musical and the unprestigious migration that inspired it, directly relevant to his biography, was consistent with Bill/ Carlos's not diminishing himself or Elena in particulars. In *Yes, Mrs. Williams*, she is redeemed from that background and remains a metaphor of a more prestigious Spanish heritage as well as a metaphor of the mysterious spontaneity of poetry; but as in "At Kenneth Burke's Place," she is also someone to redeem from the mundane cultural marginalization that conflated Elena and María. The two emerge as metaphors in the American literary imagination as a consequence of the same "weather" that Williams confronted as the artist Carlos.

In fact, an earlier important work evinced his consciousness of that culturally conflicting fifties background. The larger migration that started in 1945, the first voluntary transoceanic influx not from Europe, was part of a plan to industrialize and increase the island's middle class. Afoot was a referendum, which took place in 1951, to create a permanent, decolonizing "associate state" that would comply with the UN mandate to dismantle colonialism. The politics were supported by a public relations campaign, including photo features in *Life*, promoting this new Puerto Rico as "A Bridge between Two Cultures." In 1951 the chief proponent of this "associated" status, the island's first elected governor, spoke at Harvard, an event reported in *The New York Times*. Three months later, in response to a request for a new poem, Williams read a poem at Harvard in which he recalled a past visit to the Southwest.[10] In "The Desert Music" Williams either was influenced by or serendipitously adopted the same bridge metaphor which as Peter Middleton observes, exemplifies "Edward Said's idea of late style 'as intransigence, difficulty, and unresolved contradiction'" (169).

Midway on a bridge between the United States and Mexico, emblems of his two identities, Williams was "interjurisdictional" (CP2 274), therefore as undefined as the embryo-like figure affixed at mid-point – a man in a serape, the American stereotype of the sleepy Mexican. Middleton interprets Williams as experiencing his "poet's own identity ... fractured, as his own Hispanic roots marked by a Spanish middle name appear to leave him stranded on a border ... " (169).

Certainly on that bridge Williams was divided, between Bill and Carlos, as he had been his entire life, but as the government's spin propagandized about Puerto Rico, the bridge also joined cultures. And the embryonic figure, at once mundane, was cocooned in music, promising a redeemed emergence of the cultural stasis that he sought to achieve, being mundanely of neither culture and sublimely of both as artist, as poet, his own true identity: "I *am* a poet! I/ am.   I am.   I am a poet, I reaffirmed, ashamed" (CP2 284). One step in either direction of that bridge, of course, and he must find again "the road to Two-Gods", as Bill and Carlos, in life and in art, in baroque wordplay spoken straight ahead.

NOTES

1. Elena came to the United States as a citizen of Spain, before the Spanish American War when Puerto Rico would become an American territory and later citizenship would be extended.
2. *Writers at Work: The Paris Review Interviews, Third Series*, ed. George Plimpton (New York: Viking-Penguin, 1977), 85–86.
3. In an essay titled "A Letter," addressed to Reed Whittemore, Williams cited Pound parenthetically: "(read your Spanish lit.: 'just savages' E.P.)," *SE* 239.
4. Williams called attention to his ambiguous usage of that word by always writing it in quotation marks, "line" when referring to his poetry and cultural lineage simultaneously. The "line" also referred to the eight-syllable line favored by Spanish Golden Age poets, in which he wrote *Tituba's Children* (ML 225–300).
5. Jonathan Cohen, *By Word of Mouth: Poems from the Spanish, 1916–1965* (New York: New Directions, 2011), xxiv–xxv.
6. For more on this, please see *The Spanish American Roots of Williams Carlos Williams*, 200–05.
7. In conversation Flores good-humoredly recalled his differences with Williams, expressing regret that he didn't like his modern poems and thus having turned down publishing *Al Que Quiere!*
8. His mother's being from Mayagüez was the angle stressed by the San Juan press covering his visit.
9. *All Music Guide to Classical Music: The Definitive Guide to Classical Music*, ed. Chris Woodstra, Gerald Irennan, and Allen Schrott (San Francisco: Backbeat Books, 2005), 152.
10. Peter Middleton, "The Voices in 'The Desert Music,'" *William Carlos Williams Review* 27.2 (Fall 2007): 169–78.

13

T. HUGH CRAWFORD

Williams, science, and the body

In his autobiography William Carlos Williams notes, "as a writer I have never felt that medicine interfered with me but rather that it was my very food and drink, the very thing which made it possible for me to write" (*A* 357). As readers of Williams soon realize, his position as a doctor engaged in a community practice is inextricable from his writing, but medicine is not simply the subject matter for poems, short stories, and novels. Williams's scientific training and his daily encounters with the brute materiality of the human body – the newborn, the sick, the dying, and the dead – are central to his understanding and articulation of the world.

Born in Rutherford, New Jersey, Williams attended Horace Mann High School in New York City, and then, skipping college, enrolled directly in the Medical School of the University of Pennsylvania. In 1902 such a move was not uncommon as it was still possible to get a medical license by apprenticing with an established physician. Williams found himself in Philadelphia – the city of Medicine – where he met lifelong friends and fellow modern writers Ezra Pound and H. D., but, of equal importance, he studied medicine in the form that after the 1910 Flexner Report became standard for medical education. Penn and Johns Hopkins (Gertrude Stein's medical school) were among the leaders in turn-of-the-century medical education reform in America. When Williams studied there, those changes included four years of school, the first two with rigorous study in the basic sciences. Williams then had the privilege of practicing through what many regard as the golden age of American medicine, but, just as in the arts, the first half of the twentieth century was a time of flux, transitions in medical practice that were often driven by technological innovations and an emerging scientific perspective. Those shifts renewed the question often asked in medical history – whether the practice of medicine is a science or an art – a topic that was regularly addressed by William Osler, one of the most famous medical educators at the turn of the century and whose major text, *The Principles and Practice of*

Medicine, was one of Williams's textbooks. For Williams, it was just as fundamental a question as was the relation of medicine to his poetry.

His short story "A Night in June" addresses this question. The narrator is attending a home birth, his eighth attendance on this patient, though, as he notes, now most deliveries are in hospitals, "the equipment is far better" (*DS* 62). He waits in the kitchen, dozing with his head on the table, and dreams of an argument – art or science – concluding that he is more in the old school, that science "has crowded the stage more than is necessary" (*DS* 66). The story celebrates the contact that doctoring in the home with a long-standing patient brings, and laments the accelerated pace of a technology-driven practice, but of course Williams clearly owes much to science, as his use of pituitrin injections to accelerate her contractions indicates. And he also owes to his medical training what Marie Borroff calls his "diagnostic eye" (Borroff 62). In medical school, Williams learned the patient articulation of the particulars of the case, whether the diagnosis of a child with diphtheria or the description of a meadow in bloom.

The problem of seeing and presenting clearly pervades his texts, but he addresses it directly in his quirky book (more an odd compendium of notes written during the years 1928–1930) on educational reform called *The Embodiment of Knowledge*. Its overriding argument is that people lose the ability to see clearly because education and abstraction cloud vision. He introduces the question in what seems a straightforward example: "Children, at birth, used to be made blind by a venereal infection of the eyes, until we used silver nitrate in every case" (26). As he is trying to make the point that youths see clearly but over time education and society cloud understanding, it seems an apt metaphor. And, of course, it is significant that he chooses a medical example to make this point. What is complicated is that he describes a change in practice brought on by medical science. The antimicrobial qualities of the silver nitrate protect an infant's vision. Much of his book criticizes the celebration of science as the primary route to understanding, pointing toward works of the imagination as giving better, or more comprehensive knowledge. It is telling that the other place where the practice of using silver nitrate eyedrops appears in Williams's texts is at the end of "A Night in June" which was written just a year or two after *The Embodiment of Knowledge*. There the doctor debates with himself, with his intimate knowledge of his patient and her family and the necessity to follow medical procedure: "Oh yes, the drops in the baby's eyes. No need. She's as clean as a beast. How do I know? Medical discipline says every case must have drops in the eyes. No chance of gonorrhoea though here – but – Do it" (*DS* 68). The ambiguity of his question "How do I know?" is the subject of *The Embodiment of Knowledge*.

Historically, Williams's argument can be aligned with one of the founders of modern science, Francis Bacon, whose "Four Idols" in the *Novum Organum* lays out a method to achieve clear-sightedness by mitigating or removing the idols – theater, marketplace, tribe, cave – to achieve direct, unmediated access to the material world: "no ideas but in things" (*P* 6). *The Embodiment of Knowledge* criticizes education that abstracts knowledge from its material circumstances, lamenting the knowledge lost in such a process. In *The Evolution of Modern Medicine*, Osler makes a similar connection through Hippocrates: "A keen observer and an active practitioner, his views of disease, thus hastily sketched, dominated the profession for twenty-five centuries; indeed, echoes of his theories are still heard in the schools, and his very words are daily on our lips. If asked what was the great contribution to medicine of Hippocrates and his school we could answer – the art of careful observation" (68).

Williams's medical training emphasized careful observation of the world and resisting quick decisions based on abstract theories. His concern is that education instills those abstract frames at the expense of local, material understanding. Even though he was educated at a leading university, Williams explores local knowledge – the practices of midwives, curing with flaxseed poultices (*DS* 23), or knowing the pharmaceutical efficacy of plants, which at least in part explains his lifelong attraction to flowers and gardens. "A Morning Imagination of Russia" imagines an educated man:

> He would go
> out to pick herbs, he graduate of
> the old university. He would go out
> and ask that old woman, in the little
> village by the lake, to show him wild
> ginger. He himself would not know the plant.   (*CP*1 305)

Williams did know the plant, and many others, as he was an avid gardener. A complex relationship between medicine and gardening emerges in his writing as he often shifts seamlessly from articulating human bodies to describing flowers. *Kora in Hell* makes that complication explicit: "Pathology literally speaking is a flower garden. Syphilis covers the body with salmon-red petals. The study of medicine is an inverted sort of horticulture. Over and above all this floats the philosophy of disease which is a stern dance. One of its most delightful gestures is bringing flowers to the sick" (*I* 77–78). A peculiar statement, ending with a light-hearted quip, but he does take seriously the "stern dance" of disease, and his invocation of horticulture is an interesting move. Williams learns from his work in the garden the variability of plants, their individuality and proliferation. He also understands the local circumstances that either blight them, or help them thrive. His work as a physician in Rutherford and Passaic across a long career gave him similar local understanding. He might have a "philosophy of disease," but it is rooted in his place of practice, not in the arid abstractions of medical theories.

Clearly for Williams science alone is not the route to a completed understanding. Although direct observation is fundamental, that alone is a weak empiricism as he notes in *A Novelette:* "Science is impotent from all the viewpoints from which in its inception it seemed to promise enlightenment to the human mind. It is going nowhere but to gross and minute codification of the perceptions" (*I* 305). For Williams, knowledge must be embodied in the material world and not abstracted from it. From that perspective medicine, science, art, and the natural world are all of a piece. Although no one can accuse Williams of consistent philosophical statements – like his fellow poet from New Jersey, Walt Whitman, he also "contains multitudes" – *The Embodiment of Knowledge* does make one of his clearer statements about the relation between science and knowledge: "Science be it remembered, changes nothing, invents nothing, takes away nothing, adds nothing to the material world. How can it? It does one thing only – it brings its material into a certain relationship with the intelligence, in its relationship with man and poetry, brings man into a diagonal relationship with it" (129). One could claim that much of Williams's writing is an attempt to do the same. His poems do not so much add to the world as they articulate its furnishings: carefully, patiently, and minutely, but at the same time, bring those things into a relationship. Even though he is fully aware that words are not the things they represent, that words are things themselves, he insistently tries to present directly that materiality. "So much depends upon" his famous wheelbarrow because it is there, along with the chickens and the poet. It is in that simple (but at the same time incredibly complex) materiality that knowledge manifests.

Although innovations in medical technology often tend to move toward some form of visual display, medical practice, particularly in Williams's time, includes the exercise of all the senses. Williams does not confine his observations to the visual, but instead brings himself close to the bodies he treats. As he notes in his autobiography, "I was permitted by my medical badge to follow the poor, defeated body into those gulfs and grottos. And the astonishing thing is that at such times and in such places – foul as they may be with the stinking ischio-rectal abscesses of our comings and goings – just there, the thing, in all its greatest beauty, may for a moment be freed to fly for a moment guiltily about the room" (288–89). His practice gave the chance to encounter unexpected beauty (the "beautiful thing" section of *Paterson III* depicts a house call), but just as important, it provided contact. And he was not above berating his own desire to embrace the seemingly degraded or foul, a point made clear in his early poem "Smell!" where his "strong-ridged and deeply hollowed/nose" indiscriminately seeks out the "souring flowers of the bedraggled /poplars: a festering pulp ... " (*CP1* 92). He asks, "Must you taste everything? Must you know everything?" This is his *Embodiment of Knowledge* writ large. It can be found in the "cool of books" (*P* 96), but is also the result of direct sensory contact: sight, taste, smell, and sound. The actions of a medical examination and the celebration of the fullness of embodied experience are his source of understanding: tasting everything is the way to know something.

Not only does he embrace all the senses in embodying knowledge, Williams also recognizes the function of his own body as a living, moving entity participating in that encounter. In *Paterson*, Book II, "Sunday in the Park," Dr. Paterson articulates a walk, and in the process reveals the complexity of just such an attempt. Following such famous walking writers as Rousseau, Wordsworth, and Thoreau, Williams confronts the difficulty of detailing perceptions, thoughts, and encounters while physically moving through a landscape. What is perhaps more common in Williams are his travels by car, with his perceptions framed by a windshield and a slightly higher rate of speed. In the opening poem of *Spring and All*, or "The Young Housewife" (*CP1* 183, 57), Williams is part of a human-car assemblage with perceptions both rapid and fleeting. In "Sunday in the Park" Dr. Paterson walks, even explaining to his reader how to perform that task: "The body is tilted slightly forward from the basic standing position and the weight thrown on the ball of the foot, while the other thigh is lifted and the leg and opposite arm are swung forward (fig. 6B). Various muscles, aided" (45). This passage, which Williams excerpted from the *Journal of the American Medical Association*, is a scientific description of what becomes in Williams an artistic practice. Both pastoral ramble and flânerie, "Sunday in the Park" depicts a man describing his thoughts, perceptions, and his own body in motion through a varied landscape:

> Outside
> outside myself
> there is a world,   (43)

Williams sets the problem of articulating both interior thoughts and external experience while moving through perceptual space. At the same time, he must remind himself, as do all walkers, not to get lost in thought, but instead remain attentive to his surroundings, particularly the surface he walks. He "leaves the path, finds hard going/ across-field, stubble and matted brambles" (47). A familiar observation of novice long distance hikers is that they did not realize they would be walking hundreds of miles staring at their feet. Dr. Paterson, "– treads there the same stones/on which their feet slip as they climb" (44).

What "Sunday in the Park" reveals is that walking is another way of knowing. Observations are transitory, often involving rapid saccading vision rather than the stationary observation of the careful naturalist or the physician in an examination room. But "Sunday in the Park" is also a vision of a city in a state of decay or disease. The Doctor sees brute strength without beauty – "the ugly legs of the young girls,/pistons too powerful for delicacy!" (44) – and then stumbles onto a couple, the girl in revealing swimming attire lying,

>   – beneath
> the sun in frank vulgarity.
> Minds beaten thin
> by waste – among
>
> the working classes SOME sort
> of breakdown
> has occurred.   (51)

Williams's diagnostic eye turned onto a larger scene sees social degradation, and his judgment often veers from condemnation to fascination. But his walking perceptions drive through multiple scenes, leaving little time for judgment or therapeutic intervention. Instead the walk leads inevitably on to the next scene and a new, refreshed set of perceptions. Examination in the sick room is focused on diagnosis and a completed understanding. Walking in *Paterson* is part of what his publisher James Laughlin described as a "parataxic structure without closure," showing that Williams further recognized the tentative nature of the knowledge to be gleaned from singular encounters with a material world.

Though preoccupied with degradation, Williams, ever the doctor with a nuanced biological understanding, recognizes and articulates the relation between that and the nourishment that gives birth. This is perhaps best evident in his one of his automobile poems, the first in *Spring and All* and usually called "Spring and All." There the poet, probably on his way to or from the hospital, drives through the New Jersey meadowlands registering the emergence of plants, marking the beginning of spring. The world he describes is vaguely pathological: the road is to the "contagious hospital," and the plants, "reddish/purplish, forked, upstanding, twiggy/stuff" with "dead, brown leaves under them/lifeless vines – " (*CP1* 183). The meadow is in ferment. Williams names and details the shape and color of plants, describes their emergence, and relates them to medicine, in this case childbirth, "They enter the new world naked." Here again, the short story "A Night in June" is a poignant example as Williams further meditates on the role of touch in both medical and human relations, noting that "This woman in her present condition would have seemed repulsive to me ten years ago," but now "The flesh of my arm lay against the flesh of her knee gratefully. It was I who was being comforted and soothed". In addition, he assists her delivery by pressing with his "ungloved" hand on her abdomen and having her hold and pull his arm. He connects the joy of childbirth with the human contact such an event brings (*DS* 67).

Although medicine provides him with these opportunities, Williams does not blindly celebrate medical practice. Many of his poems and stories offer a disturbing critique of medicine, physicians, and sometimes by implication, himself. Perhaps most famous is the often-discussed short story, "The Use of Force," where the doctor is called in to diagnose a young, and, in his opinion, strikingly beautiful girl. He describes his psychic struggle with himself along with his physical struggle with this patient and her ineffectual parents, giving voice to disdain, anger, and even blind fury. He eventually succeeds in forcing a spoon past poor Mathilda's clenched teeth, revealing the membrane over her tonsils and confirming his suspicion of diphtheria. On the surface, this is a story of a physician doctoring in hard times with poor, suspicious patients, but his rage and apparent sexual attraction to his young patient, the perverse pleasure he seems to experience – "she surely rose to magnificent heights of insane fury of effort bred of her terror of me" (*DS* 58) – are profoundly disturbing.

Across his stories a complex figure emerges. Williams's narrators take on many roles – the calm obstetrician in "Mind and Body," the impatient, bigoted (but ultimately enlightened) practitioner in "A Face of Stone," and the brash, cold, but finally sympathetic pediatric ward resident in "Jean Beicke." What emerges is a doctor on the whole trying to do the right thing, owning up to his mistakes, but one who is unrelentingly critical of his own attitudes, emotions, and prejudices. Williams depicts medical success and failure, along with his own emotional trauma, with unblinking honesty. Often it is not pretty.

Without a doubt, his most sustained discussion of medicine as it was practiced in the first part of the twentieth century is "Old Doc Rivers" where he tells the story of an older, well-trained but also charismatic physician who was impaired – suffering from drug addiction and periodic bouts of depression. In the story, Rivers is an excuse for Williams to detail the vagaries of medical practice, the types of patients and illnesses encountered, but also medical malfeasance, the responsibility of fellow practitioners, and the conspiracy of silence that sometimes accompanies any professional group: "he began to slip badly in the latter years, made pitiful blunders" (*DS* 36). The narrator's wife asks, "If you know he is killing people, why do you doctors not get together and have his license taken away from him?" (*DS* 39). The doctor expresses doubt that they could. "Old Doc Rivers" also questions the charismatic element of medical authority, the magical attraction some doctors have over their patients. The story attempts to account for Rivers's popularity in the face of evidence that he is clearly a doper, making clear the distinction between being incompetent and being impaired. Ultimately Williams reads the situation through broader sociological categories: "In reality, it was a population in despair, out of hand, out of discipline, driven about by each other blindly believing in the miraculous, the drunken, as it may be" (40). Rivers ends up "a local shrine" (40) because of his idiosyncrasy, his instinct, his art. Even though he had studied in the great clinics of Europe, Rivers's medicine was an art not crowded too much by science.

In addition to impairment, Williams also addresses disability. He had patients who suffered from congenital defects ("The Girl with a Pimply Face"), or were maimed in industrial accidents ("The Paid Nurse"). Many of the inhabitants of the region were debilitated by chronic poverty (physical, emotional, and intellectual), including the housemaid, Elsie, who "express-[es] with broken// brain the truth about us" (*CP1* 218). He also struggles with his own disability. In 1951 he suffered the first of the number of strokes which, while slurring his speech and reducing his mobility, also prompted some of his finest contemplative work, such as "Asphodel, That Greeny Flower," a long poem about love, knowledge, understanding, and memory. There Williams details the things he learned in books, in the classics, and expresses frustration about attaining knowledge, of getting to the understanding poetry can give, but from which "men die miserably every day/ for lack/ of what is found there" (*CP2* 318). Significantly, the access point to this revelation is the smell of flowers. The opening pages are awash with the odor of various flowers, each of which bring "a whole flood/ of sister memories!" (*CP2* 312). Here, unlike his early "Smell!", the odors do not prompt desire nor signal spring. Instead they mark the passing of a life, the loss of time: "Listen while I talk on/against time" (311).

Addressing his wife he goes on to detail moments they had shared in their long life together, proclaiming his many failings, begging forgiveness, offering up a poem to capture that lost time and to celebrate what remains. But it is a sober celebration with the poem ending not just with a sense of lost time but also, once again, with embodiment:

It is late
    but an odor
        as from our wedding
            has revived for me
    and begun again to penetrate
        into all crevices
            of my world.   (337)

In a way, this is an inversion of the opening of *Paterson*, Book II, where Dr. Paterson asserts: Outside/outside myself/ there is a world (43). "Asphodel, That Greeny Flower" was originally written to be part of *Paterson*, Book V, but the flower's odor is not ripe festering rot nor disease but instead "is a curious odor,/ a moral odor" (312). Williams finds himself at a nexus – facing disability, the possible dissolution of his marriage (his stroke prompted revelations to his wife Floss of a number of indiscretions (Mariani 665), but poetically he also finds himself on interesting ground, calling up Greek texts while, at the same time, remembering his own excursions into nature cataloging flowers. Perhaps most significant is the role smell once again plays in the production of his mood and self-understanding. The scene of the doctor (a self-contained Dr. Paterson) recognizing there was a world out there "Subject to my incursions" (*P* 43) highlights the threshold he regularly crossed – doorways, physical examinations, and of course his presence at birth, one of the most important of thresholds. His stroke brings on another penetration – a moral odor – one that demanded contemplation and slow circumspection, something he delivers in the poem.

But the asphodel is also the flower of death. He notes that they grow in Hades, calling up his own personal hell: his anxiety about his marriage and his own disability, and of course, his own mortality. Clearly, as a physician, he confronted death regularly and, typical of Williams, his attitude moved from brash dismissal to genuine pathos. Early in his career he takes up the ritual of American death. His 1916 "Tract" is an address where he will "teach you my townspeople" (*CP*1 72) concluding with apparent success: "Go now/I think you are ready" (74). His lesson is pointed: death is death, and no amount of pomp will change that simple fact. No hearse, just a wagon, no "silk hat," no tailored driver. The brute simplicity of a farm wagon for a body that will soon be rained down with "pebbles and dirt and what not" (*CP*1 73–74). Williams's actual descriptions of death can be both brutal and decidedly poetic. In "Danse Pseudomacabre," he details the death of a baby from meningitis, once again linking pathology to flowers: "The lips are blue. The mouth puckers as for some diabolic kiss. It twitches, twitches faster and faster, up and down. The body slowly grows rigid and begins to fold itself like a flower folding again" (*DS* 90). Most often though, Williams refuses to sentimentalize death. Births are accompanied by joy, death is emptied of significance, a strategy clearly evident in "Death" where he repeatedly berates a dead man, calling him a bastard, insufferable, and a liar, noting that these are not qualities describing the living man, but are simple characteristics of a corpse: "He's a bastard because// there's nothing/ legitimate in him any/more/ he's dead" (*CP1* 346–47). "Death" is all the more striking for its lack of sentimentality in its original version (published in *Blues*, Fall 1930) where the dead body is clearly that of his father (*CP1* 530).

His 1927 poem "The Dead Baby," leaves out the body, detailing instead the scene in the home where the parents prepare themselves for the arrival of their dead child's corpse. It is a familiar scene in his work: a cursory description of a simple uncarpeted house and its primary inhabitants, in this case, an unconsoled mother and her "wellspoken, pitiful" husband (*CP1* 268). Parents of patients often appear in Williams's texts, as obstacles to be overcome ("The Use of Force"), or, as in this poem, humans in need. However, Williams's response to the situation remains matter-of-fact, encouraging activity – sweeping – and a degree of resignation to the "force of the facts."

> here is one who has gone up
> (though problematically)
> to heaven, blindly
> by force of the facts –
> a clean sweep
> is one way of expressing it –   (268)

Again he questions funereal practices and our uncertain relationship with dead bodies, picturing the soon-to-arrive corpse as "a white model of our lives/ a curiosity – / surrounded by fresh flowers" (268).

Many of his short stories depict a physician keeping professional distance from disease and death, often with a macabre sense of humor. He describes poor dying Jean Beicke as "such a scrawny, misshapen, worthless piece of humanity that I had said many times that somebody ought to chuck her in the garbage chute" (*DS* 74). What is equally clear is that this is a brittle shell, an attempt to keep emotional distance from Jean's inexplicable death. In those same stories he often articulates his patients' family's fear of disease and death. The parents of Mathilda in "The Use of Force," in the midst of that out-of-control scene, become "contemptible" because of their anxiety and solicitousness (*DS* 58). "Comedy Entombed" shows another side. There the doctor has been called to a patient who has gone into premature labor. The mother of four sons, her husband was hoping for a daughter. After delivering a stillborn *in caul* fetus, she ends up poking fun at her husband about the sympathetic pains he seemed to have experienced during her labor. While clearly not a happy nor carefree moment, the story does call attention to the circumstances of birth and death in the population Williams treats. No one sentimentalizes the scene. All (except perhaps the husband) treat the baby's death as part of the larger circumstances of a life lived in poverty.

William Carlos Williams died in 1963. His last book of poems *Pictures from Brueghel*, published in 1962, has in places the tone of a poet approaching death. Much of Williams's work across his career reflects the frenetic pace of his life as a pediatrician. There were idyllic peaceful moments caught going to or from a house call, or those moments attending birth where "The peace of the room was unchanged. Delicious" (*DS* 65), but more often there was the frantic writing-on-the-run that characterizes much of his work as a young doctor (see in particular "The Simplicity of Disorder" in *A Novelette* which depicts the chaos of doctoring in the 1929 influenza epidemic [*I* 275–79]). *Pictures from Brueghel* is slower, patiently descriptive, and contemplative. On his death, Williams was buried at Hillside Cemetery in his hometown of Rutherford in a ceremony that included the reading of "Tract." In *Pictures* there is a short poem called "The Children" (*CP2* 402–03) where he reminiscences about searching for flowers in the same Hillside cemetery woods, perhaps when he was younger, or possibly with his own grandchildren whom he describes in a series of short sketches in the pages immediately preceding this poem. They would sometimes find yellow violets, but if not, then "big blue/ones" and they would seek out the graves of children to decorate. There is a quiet poignance in this scene – pointing as it does to a career attending the birth and sometimes death of children, but also one that celebrates the vibrancy of the biological world. As he said to Floss in "Asphodel":

> We lived long together
> a life filled,
> if you will,
> with flowers. (310)

Williams lived a life filled with bodies. He knew them as patients, as objects of science, and as the material for poetry. He also knew them as flowers.

Works cited

Bell, Barbara Currier. "'The Use of Force' and First Principles in Medical Ethics." *Literature and Medicine* 3 (1984): 143–51.
Borroff, Marie. "William Carlos Williams: The Diagnostic Eye." In *Medicine and Literature*, edited by Enid Rhodes Peschel. New York: Neale Watson, 1980, pp. 56–65.

Bremen, Brian A. *William Carlos Williams and the Diagnostics of Culture*. New York: Oxford University Press, 1993.

Clark, Miriam Marty. "Art and Suffering in Two Late Poems by William Carlos Williams." *Literature and Medicine* 23.2 (2004): 226–40.

Crawford, T. Hugh. *Modernism, Medicine, & William Carlos Williams*. Norman: University of Oklahoma Press, 1993.

Flexner, Abraham. *Medical Education in the United States and Canada*. New York: The Carnegie Foundation for the Advancement of Teaching, 1910. Reprint. New York: Arno Press, 1972.

Laughlin, James. "Interview," *William Carlos Williams*, Voices and Visions, PBS, 1986.

Monteiro, George. "Doc Rivers, Rogue Physician." *William Carlos Williams Review* 17.2 (Fall 1991): 52–58.

Osler, William. *The Evolution of Modern Medicine*. New Haven, CT: Yale University Press, 1921.

Poirier, Suzanne. "The Physician and Authority: Portraits by Four Physician-Writers." *Literature and Medicine* 2 (1983): 21–40.

Snyder, Sharon L., and David T. Mitchell. "Disability Haunting in American Poetics." *Journal of Literary & Cultural Disability Studies* 1.1 (2007): 1–12.

Surman, Diana Collecutt. "Towards the Crystal: Art and Science in Williams' Poetic." In *William Carlos Williams: Man and Poet*, edited by Carroll F. Terrell. Orono, Maine: National Poetry Foundation, 1983, pp. 187–207.

Willms, Janice, and Henry Schneiderman. "The Ethics of Impaired Physicians: Wolfe's Dr. McGuire and Williams's Dr. Rivers." *Literature and Medicine* 7 (1988): 123–31.

14

JOHN LOWNEY

Williams: the new poetries and legacy

No modernist poet has had a greater impact on postmodernist American poetry than William Carlos Williams. His experimentation with poetic language, his dedication to formal innovation, and his literary engagement with the visual arts have influenced open-form poetics from the Objectivists through more recent Language poetry. As conversant as he was with international avant-garde movements in the literary as well as visual arts, Williams also insisted on the relation of art to the artist's locality. As his short stories, novels, plays, and autobiographical writings also demonstrate, his democratic commitment to articulating the everyday struggles of working- and middle-class life that he encountered in his medical practice has also appealed to readers worldwide. He underscores this commitment through his attention to vernacular forms of expression and through his social and geographical explorations of his locality, from the suburban New Jersey sites of his early lyrics to the apocalyptic urban scenes of his ambitious long poem, *Paterson*. As he wrote in his introduction to *The Wedge* (1944), "There is no poetry of distinction without formal invention, for it is in the intimate form that works of art achieve their exact meaning . . . to give language its highest dignity, its illumination in the environment to which it is native" (*CP2* 55). Williams's correlation of formal invention with the sociolinguistic milieu in which it emerges remains his most distinctive legacy as a modernist poet. As the testimony and practice of subsequent poets suggests, however, his legacy is complicated by the breadth and longevity of his experimentation. While Williams's experimental approach to language and form is most evident in his early avant-garde sequences (*Kora in Hell, Spring and All*, and "The Descent of Winter"), he continued to experiment with lyric form after World War II. The collections that enact his development of the triadic "variable foot," *The Desert Music* and *Journey to Love*, include some of his most moving considerations of memory, love, and mortality. Williams's significance has been debated since the later years of his life in little magazines, scholarly journals and books, anthologies, and digital media. It has

188

also been addressed through a multitude of poems that honor, parody, or otherwise invoke his life and poetry, as the recent collection *Visiting Dr. Williams* exemplifies.[1] The question of Williams's legacy, then, is a question of *which* Williams should be remembered. This question remains so meaningful because it is also a question of which modernism, or modernisms, should be remembered.

In the 1983 Modern Language Association "Poets' Centennial Tribute to William Carlos Williams," Charles Bernstein concluded: "In the end, Williams may be a token inclusion in a canon that excludes what he stands for."[2] Bernstein decries how Williams's acceptance in academic canons of poetry has been based on a limited selection of poems, taken out of context, rather than on the experimental process of his writing and its impact on postmodern poetry. As Bernstein writes, Williams insisted that "no theory has any value except as enacted in a practical or particular context ... in the language practices of living ... communities."[3] In distinguishing Williams's poetics from those of "official verse culture," Bernstein speaks to his own practice as a Language poet as well as to Williams's professed skepticism about the academy.[4] In emphasizing the critical value of Williams's marginalized position in literary history, Bernstein also recalls Donald Allen's preface to *The New American Poetry* (1960). Allen cites "the practice and precepts" of Pound and Williams as the primary influences for the Black Mountain, San Francisco Renaissance, Beat, and New York School poets, who are otherwise united by their "total rejection of all those qualities typical of academic verse."[5] It is no surprise, then, that Frank O'Hara would cite Williams, along with Walt Whitman and Hart Crane, as the only American poets who are "better than the movies."[6] And while Williams is less frequently associated with black vernacular poetics, Amiri Baraka defines him as the "common denominator" for the New American Poetry, "because he wanted American Speech, a mixed foot, a variable measure. He knew American life had outdistanced the English rhythms and their formal meters." His was "the language of this multinational land, of mixed ancestry."[7] Along with Whitman, Pound, and Olson, Williams has been widely acknowledged for his influential commitment to an experimental open-form poetics. Given the familiarity of this literary historical narrative, it is perhaps surprising to recall Robert Lowell's 1964 acknowledgement of Williams, in an unlikely triad with Allen Tate and Elizabeth Bishop, as a primary influence for his poetry.[8] It was Lowell, after all, who defined the opposition of the "raw" and the "cooked" when comparing the free-verse, oral poetics of the Beats to the more traditional formalist poetics favored by the New Criticism.[9] Williams's legacy is more complex, then, than the presumed opposition of Allen Ginsberg and Allen Tate, even if Tate did consider Williams "of the lunatic fringe."[10] His legacy is furthermore more complex than the opposition of Donald Allen and Donald Hall, the respective editors of the warring "raw" and "cooked" anthologies, *The New American Poetry* and *The New Poets of England and America* (1957). Beginning with the reconsideration of Williams in the 1950s, this essay will emphasize how Williams's poetry has remained so vital because of the provocative questions it enacts about what is "new," what is "American," and what is "poetry."[11]

By the time Williams had won the National Book Award for *Paterson Three* in 1950, his formidable presence as a writer was impossible to ignore. In addition to *Paterson* (1946–1951), his *Collected Later Poems* (1950), *Collected Earlier Poems* (1951), *Make Light of It: Collected Stories* (1950), and *Autobiography* (1951) were all published as he approached his seventieth birthday. These retrospective volumes would be followed by acclaimed volumes of new lyric poems, *The Desert Music* (1954) and *Journey to Love* (1955), which featured Williams's new metric, the triadic line pattern based on his concept of the variable foot. This new metric as well as the digressive, allusive, and meditative voice that characterized his early 1950s lyric poetry would further challenge preconceptions of Williams as the imagist poet most familiarly associated with "The Red Wheelbarrow." Given this evidence of his long career as a writer and his ongoing creativity, Williams's reputation became widely debated among poets in the 1950s. By the 1960s his work would attract considerable academic attention. Williams also played an active role in defining his legacy, through his correspondence and interaction with younger writers and through more overt acts of recognition such as his lengthy quotation of Charles Olson's essay "Projective Verse" in his *Autobiography*, his introduction to *Howl* and adoption of Allen Ginsberg as his poetic "son" in *Paterson*, and his quotation of Gilbert Sorrentino's prose and Marcia Nardi's letters in *Paterson*. Like his poetic "sons" and "daughters," Williams actively promoted his poetics as an alternative to the legacy of T. S. Eliot.

Williams's impact on the New American Poetry is most evident in such prominent little magazines as *Origin, Black Mountain Review, Yūgen,* and *Floating Bear*. These little magazines were important not only for publishing new poets but also for fostering alternative literary communities, for creating contacts among poets and a shared sense of purpose. *Origin*, edited by Cid Corman, was especially significant in setting an example for subsequent little magazines: in its first series (1951–1957) it introduced poets whose experimentation with vernacular poetics and composition by field extended the precedent of Williams and Olson and implicitly challenged the high modernist aesthetic principles defined by the New Criticism. In featuring poets such as Charles Olson, Robert Creeley, Robert Duncan, Paul Blackburn, Larry Eigner, and Denise Levertov, *Origin* transformed literary history as it shaped future poetry, reinterpreting modernism through the tradition of Pound and Williams. *Black Mountain Review* (1954–1957), edited by Creeley, would further define the poetics that became identified with the Black Mountain School. Because of his long history of supporting little magazines, Williams understood their formative role in creating literary groups and movements. His writing was prominently featured in *Origin*, which published his poetry (including "The Desert Music"), letters (to Creeley and Corman), and his essay "On Measure," as well as tributes to and discussions of his work, including Creeley's poem, "For W. C. W."[12]

Yūgen was also exceptionally important for the New American Poetry because it published poetry from all of the literary groups represented in Allen's anthology as well as substantial selections from the "New Black Poetry." Williams published only one poem in *Yūgen*, but his presence was ubiquitous in this journal edited by Amiri Baraka (Leroi Jones) and Hettie Cohen from 1958 to 1962, and its successor, *Floating Bear*, edited by Baraka and Diane Di Prima.[13] Williams's precedent was evident in the poetry and poetics of such writers as Olson and Creeley, Ginsberg and Kerouac, O'Hara and Ashbery, as well as African American poets such as Tom Postell, Steve Jonas, and Baraka. When Williams's "A Formal Design" was published in *Yūgen* 5 (1959), the biographical note for this "New Contributor" wryly underscored his importance: "William Carlos Williams, as an instructor at Brooklyn College sd., 'has had an amazing influence on the yng.'"[14] The volume that begins with "A Formal Design" exemplifies the vernacular mix of the "multinational land" that Baraka identified with Williams: following Williams's poem is a long excerpt of Ginsberg's "Kaddish," Barbara Guest's "Sunday Evening," and a remarkably diverse selection of poems, including translations of Rainer Gerhardt and Cesar Vallejo. The mix of styles in *Yūgen* is also considerably surrealist, from blues lyrics and sound poems to the cutups of Ashbery and William Burroughs, recalling Williams's more experimental writing in *Kora in Hell* and *Spring and All* more than his later poetry. *Yūgen* also recalls modernists such as Gertrude Stein and Lorca, and when Williams and Pound are placed in dialogue with modernists who are not necessarily "American" as well as with younger poets who are African American, their "practice and precepts" are revised and reinvented, in a way that suggests more expansive possibilities for imagining poetic communities and networks than Allen's anthology.

Williams's impact on the "New Black Poetry" is not widely acknowledged, despite the testimony of Baraka, the only African American poet represented in Allen's anthology and the most important figure in black experimental poetry of the 1960s. Despite the important scholarship of Nathanael Mackey, Aldon Nielsen, and James Smethurst, the interaction of the "New American Poetry" and the "New Black Poetry" has received limited attention in historical scholarship on "contemporary" or "postmodern" poetry.[15] Baraka's role was especially important, as a poet who invoked the "American idiom" of Williams with the vernacular traditions of the blues and jazz, and as an editor who fostered an interracial avant-garde on the pages of *Yūgen* and *Floating Bear*. Baraka's subsequent commitment to the "Black Aesthetic" of course complicates claims for his earlier role, and Williams's precedent is most evident in his first book, *Preface to a Twenty Volume Suicide Note* (1961). Baraka cited Williams's importance for his poetic practice throughout his life, however, from his statement on poetics in *The New American Poetry*, "How You Sound??" to his introductory statement for his later long poem, *Why's/Wise* (1990), where he cites *Paterson* along with Olson's *Maximus Poems* and Melvin Tolson's *Libretto for the Republic of Liberia* as analogues for his poem.[16] Baraka's fashioning of Williams as a poet whose vernacular diction and formal experimentation correspond with black vernacular forms has had a substantial impact on African American poetry, as poets such as Stephen Jonas, A. B. Spellman, Clarence Major, and Nathaniel Mackey exemplify.[17]

Williams had already had a significant but less widely recognized impact on poets of the generation prior to the New American Poetry. As a correspondent, reader of manuscripts, reviewer of books, and contributor to magazines and anthologies, he played a crucial role for emerging poets who would receive public acclaim much later than his initial support. Most notably, his support as a friend and collaborator with Louis Zukofsky was important for the younger poet's early career and for the important 1932 *An 'Objectivists' Anthology*, which included then obscure writers such as Basil Bunting, George Oppen, Carl Rakosi, and Charles Reznikoff. Williams contributed eighteen poems to the anthology and wrote a substantial review for *The Symposium* as well as a positive review of Oppen's first book, *Discrete Series*, in *Poetry* (1934).[18] One of the younger poets featured in the Objectivist anthology was Kenneth Rexroth, who would become better known as a leading figure in the postwar San Francisco Renaissance. Williams first met Rexroth in 1929 when he was twenty-four years old and subsequently corresponded with him about his poetry, despite skepticism about his mystical inclinations, and wrote an appreciative review of his 1944 *The Phoenix and the Turtle*.[19] Another poet whose early accomplishment Williams recognized was Muriel Rukeyser, who in the 1930s was associated with the Popular Front Left and who later would become better known as an influential feminist poet. Although Williams expressed reservations about poetry written explicitly for a "cause," his 1938 *New Republic* affirmation of Rukeyser's documentary poetics in *USi* anticipates subsequent experiments with documentary materials in long poems, most notably his own work-in-progress, *Paterson*.[20] Williams met Olson as early as 1939 and corresponded with him afterward.[21] He read drafts of *The Maximus Poems* as he was writing *Paterson*, discussing especially the challenge of conveying a vital local history. Williams's quotation of "Projective Verse" in his *Autobiography* was at once a tribute to Olson's theoretical acumen and an affirmation of their shared sense of purpose. It was also a public affirmation of their shared impact on writers such as Robert Creeley, whose early poetry and essays are especially notable for their astute considerations of Williams's poetics. Finally, Williams was a decisive reader and mentor for a poet who was initially more traditional in his language and form, Theodore Roethke. After their meeting in 1940, Roethke initiated a correspondence with Williams and ultimately accepted his advice to open his poetry to the language and rhythms of everyday speech, most notably in his 1951 book *Praise to the End!*, which he dedicated to Williams and Kenneth Burke.[22] As these examples suggest, Williams was often prescient in his support for younger poets who learned from his advice and subsequently flourished. Of course, the examples of Zukofsky, Olson, and to some extent Rukeyser also suggest the mutuality of these relationships: Williams played the role of mentor but was also open to what he could learn from their poetry, especially as he was composing *Paterson*.

James Breslin has written that in his support for younger poets, Williams was often regarded "either as the affectionate, tolerant, and homespun patron saint of contemporary poetry or as a mindlessly indiscriminate zealot ready and willing to write a puff at the drop of a chapbook."[23] His exuberant praise for otherwise obscure figures such as H. H. Lewis, Merrill Moore, and Nardi suggests how he understood the world of poetry in more cooperative than competitive terms. And his appreciative reviews of poets as different as Laura Riding, Parker Tyler, and Irving Layton defy skeptical assessments of his self-promotional interests as a critic.[24] Williams's impact on younger writers is paradoxical, though, as Baraka exemplifies in a 1960 interview. He said that Williams taught him "mostly how to write in my own language – how to write the way I speak rather than the way I think a poem ought to be written."[25] To write like Williams, then, is to write in a "language" that is not Williams's. It might seem strange that Baraka develops his black vernacular poetics through the example of white avant-garde writers such as Williams and Olson.[26] Williams, however, made similar claims about Whitman in "America, Whitman, and the Art of Poetry" (1917): "The only way to be like Whitman is to write *unlike* Whitman."[27] Recognizing

Whitman's colossal precedent for American free-verse poetry, Williams also acknowledges the impossibility of his own assertion: "Let me at least realize that to be a poet one must be himself!" He then asks, "'Be himself?' What the devil difference does it make to anyone whether a man is himself or not so long as he write good poetry."[28] While insisting on a distinction between the poet and his poetry, Williams suggests not only the "contradiction" that informs "Song of Myself" ("I am large, I contain multitudes"), but also the elision of personality and poetry that would become so prominent in poetry that emulates Williams's writing.

Of the many poets whom Williams supported and influenced, no one seems more unlikely, and less like Whitman, than Robert Lowell. Lowell's interest in Williams's poetry actually began prior to his first book, though, when he attended Harvard and met fellow student James Laughlin in the 1930s. Laughlin introduced Lowell to Williams's poetry as he was beginning to contact Williams to publish his writing with New Directions. While Laughlin's commitment to Williams's writing played an inestimable role in sustaining his legacy, the colloquial, free verse poems that Lowell initially wrote were discouraged by his Harvard mentors, and he eventually left Harvard and studied with Tate.[29] Lowell would cite Tate and Williams as dual role models throughout his career, but there was little evidence of Williams's poetics in *Lord Weary's Castle* (1946), which established Lowell as an exemplary formalist poet. The transformation of Lowell into the poet who became famously identified with "confessional" poetry a decade later, though, had everything to do with his engagement with Williams and his poetics. Lowell was especially enthusiastic about *The Desert Music* and *Journey to Love*, with their more personal tone and subject matter and their more direct expression of emotion than he associated with the modernist idea of the poem as an impersonal object. Lowell became personally close to Williams in the 1950s as he sought his advice, and he eventually adapted Williams's insistence on the "American idiom" to his family history in *Life Studies* (1959), which won the National Book Award the following year and remains Lowell's most renowned achievement. Lowell's patrician New England "American idiom" is hardly the idiom of his mentor, but *Life Studies* is distinguished by a more conversational tone than Lowell's earlier poetry, even as colloquial speech is blended within more conventional poetic diction. The autobiographical and sometimes excruciatingly personal subject matter of *Life Studies* likewise can be attributed to Lowell's reading of Williams, including his family chronicles (especially *In the Money*) as well as his late poems. Williams is not routinely associated with "confessional poetry," but his catalytic effect on Lowell's development suggests how his influence exceeds the most familiar parameters of literary history.

Williams more familiarly mentored another poet who famously transformed American poetry in the 1950s, Allen Ginsberg. Williams's introduction to *Howl and Other Poems* (1956) affectionately commemorates his long association with the poet and his necessary "belief in the art of poetry that has gone hand in hand with this man into his Golgotha."[30] Ginsberg in turn recalls Williams in the lineation and imagery of a poem like "In back of the real," which, like the earlier poems of *Empty Mirror*, contrasts so dramatically with what Ginsberg characterized as the longer "Hebraic-Melvillean bardic breath" lines of "Howl."[31] The fact that Williams had such an important effect on two of the most iconic volumes of 1950s poetry, *Life Studies* and *Howl*, attests to his remarkable effect on postwar American poetry. Lowell, after all, remains reserved and ironic even when immersed in disturbing moments of family drama. Ginsberg, on the other hand, "howls" prophetically on behalf of the Beat generation, translating intensely painful personal experience into prophetic revelations.[32] His visionary poetics seem far removed from the more "measured" introspection of Williams's late lyrics, but Ginsberg, too, arrived at his prophetic vision of "America" via Rutherford. As Williams documents in *Paterson Four*, Ginsberg, who grew up in Paterson, first approached him for guidance in 1950, when he was twenty-three. Williams worked intensively with him as he was transforming journal entries into the poems that would be collected in *Empty Mirror*, encouraging him to transcribe the lines "according to how they might be spoken, and where I might take a breath."[33] Ginsberg recalls how this process of composition was one of discovering form, a process that he eventually adapts to the testimonial and prophetic modes of *Howl*. If the idea of the line as breath unit suggests Olson's concept of lineation more than Williams's, the idea of form as discovery was intrinsic to Williams's poetry, even as the content and tone of "Howl" or "America" were dramatically different from either *Paterson* or Williams's late lyrics. If for Williams, "the only way to be like Whitman is to write *unlike* Whitman," in Ginsberg's case, the only way to be like Williams is to write more *like* Whitman.

The "New American Poet" who was perhaps most affected by Williams's poetics in the 1950s and early 1960s was a poet who grew up in England, Denise Levertov. She was also one of the few women represented in Allen's anthology.[34] Levertov moved to the United States with her husband, the American writer Mitchell Goodman, shortly after first reading Williams in Paris after the publication of her first book, *The Double Image* (1946). She subsequently corresponded with Williams and studied his poetry as she was raising her child. Williams's mentorship role with Levertov was as transformative as his impact on Lowell, but this impact was of course complicated by the gendered dynamic of this relationship. As Linda Kinnahan has written, Williams is usually associated with the idea of the "female" as "the material upon and from which the poet works," but as early as *In the American Grain*, he also conceptualizes the "feminine" as that which is "excluded and oppressed and silenced" but also a source of "disruptive resistance to masculinist containment."[35] Williams's interactions with women writers also suggest these contradictions. On the one hand, he expressed admiration for innovative modernist women writers such as H. D., Mina Loy, Marianne Moore, and Gertrude Stein: the essays on Moore (1925) and Stein (1930) that are reprinted in *Imaginations* are among the most compelling articulations of his own aesthetics in the 1920s. On the other hand, he could be patronizing or even appropriative in his interactions with younger women writers: the most notorious example is his incorporation of Marcia Nardi's correspondence in *Paterson*.[36] In his correspondence with Levertov, his role was paternal, at times condescending but generally encouraging, as Levertov became increasingly familiar with the possibilities and limitations of Williams's concept of "the American idiom."[37] His advice about language, syntax, and lineation is especially evident in *Here and Now* (1957) and *Overland to the Islands* (1958), which also take up his thematic preoccupations, as poems such as "Pure Products" and "Overland to the Islands" exemplify. Yet, in her exploration of domestic space, as a site of limits but also of maternal power, Levertov also enacts a struggle that is familiar in women's poetry, the negotiation of masculine poetic traditions. This struggle to negotiate Williams's iconoclastic appeal as a poet *and* his masculine authority is also evident in more experimental female poets such as Hilda Morley, Kathleen Fraser, and Alice Notley. Levertov's poetic process of reconciling her domestic experience as a woman with Williams's poetics is, then, also a process of exploring contradictory subject positions for the female poet. Her engagement with his poetry ultimately produces a feminized Williams that differs dramatically from the masculinist poet most often associated with the New American Poetry. The poetry she identifies with her mentor, she later writes in "Great Possessions," is decidedly not the poetry of "notations" that becomes so familiar in the 1960s, but a poetry that enacts "that energetic, compassionate, questioning spirit that infused even the most fragmentary of Williams's poems."[38]

As Levertov writes in "Great Possessions," the significance of Williams's poetry was distorted by his popularity and apparent accessibility, whether in the literature classroom or the creative writing workshop. While the struggle to recover an avant-garde Williams would take on greater urgency and precision with the emergence of the Language writers, the question of his reputation was already a source of debate – and parody – among the New York Poets by the early 1960s. The best known parody of the Williams poem most often parodied, "This Is Just to Say," was written by Kenneth Koch and published in his 1962 book *Thank You and Other Poems*. "Variations on a Theme by William Carlos Williams" begins with the unforgettable lines: "I chopped down the house that you had been saving to live in next summer. / I am sorry, but it was morning, and I had nothing to do / and its wooden beams were so inviting."[39] This affectionately irreverent demolition of the house of Williams proceeds to increasingly absurd variations. A more abstract and more digressive allusion to Williams's poetics appears in the more abstract and more digressive poetry of John Ashbery, specifically in the mock-triadic verses of "The Thief of Poetry," a wonderfully self-reflexive enactment of wandering memory from *Houseboat Days* (1975).[40] The poet who is most emphatically serious in his comic evocations of Williams, however, is Frank O'Hara. While he only somewhat sarcastically praises Williams in his mock-manifesto "Personism," his invocation of Williams to celebrate the impending marriage of his artist friends Jane Freilicher and Joe Hazan is more typical in its understated rhetorical complexity:

> It's so
> original, hydrogenic, anthropomorphic, fiscal, post-anti-esthetic,
>   bland, unpicturesque and WilliamCarlosWilliamsian!
> it's definitely not 19th Century, it's not even Partisan Review, it's
>   new, it must be vanguard![41]

Like "Personism," "Poem Read at Joan Mitchell's" gently mocks the pretention of avant-garde proclamations as well as the institution of marriage. And the characterization of this marriage as "WilliamCarlosWilliamsian" likewise mocks both a presumably shared affection for Williams and the branding of his name as a "vanguard" writer. This example of O'Hara's occasional "lunch poems," like his poetry more generally, furthermore implicitly mocks the heteronormative construction of Williams as a "New American" poet. O'Hara's "post-anti-esthetic" poetry, like the poetry of New York peers such as Koch, Ashbery, Guest, and James Schuyler, instead recalls a less determinate, more hybrid version of Williams, the Williams whose early writing is deeply engaged with the artistic vanguard of Paris as much as New York. As writers who were professionally immersed in the New York modern art world, O'Hara and Ashbery were especially attuned to Williams's formative interaction with the visual arts and the significance of his reputation within the "poetry wars" of the 1950s and 1960s.

As Williams became more widely acknowledged in academic canons of modernist poetry by the 1970s, his significance as a poet would continue to be contested by scholars dismissive of his poetics (such as Helen Vendler, Harold Bloom, and Donald Davie), by advocates of his poetry in creative writing programs, and by an emerging generation of poets who argued for avant-garde alternatives to the "workshop poem" increasingly identified with Williams. The republication of Williams's earlier writing, most notably in *Imaginations* (1970), was especially important for reconsidering his poetics. This reconsideration of Williams was also specifically affected by several coinciding developments: the reemergence of the Objectivist poets, the formation of a new avant-garde movement known as "Language" writing, and the growing prominence of feminist poetry.

The reconsideration of Williams after his death in the 1960s coincided with what Ron Silliman has defined as "third phase objectivism," which, if not a renewed literary movement, was a return of the Objectivist poets to the public eye.[42] The public reemergence of writers such as Reznikoff, Zukofsky, Oppen, Rakosi, Bunting, and Lorine Niedecker in the 1960s prompted a reexamination of both the Objectivist movement of the 1930s (the first phase) and its subsequent postwar absence from literary history (the second phase). The reemergence of poetry that was both politically radical and formally experimental also challenged histories of US poetry that either ignored or dismissed poetry informed by Marxism. Given Williams's involvement with such projects as *An "Objectivists" Anthology* and the Objectivist Press, it is not surprising that he would figure prominently in the Objectivist poetry of the 1960s. Both Zukofsky and Oppen articulate Williams's literary historical significance in essays that were published in that decade. Zukofsky underscores the social precision of Williams's linguistic objectification in essays such as "Sincerity and Objectification" and "American Poetry 1920–1930," reprinted in *Prepositions*.[43] Oppen's articulation of Williams's legacy in "The Mind's Own Place" critiques his appropriation by the younger generation of the New American Poetry.[44] Like Zukofsky, Oppen celebrates the proto-Objectivist poet of *Spring and All* as he contests constructions of Williams's reputation that obscure his early accomplishment. Two important poetic sites of their engagement with Williams's poetics also assert an Objectivist legacy for his writing: Zukofsky's long poem *A*, specifically the elegiac commemoration of Williams in *A* 15–17, and Oppen's serial poem "Of Being Numerous." While the more conventional elegiac form of *A* 15 heightens the loss of Williams through its simultaneous reflection on the assassination of President Kennedy, *A* 17, "A Coronal" (dedicated to Floss Williams) is a collage comprising writings by Zukofsky and Williams that celebrates the lasting significance of Williams's example and friendship. Oppen also addresses the social implications of Williams's formal innovations in his intertextual allusions to Williams. The contested legacy of Williams's poetics is embedded within the dialogic structure of "Of Being Numerous," which addresses the Vietnam War and interrogates the cultural contradictions resulting from the exceptionalist myth of "America," so often (and so often misleadingly) associated with Whitman and Williams.

Williams's legacy as an avant-garde poet became especially important to the generation of experimental poets emerging in the 1970s. What came to be known as Language poetry by the 1980s was in part a response to Williams's writing, as it was represented in academic accounts of modern poetry, in the generation of poets associated with the New American Poetry, and in the renewed attention to Objectivism. While Williams had become an established figure in the growing number of creative writing programs in the United States, the publication of *Imaginations* in 1970 presented a radically experimental alternative to the familiar image of the plain-spoken American lyric poet. Sequences such as *Kora in Hell, Spring and All*, and "The Descent of Winter" demonstrated Williams's engagement with European avant-garde movements such as cubism, futurism, and dada as well as US movements such as precisionism. The hybrid form of these sequences, mixing poetry and critical prose, furthermore underscores Williams's serious interest in literary and social theory, which is also evident in the 1920s essays collected in *Imaginations*. If the New American poets – especially the Black Mountain poets – most often cited *The Wedge* as a foundational text for their open-form, speech-based poetics, the Language poets cite Williams's 1920s sequences, most notably *Spring and All*. In his introduction to the 1986 anthology of Language poetry, *In the American Tree*, Ron Silliman makes a clear distinction between Language poetry and the previous generation of the New American Poetry, which he identifies by "an insistence on the centrality of the influence of William Carlos Williams and a preference for poetry that, read aloud, sounded spoken."[45] In contrast with the projectivist poetics of the New American Poetry, Silliman underscores the theoretical interest in textuality, signification, and the materiality of written language shared by the mostly New York and San Francisco poets affiliated with journals such as *This, Hills, Roof*, and especially *L=A=N=G=U=A=G=E* in the 1970s and early 1980s. As suggested by the title of *In the American Tree*, the title also of the anthology's introductory poem by Kit Robinson, Language poetry itself acknowledges the influence of Williams, but the Williams of the 1920s, the Williams in dialogue with Stein and Zukofsky. *In the American Tree* also includes important poets who predate the Language movement but who likewise extend Williams's experimental poetics, such as Clark Coolidge, Michael Palmer, and Susan Howe.

As Alan Golding documents, Williams's significance for Language writing is most evident in the theoretical writings of poets such as Silliman, Bob Grenier, Bob Perelman, and Charles Bernstein, as well as in the feminist experimentalism of poets such as Rachel Blau DuPlessis, Alice Notley, Lyn Hejinian, and Rae Armantrout. Grenier's 1971 essay "On Speech" is one of the earliest critiques of speech-based poetics that cites *Spring and All* as an alternative example. Silliman's prose poetry and essays in the late 1970s and 1980s are especially important for their engagement with Williams's prose poetry. Most notably, his influential 1980 essay "The New Sentence" looks at *Kora in Hell*, along with Stein's *Tender Buttons*, as one of the earliest examples of important American prose poems. Perelman likewise positions Williams prominently within his genealogy of Language writing in *The Marginalization of Poetry* (1996). Bernstein writes about the radical implications of Williams's experimental poetry frequently, whether directly in his essays or less directly in his intertextual evocations of his poetry, in volumes such as *Content's Dream* (1986) and *A Poetics* (1992).[46] His poem "For Bill Charley Bill on Memorial Day," included in *Visiting Dr. Williams*, is an especially cogent – and cogently comic – defense of the Language writers' Williams, the more unpredictable free-verse Williams of *Spring and All* rather than the later Williams of the "variable foot":

> There's no
>
> formula for
> poetry: constraints
>
> or not
> countable rhythms
>
> or uncountable
> (and unaccountable)
>
> ones.[47]

Williams figures more ambivalently in feminist writing associated with the Language movement. The question of his legacy takes on renewed importance for women writers in the 1970s and 1980s largely because Williams's belated inclusion in academic canons of modernism coincides with increasing attention to women's poetry, including modernist women's poetry. Lyn Hejinian, whose acclaimed prose poetry sequence *My Life* can be related to Williams's earlier serial prose poems, wrote a 1982 review of Paul Mariani's biography of Williams that criticized his predominantly thematic interpretation of the poetry. She argued instead for the influence of his "poetics in which the word is the concrete perceptible fact and the structure is tantamount to statement."[48] If this self-reflexive Williams is the figure most frequently constructed in Language writing, the gender politics of his writing are more problematic. Rachel Blau DuPlessis, who is as knowledgeable about Objectivist poetry as about modernist and postmodernist women's poetry, qualifies her appreciation of Williams in her 1984 essay "Pater-daughter," where she notes Williams's conventional language of gender even in radically experimental texts such as *Spring and All*. As a poet who was herself writing long serial poems in the 1980s, most notably *Drafts*, she underscores the challenge of adapting Williams's poetics and seeking moments of gender instability in his poetry that contradict more predictable binary oppositions.[49] Another poet who has addressed Williams's legacy for women poets is Alice Notley, in her talk that was later published by Hejinian's Tuumba Press, "Doctor Williams' Heiresses." Notley, who is more often associated with the New York School than with Language poetry, playfully critiques genealogical constructs of "the Williams tradition" while enacting how she as a woman can subversively adapt his poetics. Such an intertextual engagement with Williams's poetics is also implicit in her underground (subway) invocation of the Kora myth in her long poem *The Descent of Alette* (1992).[50] Finally, Rae Armantrout, the feminist West Coast Language poet who dramatically extends the methods of Williams's transformation of the lyric – his syntax, lineation, and formal compression – also ironically adapts his emphasis on observation. Through compact, enjambed lines that suggest multiple significations, Armantrout's poetry is as likely to underscore the social construction of gendered subjectivity as the incongruity of mass-mediated domestic life.

From the Objectivists to the Language poets, Williams's poetry is invoked for the social criticism implicit in its linguistic and formal innovations. This is also true for poets who are not so easily categorized. Williams has become as likely to be read as a transnationalist poet as a localist poet, given the international dimensions of his life and writing, including his work as a translator, and the multilingual sources of his "American idiom." Williams's localist modernism, as Eric White has written, is also a transnationalist modernism,[51] and this translocalist dynamic informs the projects of poets as different as Lorine Niedecker, Charles Tomlinson, or Victor Hernández Cruz. I will conclude with one example of a contemporary poet who suggests the transnationalist implications of Williams's poetics for the twenty-first century. This poet is Lawrence Joseph, whose 2005 book *Into It* addresses the 2001 terrorist attacks on the World Trade Center from multiple perspectives: as a lower Manhattan resident, as an Arab American, and as a lawyer-poet.[52] Joseph invokes Williams's precedent for his poetics in an earlier poem, "Some Sort of Chronicler I Am":

> Has anyone considered
> during the depression of 1921
>
> Carlos Williams felt a physician's pain,
> vowed to maintain the most compressed
>
> expression of perceptions and ardors
> —intrinsic, undulant, physical movement—
>
> revealed in the speech he heard around him
> (dynamization of emotions into imagined
>
> form as a reality in itself).[53]

Williams as a poet of social crisis, whose formal complexity emerges from an empathetic response to his patients' expression of pain, is intertextually invoked more opaquely in the wake of 9/11. *Into It* similarly recalls the Williams of the 1920s, the writer of *In the American Grain* as well as *Imaginations*, whose insights into the xenophobic violence of US nationalism take on new significance post-9/11. Joseph underscores the transnationalism of Williams's localism, as he relates the devastation of his Manhattan location to his prior experience in the city of his birth, Detroit, to his family history in Lebanon and Syria, and to US military incursions in Iraq and elsewhere. For Joseph, as for previous writers who have been challenged by the "compressed // expression" of Williams's poetry and prose, the often dissonant "speech he heard around him" continues to resonate, not only in "American" poetry, but also in unexpected locations worldwide.

NOTES

1. Sheila Coghill and Thom Tammaro, eds., *Visiting Dr. Williams: Poems Inspired by the Life and Work of William Carlos Williams* (Iowa City, IA: University of Iowa Press, 2011).
2. Charles Bernstein, "The Academy in Peril: William Carlos Williams Meets the MLA," in *Content's Dream: Essays 1975–1984* (Los Angeles, CA: Sun & Moon Press, 1986), 246.
3. Bernstein, "The Academy in Peril," 250–51.
4. Williams' most sustained critique of American education is *The Embodiment of Knowledge*, which he wrote in 1928–1930, but which was not published until 1974. See Williams, *The Embodiment of Knowledge* (New York: New Directions, 1974).

5. Donald M. Allen, Preface to *The New American Poetry*, ed. Donald M. Allen (New York: Grove Press, 1960), xi.

6. Frank O'Hara, "Personism: A Manifesto" (1961), in *The Collected Poems of Frank O'Hara*, ed. Donald Allen (Berkeley, CA: University of California Press, 1995), 498.

7. Imamu Amiri Baraka, *The Autobiography of LeRoi Jones* (New York: Freundlich Books, 1984), 159.

8. In a 4 October 1964 *New York Times Book Review* interview with Stanley Kunitz, Lowell said: "The poets who most directly influenced me were Allen Tate, Elizabeth Bishop and William Carlos Williams." Quoted in Stephen Gould Axelrod, *Robert Lowell: Life and Art* (Princeton, NJ: Princeton University Press, 1978), 19.

9. In his acceptance speech for the 1960 National Book Award he received for *Life Studies*, Lowell said: "Two poetries are now competing, a cooked and a raw. The cooked, marvelously expert, often seems laboriously concocted to be tasted and digested by a graduate seminar. The raw, huge blood-dripping gobbets of unseasoned experience are dished up for midnight listeners. There is a poetry that can only be studied, and a poetry that can only be declaimed, a poetry of pedantry, and a poetry of scandal." Quoted in Jed Rasula, *The American Poetry Wax Museum: Reality Effects, 1940–1990* (Urbana, IL: National Council of Teachers of English, 1996), 233. See Rasula's incisive discussion of the 1950s "anthology wars" in *The American Poetry Wax Museum*, 223–46.

10. When Williams mentions Tate in his *Autobiography*, he characterizes him as "Allen Tate, whom I had always despised, and who in his turn had always considered me of the lunatic fringe," although they eventually became friendly with each other. See *A* 312.

11. For a fuller examination of Williams and the New American Poetry, see John Lowney, *The American Avant-Garde Tradition: William Carlos Williams, Postmodern Poetry, and the Politics of Cultural Memory* (Lewisburg, PA: Bucknell University Press, 1997). For recent considerations of the lasting significance of Allen's anthology, see John R. Woznicki, ed., *The New American Poetry: 50 Years Later* (Bethlehem, PA: Lehigh University Press, 2014). Especially pertinent is the essay by Paul Cappucci, "'Trying to Build on Their Elders' Work: The Correspondence of Donald Allen and William Carlos Williams," in Woznicki, 15–28. Another valuable collection of essays on Williams' legacy is Ian Copestake, ed., *The Legacy of William Carlos Williams: Points of Contact* (Newcastle: Cambridge Scholars Press, 2007).

12. For a thorough analysis of the importance of *Origin*, see Alan Golding, *From Outlaw to Classic: Canons in American Poetry* (Madison, WI: University of Wisconsin Press, 1995), 114–43.

13. See Nielsen on the significance of Baraka's role as editor of these little magazines: Aldon Lynn Nielsen, *Writing Between the Lines: Race and Intertextuality* (Athens, GA: University of Georgia Press, 1994), 214–51.

14. "New Contributors," *Yūgen* 5 (1959), 39.

15. Nathaniel Mackey, *Discrepant Engagement: Dissonance, Cross-Culturality, and Experimental Writing* (Cambridge: Cambridge University Press, 1993); Aldon Lynn Nielsen, *Black Chant: Languages of African-American Postmodernism* (Cambridge: Cambridge University Press, 1997);

James Smethurst, *The Black Arts Movement: Literary Nationalism in the 1960s and 1970s* (Chapel Hill, NC: University of North Carolina Press, 2005).

16. Amiri Baraka (LeRoi Jones), "'How You Sound??'" in *The New American Poetry*, 424–25; Baraka, Introduction to *Why's/Wise, in The LeRoi Jones/ Amiri Baraka Reader*, ed. William Harris (New York: Thunder's Mouth Press, 1991), 480.

17. See Aldon Lynn Nielsen, "William Carlos Williams and the New Black Poetries," *Sagetrieb* 18.2 & 3 (2002), 283–95.

18. William Carlos Williams, *"An 'Objectivists' Anthology*, Edited by Louis Zukofsky" (1933), reprinted in *STS* 42–46; Williams, "The New Poetical Economy: George Oppen's *Discrete Series*" (1934), reprinted in *STS* 55–59.

19. Williams, "In Praise of Marriage: Kenneth Rexroth's *The Phoenix and the Tortoise*" (1945), reprinted in *STS* 132–38. On their first meeting, see Mariani 292.

20. Williams, "Muriel Rukeyser's *US1*" (1938), reprinted in *STS* 89–91.

21. According to Mariani, Olson first met Williams at Ford Madox Ford's "Les Amis de William Carlos Williams" group in New York. See Mariani 424.

22. On Williams and Roethke, see Robert Kusch, *"My Toughest Mentor": Theodore Roethke and William Carlos Williams (1940–1948)* (Lewisburg, PA: Bucknell University Press, 1999).

23. Breslin, "Introduction: The Presence of Williams in Contemporary Poetry," *STS* 7.

24. These reviews are all included in *STS*.

25. David Ossman, "LeRoi Jones: An Interview on *Yugen*" (1960), in *Conversations with Amiri Baraka*, ed. Charlie Reilly (Jackson, MS: University Press of Mississippi, 1994), 6.

26. William J. Harris discusses this paradox in *The Poetry and Poetics of Amiri Baraka: The Jazz Aesthetic* (Columbia, MO: University of Missouri Press, 1985), especially 34–66.

27. William Carlos Williams, "America, Whitman, and the Art of Poetry" (1917), reprinted in *William Carlos Williams Review* 13.1 (Spring 1987): 2.

28. Williams, "America, Whitman, and the Art of Poetry," 3.

29. On Lowell's interactions with Williams and his writing, see Axelrod, especially 84–100.

30. William Carlos Williams, "Howl for Carl Solomon," in Allen Ginsberg, *Howl and Other Poems* (San Francisco, CA: City Lights Books, 1956), 8.

31. Allen Ginsberg, "Notes for *Howl* and Other Poems," in Allen, *The New American Poetry*, 415.

32. Breslin develops this contrast in *From Modern to Contemporary: American Poetry, 1945–1965* (Chicago: University of Chicago Press, 1984), 110–12.

33. Allen Ginsberg, "Early Poetic Community" (with Robert Duncan), in *Allen Verbatim: Lectures on Poetry, Politics, Consciousness*, ed. Gordon Ball (New York: McGraw-Hill, 1974), 140.

34. The other women represented are Helen Adam, Madeline Gleason, and Barbara Guest.

35. Linda A. Kinnahan, *Poetics of the Feminine: Authority and Literary Tradition in William Carlos Williams, Mina Loy, Denise Levertov, and Kathleen Fraser* (Cambridge: Cambridge University Press, 1994), 7–8.

36. See *Paterson I*, 7 and *Paterson II*.
37. See Christopher MacGowan, ed., *The Letters of Denise Levertov and William Carlos Williams* (New York: New Directions, 1998). Levertov's 21 September 1960 letter exemplifies her resistance to Williams' prescriptive claims for "the American idiom." She notes that her own formative linguistic experience was not "English" but "European," as her father was Russian Jewish and her mother was Welsh and had lived for many years in central Europe (100).
38. Denise Levertov, "Great Possessions," in *The Poet in the World* (New York: New Directions, 1973), 90.
39. Kenneth Koch, "Variations on a Theme by William Carlos Williams," reprinted in *Visiting Dr. Williams*, 89.
40. John Ashbery, "The Thief of Poetry," reprinted in *Visiting Dr. Williams*, 7–12.
41. Frank O'Hara, "Poem Read at Joan Mitchell's," in *The Collected Poems of Frank O'Hara*, 265.
42. Ron Silliman, "Third Phase Objectivism," *Paideuma* 10 (Spring 1981): 85–89.
43. Louis Zukofsky, *Prepositions: The Collected Critical Essays of Louis Zukofsky* (London: Rapp and Carroll, 1967). "Sincerity and Objectification," from *Poetry* (Feb. 1931), appears in revised form in *Prepositions* titled "An Objective."
44. George Oppen, "The Mind's Own Place," *Kulchur* 10 (Summer 1963), 2–8.
45. Ron Silliman, "Language, Realism, Poetry," introduction to *In the American Tree* (Orono, ME: National Poetry Foundation, 1986), xv.
46. Alan Golding discusses these Language texts in "'What about all this writing?': Williams and Alternative Poetics," *Textual Practice* 18.2 (2004): 265–82. See also Hank Lazer, "Language Writing; or, Literary History and the Strange Case of the Two Dr. Williamses," in Lazer, *Opposing Poetries, Volume 2: Readings* (Evanston, IL: Northwestern University Press, 1996), 19–28.
47. Charles Bernstein, "For Bill Charley Bill on Memorial Day," reprinted in *Visiting Dr. Williams*, 22–23.
48. Lyn Hejinian, "An American Opener," *Poetics Journal* 1 (1982), quoted in Golding, "'What about all of this writing?'" 278.
49. Golding, "'What about all of this writing?'" 274.
50. See Julia Bloch, "Alice Notley's Descent: Modernist Genealogies and Gendered Literary Inheritance," *Journal of Modern Literature* 35.3 (Spring 2012): 1–24.
51. Eric B. White, *Transatlantic Avant-Gardes: Little Magazines and Localist Modernism* (Edinburgh: Edinburgh University Press, 2013).
52. Lawrence Joseph, *Into It* (New York: Farrar, Straus and Giroux, 2005).
53. Lawrence Joseph, "Some Sort of Chronicler I Am," in *Codes, Precepts, Biases, and Taboos: Poems 1973–1993* (New York: Farrar, Straus and Giroux, 2005), 161–62.

FURTHER READING

Biographies

Baldwin, Neil. *To All Gentleness: William Carlos Williams: The Doctor Poet.* New York: Atheneum Books, 1984.

Coles, Robert and Thomas Roma. *House Calls with William Carlos Williams, MD.* Brooklyn: powerHouse Books, 2008.

Creeley, Robert. "A Visit with Dr. Williams." *Sagetrieb* 3.2 (Fall 1984): 27–35.

Laughlin, James. *Remembering William Carlos Williams.* New York: New Directions, 1995.

Leibowitz, Herbert. *"Something Urgent I Have to Say to You": The Life and Works of William Carlos Williams.* New York: Farrar Straus and Giroux, 2011.

Mariani, Paul. *William Carlos Williams: A New World Naked.* New York: McGraw-Hill, 1981.

Wagner, Linda Welshimer, ed. *Interviews with William Carlos Williams: "Speaking Straight Ahead."* New York: New Directions, 1976.

Whittemore, Reed. *William Carlos Williams, Poet from Jersey.* Boston: Houghton Mifflin, 1975.

Letters

The American Idiom: A Correspondence. William Carlos Williams and Harold Norse. Ed. John J. Wilson. San Francisco: Bright Tyger Press, 1990.

The Correspondence of William Carlos Williams and Louis Zukofsky. Ed. Barry Ahearn. Middletown: Wesleyan University Press, 2003.

The Humane Particulars: The Collected Letters of William Carlos Williams and Kenneth Burke. Ed. James H. East. Columbia: University of South Carolina Press, 2003.

The Last Word: Letters between Marcia Nardi and William Carlos Williams. Ed. Elizabeth M. O'Neil. Iowa City: University of Iowa Press, 1994.

The Letters of Denise Levertov and William Carlos Williams. Ed. Christopher MacGowan. New York: New Directions, 1998.

The Letters of Williams Carlos Williams to Edgar Irving Williams, 1902–1912. Ed. Andrew J. Krivak. Madison: Fairleigh Dickinson University Press, 2009.

Pound/Williams: Selected Letters of Ezra Pound and William Carlos Williams. Ed. Hugh Witemeyer. New York: New Directions, 1996.

The Selected Letters of William Carlos Williams. Ed. John C. Thirlwall. New York: McDowell, Obolensky, 1957.

William Carlos Williams and Charles Tomlinson: A Transatlantic Connection. Ed. Barry Magid and Hugh Witemeyer. New York: Peter Lang, 1999.

William Carlos Williams and James Laughlin: Selected Letters. Ed. Hugh Witemeyer. New York: Norton, 1989.

William Carlos Williams and John Sanford: A Correspondence. Ed. Lin Rolens. Santa Barbara: Oyster Press, 1984.

Criticism and bibliography

Ahearn, Barry. *William Carlos Williams and Alterity: The Early Poetry.* Cambridge: Cambridge University Press, 1994.

Angoff, Charles, ed. *William Carlos Williams.* Rutherford: Fairleigh Dickinson University Press, 1974.

Baldwin, Neil and Steven L. Myers. *The Manuscripts and Letters of William Carlos Williams in the Poetry Collection of the Lockwood Memorial Library, State University of New York at Buffalo, a Descriptive Catalogue.* Boston: G.K. Hall, 1978.

Beck, John. *Writing the Radical Center: William Carlos Williams, John Dewey, and American Cultural Politics.* Albany: SUNY Press, 2001.

Bernstein, Michael. *The Tale of the Tribe: Ezra Pound and the Modern Verse Epic.* Princeton: Princeton University Press, 1980.

Berrien, Edith Heal, Barbara Perkins, and George Perkins. "Descriptive List of Works from the Library of William Carlos Williams at Fairleigh Dickinson University." Ed. Peter Schmidt. *William Carlos Williams Review* X.2 (Fall 1984), 30–53.

Berry, Eleanor. "Williams' Development of a New Prosodic Form – *Not* the 'Variable Foot,' but the 'Sight-Stanza.' " *William Carlos Williams Review* 7.2 (Fall 1981): 21–30.

"The Williams-Oppen Connection." *Sagetrieb* 3.2 (Fall 1984): 99–116.

"William Carlos Williams' Triadic-Line Verse: An Analysis of Its Prosody." *Twentieth Century Literature* 35.3 (Fall 1989): 364–88.

Berry, Wendell. *The Poetry of William Carlos Williams of Rutherford.* Berkeley: Counterpoint, 2011.

Bloom, Harold. *Bloom's Major Poets: William Carlos Williams, Comprehensive Research and Study Guide.* Broomall: Chelsea House, 2002.

Bremen, Brian A. *William Carlos Williams and the Diagnostics of Culture.* New York: Oxford University Press, 1993.

Breslin, James E. B. *William Carlos Williams: An American Artist.* New York: Oxford University Press, 1970.

"William Carlos Williams and Charles Demuth: Cross-Fertilization in the Arts." *Journal of Modern Literature* VI.2 (April 1977): 248–63.

From Modern to Contemporary: American Poetry, 1945–1965. Chicago: University of Chicago Press, 1984.

Bufithis, Philip. "William Carlos Williams Writing against *The Waste Land*." *Sagetrieb* 8.1–2 (1989): 215–23.

Callan, Ron. *William Carlos Williams and Transcendentalism: Fitting the Crab in a Box*. New York: St. Martin's Press, 1992.

Cappucci, Paul R. *William Carlos Williams' Poetic Response to the 1913 Paterson Silk Strike*. Lewiston: Edwin Mellen Press, 2002.

William Carlos Williams, Frank O'Hara and the New York Art Scene. Madison: Fairleigh Dickinson University Press, 2010.

Churchill, Suzanne W. *The Little Magazine* Others *and the Renovation of Modern American Poetry*. Aldershot: Ashgate, 2006.

Cirasa, Robert J. *The Lost Works of William Carlos Williams*. Madison: Fairleigh Dickinson University Press, 1995.

Clarke, Bruce. "The Fall of Montezuma: Poetry and History in William Carlos Williams and D. H. Lawrence." *William Carlos Williams Review* 12.1 (Spring 1986): 1–12.

Cohen, Milton A. *Beleaguered Poets and Leftist Critics: Stevens, Cummings, Frost, and Williams in the 1930s*. Tuscaloosa: University of Alabama Press, 2010.

Coles, Robert. *William Carlos Williams: The Knack of Survival in America*. New Brunswick: Rutgers University Press, 1975.

Connaroe, Joel. *William Carlos Williams' Paterson: Language and Landscape*. Philadelphia: University of Pennsylvania Press, 1970.

Conrad, Bryce. *Refiguring America: A Study of William Carlos Williams' In the American Grain*. Urbana: University of Illinois Press, 1990.

Copestake, Ian D., ed. *Rigor of Beauty: Essays in Commemoration of William Carlos Williams*. Bern: Peter Lang, 2004.

ed. *The Legacy of William Carlos Williams: Points of Contact*. Newcastle: Cambridge Scholars Publishing, 2007.

The Ethics of William Carlos Williams's Poetry. Rochester: Camden House, 2010.

Crawford, T. Hugh. *Modernism, Medicine, & William Carlos Williams*. Norman: University of Oklahoma Press, 1993.

Cushman, Stephen. *William Carlos Williams and the Meanings of Measure*. New Haven: Yale University Press, 1985.

Diggory, Terence. *William Carlos Williams and the Ethics of Painting*. Princeton: Princeton University Press, 1991.

Dijkstra, Bram. *The Hieroglyphics of a New Speech: Cubism, Stieglitz, and the Early Poetry of William Carlos Williams*. Princeton: Princeton University Press, 1969.

Doyle, Charles, ed. *William Carlos Williams, The Critical Heritage*. London: Routledge & Kegan Paul, 1980.

William Carlos Williams and the American Poem. New York: St. Martin's Press, 1982.

Driscoll, Kerry. *William Carlos Williams and the Maternal Muse*. Ann Arbor: UMI Research Press, 1987.

"Inversions, Evasions, Strange Machinations of Desire: William Carlos Williams and the Baroness Revisited." *Sagetrieb* 18.2–3 (2002): 43–77.

Duffey, Bernard. *A Poetry of Presence: The Writing of William Carlos Williams*. Madison: University of Wisconsin Press, 1986.

Durgin, Patrick F. "Post-Language Poetries and Post-Ableist Poetics." *Journal of Modern Literature* 32.2 (2009): 159–84.

Fedo, David A. *William Carlos Williams: A Poet in the American Theater*. Ann Arbor: UMI Research Press, 1983.

Fisher-Wirth, Ann W. *William Carlos Williams and Autobiography, The Woods of His Own Nature*. University Park: Pennsylvania State University Press, 1989.

Frail, David. *The Early Politics and Poetics of William Carlos Williams*. Ann Arbor: UMI Research Press, 1987.

Fredman, Stephen. *Poet's Prose: The Crisis in American Verse*. New York: Cambridge University Press, 1983.

Gable, Craig A., ed. *A Concordance to the Poetry of William Carlos Williams*. Lewiston: Edwin Mellen Press, 2012.

Gelpi, Albert. *A Coherent Splendor: The American Poetic Renaissance*. Cambridge: Cambridge University Press, 1998.

Gilbert, Sandra M. "Purloined Letters: William Carlos Williams and 'Cress.'" *William Carlos Williams Review* XI.2 (Fall 1985): 5–15.

Giorcelli, Cristina and Maria Anita Stefanelli, eds. The Rhetoric of Love in *The Collected Poems of William Carlos Williams*. Rome: Edizioni Associate, 1993.

Gish, Robert F. *William Carlos Williams: A Study of the Short Fiction*. Boston: Twayne, 1989.

Graham, Theodora R. "'Her Heigh Compleynte': The Cress Letters of Williams Carlos Williams' *Paterson*." In *Ezra Pound & William Carlos Williams: The University of Pennsylvania Conference Papers*. Ed. Daniel Hoffman. Philadelphia: University of Pennsylvania Press, 1983: pp. 164–193.

Guimond, James. *The Art of William Carlos Williams, A Discovery and Possession of America*. Urbana: University of Illinois Press, 1968.

Hahn, Stephen. "'It was ... civilization I was after': George Tice, William Carlos Williams, and the Archaeology of Paterson." *The Literary Review* 50.4 (Summer 2007): 62–82.

Halter, Peter. *The Revolution in the Visual Arts and the Poetry of William Carlos Williams*. Cambridge: Cambridge University Press, 1994.

Hatlen, Burton and Demetres Tryphonopoulos, eds. *William Carlos Williams and the Language of Poetry*. Orono: National Poetry Foundation, 2002.

Hoffmann, Daniel, ed. *Ezra Pound and William Carlos Williams: The University of Pennsylvania Conference Papers*. Philadelphia: University of Pennsylvania Press, 1983.

Juhasz, Suzanne. *Metaphor and the Poetry of Williams, Pound, and Stevens*. Lewisburg: Bucknell University Press, 1974.

Kallet, Marilyn. *Honest Simplicity in William Carlos Williams' "Asphodel, That Greeny Flower."* Baton Rouge: Louisiana State University Press, 1985.

Kenner, Hugh. *A Homemade World: The American Modernist Writers*. New York: Knopf, 1975.

Kinnahan, Linda A. *Poetics of the Feminine: Authority and Literary Tradition in William Carlos Williams, Mina Loy, Denise Levertov, and Kathleen Fraser*. Cambridge: Cambridge University Press, 1994.

Koch, Vivienne. *William Carlos Williams*. Norfolk: New Directions, 1950.

Koehler, G. Stanley. *Countries of the Mind: The Poetry of William Carlos Williams*. Lewisburg: Bucknell University Press, 1998.

Kusch, Robert. *"My Toughest Mentor," Theodore Roethke and William Carlos Williams (1940–1948)*. Lewisburg: Bucknell University Press, 1999.

Kutzinski, Vera M. *Against the American Grain: Myth and History in William Carlos Williams, Jay Wright and Nicolás Guillén*. Baltimore: Johns Hopkins University Press, 1987.

Larson, Kelli A. *Guide to the Poetry of William Carlos Williams*. New York: G. K. Hall, 1995.

Lenhart, Gary. *The Teachers & Writers Guide to William Carlos Williams*. New York: Teachers & Writers Collaborative, 1998.

Lloyd, Margaret Glynne. *William Carlos Williams's Paterson: A Critical Reappraisal*. Rutherford: Fairleigh Dickinson University Press, 1980.

Loevy, Stephen Ross. *William Carlos Williams's A Dream of Love*. Ann Arbor: UMI Research Press, 1983.

Lowney, John. *The American Avant-Garde Tradition: William Carlos Williams, Postmodern Poetry, and the Politics of Cultural Memory*. Lewisburg: Bucknell University Press, 1997.

MacGowan, Christopher. *William Carlos Williams' Early Poetry: The Visual Arts Background*. Ann Arbor: UMI Research Press, 1984.

Mariani, Paul. *William Carlos Williams: The Poet and His Critics*. Chicago: American Library Association, 1975.

Markos, Donald W. *Ideas in Things: The Poems of William Carlos Williams*. Rutherford: Fairleigh Dickinson University Press, 1994.

Marling, William. *William Carlos Williams and the Painters, 1909–1923*. Athens: Ohio University Press, 1982.

Marsh, Alec. *Money and Modernity: Pound, Williams, and the Spirit of Jefferson*. Tuscaloosa: University of Alabama Press, 1998.

Martz, Louis, L. *Many Gods and Many Voices: The Role of the Prophet in English and American Modernism*. Columbia: University of Missouri Press, 1998.

The Poem of the Mind: Essays on Poetry, English and American. Oxford: Oxford University Press, 1966.

Marzán, Julio. *The Spanish American Roots of William Carlos Williams*. Austin: University of Texas Press, 1994.

Mazzaro, Jerome. *William Carlos Williams: The Later Poems*. Ithaca: Cornell University Press, 1973.

Miki, Roy. *The PrePoetics of William Carlos Williams: Kora in Hell*. Ann Arbor: UMI Research Press, 1983.

Miller, J. Hillis. *Poets of Reality: Six Twentieth-Century Writers*. Cambridge: Harvard University Press, 1965.

ed. *William Carlos Williams: A Collection of Critical Essays*. Englewood Cliffs: Prentice Hall, 1966.

Monacell, Peter. "In the American Grid: Modern Poetry and the Suburbs." *Journal of Modern Literature* 35.1 (2011): 122–42.

Morris, Daniel. *The Writings of William Carlos Williams: Publicity for the Self*. Columbia: University of Missouri Press, 1995.

Nolan, Sarah. "'The Poem is the World': Re-Thinking Environmental Crisis Through William Carlos Williams' *Paterson*." *UnderCurrents* 18 (2014): 38–43.

Oliphant, Dave and Thomas Zigal, eds. *WCW & Others, Essays on Williams Carlos Williams and his Association with Ezra Pound, Hilda Doolittle, Marcel*

Duchamp, Marianne Moore, Emanuel Romano, Wallace Stevens, and Louis Zukofsky. Austin: Harry Ransom Humanities Research Center, 1985.

Paul, Sherman. *The Music of Survival: A Biography of a Poem by William Carlos Williams*. Urbana: University of Illinois Press, 1968.

Perleman, Bob. "A Williams Sound-Script: Listening to 'The Sea-Elephant.' " *English Studies in Canada* 33.4 (December 2007): 37–53.

Perloff, Marjorie. *The Poetics of Indeterminacy: Rimbaud to Cage*. Princeton: Princeton University Press, 1981.

The Dance of the Intellect: Studies in the Poetry of the Pound Tradition. Cambridge: Cambridge University Press, 1985.

Peterson, Walter Scott. *An Approach to* Paterson. New Haven: Yale University Press, 1967.

Qian, Zhaoming. *Orientalism and Modernism: The Legacy of China in Pound and Williams*. Durham: Duke University Press, 1995.

Rapp, Carl. *William Carlos Williams and Romantic Idealism*. Hanover: University Press of New England, 1984.

Rehder, Robert. *Stevens, Williams, Crane and the Motive for Metaphor*. New York: Palgrave Macmillan, 2005.

Riddel, Joseph N. *The Inverted Bell: Modernism and the Counterpoetics of William Carlos Williams*. With a New Postscript by the Author. Baton Rouge: Louisiana State University Press, 1991.

Rodgers, Audrey T. *Virgin and Whore: The Image of Women in the Poetry of William Carlos Williams*. Jefferson: McFarland, 1987.

Sankey, Benjamin. *A Companion to William Carlos Williams's* Paterson. Berkeley: University of California Press, 1971.

Sayre, Henry M. *The Visual Text of William Carlos Williams*. Urbana: University Of Illinois Press, 1983.

Schmidt, Peter. *William Carlos Williams, the Arts, and Literary Tradition*. Baton Rouge: Louisiana State University Press, 1988.

Sharpe, William Chapman. *Unreal Cities: Urban Configuration in Wordsworth, Baudelaire, Whitman, Eliot and Williams*. Baltimore: Johns Hopkins University Press, 1990.

Steinman, Lisa M. *Made in America: Science, Technology, and American Modernist Poets*. New Haven: Yale University Press, 1987.

Tapscott, Stephen. *American Beauty: William Carlos Williams and the Modernist Whitman*. New York: Columbia University Press, 1984.

Tashjian, Dickran. *Skyscraper Primitives: Dada and the American Avant-Garde, 1910 – 1925*. Middletown: Wesleyan University Press, 1975.

William Carlos Williams and the American Scene, 1920 – 1940. New York: Whitney Museum of American Art, 1978.

Terrell, Carroll F., ed. *William Carlos Williams: Man and Poet*. Orono: National Poetry Foundation, 1983.

Tichi, Cecelia. *Shifting Gears: Technology, Literature, Culture in Modernist America*. Chapel Hill: University of North Carolina Press, 1987.

Tomlinson, Charles, ed. *William Carlos Williams: A Critical Anthology*. Harmondsworth: Penguin, 1972.

Townley, Rod. *The Early Poetry of William Carlos Williams*. Ithaca: Cornell University Press, 1975.

Wagner, Linda Welshimer. *The Poems of William Carlos Williams: A Critical Study*. Middletown: Wesleyan University Press, 1964.

The Prose of William Carlos Williams. Middletown: Wesleyan University Press, 1970.

William Carlos Williams: A Reference Guide. Boston: G. K. Hall, 1978.

Wallace, Emily Mitchell. *A Bibliography of William Carlos Williams*. Middletown: Wesleyan University Press, 1968.

Wallaert, Josh. "The Ecopoetics of Perfection: William Carlos Williams and Nature in *Spring and All*." *ISLE: Interdisciplinary Studies in Literature and Envioronment* 12.1 (2005): 79–98.

Weaver, Mike. *William Carlos Williams: The American Background*. Cambridge: Cambridge University Press, 1971.

Whitaker, Thomas R. *William Carlos Williams*. Rev. Ed. Boston: Twayne, 1989.

White, Eric B. *Transatlantic Avant-Gardes: Little Magazines and Localist Modernism*. Edinburgh: Edinburgh University Press, 2013.

Williams, William Carlos. *Many Loves and Other Plays*. New York: New Directions, 1961.

translator. Philippe Soupault. *Last Nights of Paris*. New York: Full Court Press, 1982.

Something to Say: William Carlos Williams on Younger Poets. Ed. James E. B. Breslin. New York: New Directions, 1985.

William Carlos Williams: The Collected Recordings. Ed. Richard Swigg. Twenty Audio-Cassette Tapes. Keele University, England, 1993. Available online at PennSound, http://writing.upenn.edu/pennsound/x/Williams-WC.php.

Poems [1909]. Introduction by Virginia M. Wright-Peterson. Urbana: University of Illinois Press, 2002.

By Word of Mouth: Poems from the Spanish, 1916–1959. Ed. Jonathan Cohen. New York: New Directions, 2011.

INDEX

Joseph, Lawrence, 201–2
Joyce, James, 26, 32–34, 83–84, 96, 102,
    135, 136

Kandinsky, Wassily, 49
Kerouac, Jack, 1, 191
Koch, Kenneth, 5, 197
Kreymborg, Alfred, 3, 28–29, 32, 38, 40, 55

Language Poetry, 188, 198–201
Laughlin, James, 1, 4–5, 7, 34, 91, 95–96, 97,
    115, 181, 194
Levertov, Denise, 1, 5, 7, 115, 191, 195–96
Lewis, H.H., 90, 193
little magazines
    Black Mountain Review, 190, 191
    Blast, 71–72, 91
    Blues, 185
    Broom, 26, 28, 32
    Contact, 2, 7, 9, 14–16, 32, 71, 95, 135
    The Dial, 9, 14, 15, 20, 25, 28, 31
    The Egoist, 2, 14, 27–28, 144
    Exile, 82
    Floating Bear, 190–92
    The Glebe, 28
    Harvard Advocate, 95
    The Little Review, 2, 14, 28, 32, 33, 135
    The Lyric, 79
    The Magazine, 91, 97
    The New Anvil, 91
    The New Masses, 71, 72, 77, 83, 91, 93
    Origin, 190, 191
    Others, 2, 3, 7, 14, 28–30, 32, 38, 40
    Pagany, 94–95, 97
    The Paris Review, 163
    Partisan Review, 66, 71, 77–78
    Poetry, 1, 3, 14, 28, 35, 189
    The Symposium, 192
    transatlantic review, 26, 28, 33
    transition, 26, 82
    Yūgen, 190–92
Lorca, Frederico García, 168–69, 191
Lowell, Robert, 1, 5, 112, 119, 140, 189,
    194–95
Loy, Mina, 28–29, 32, 38, 196

Mariani, Paul, 5, 17, 90, 93–95, 98, 101, 104,
    106, 107, 112, 115, 135, 146, 162, 167,
    173, 200
Martz, Louis, 107, 136
Matos, Luis Palés, 168, 172, 173
McAlmon, Robert, 3, 14–16, 32–33, 53, 68,
    116, 135, 136

Moore, Marianne, 1, 28, 29, 30, 32, 54–55,
    72, 106, 196
Music and Women (Drinker), 150–56

Nardi, Marcia, 7, 94, 104, 147, 190, 193, 196
Neruda, Pablo, 168, 169
Niedecker, Lorine, 35, 198, 201
Notley, Alice, 196, 200, 201

O'Hara, Frank, 5, 189, 191, 197
Objectivists, 35, 188, 192, 198, 201
Olson, Charles, 1, 5, 101, 113, 189, 190–91,
    192–93, 195
The Open Window (Gris), 61–63
Oppen, George, 35, 55, 91, 192, 198–99
Osler, William, 176, 178

Perloff, Marjorie, 17, 21, 86, 101, 106, 112,
    121, 145
Picasso, Pablo, 38, 122–23, 136
Poe, Edgar Allan, 15, 131
Pound, Ezra, 1–5, 7, 24–28, 32, 34–35,
    38, 54, 55–56, 66, 67–68, 71, 73–74,
    75, 79, 82, 83–84, 86, 91, 93, 95, 102,
    104, 106, 134, 136, 163, 167, 176, 189,
    191, 212
pragmatism, 9, 100
Precisionism, 56, 199
projective verse, 83

Ray, Man, 3, 28, 32, 38
Rexroth, Kenneth, 192
Reznikoff, Charles, 35, 192, 198
Rodriguez, Richard, 165
Roethke, Theodore, 193
Rukeyser, Muriel, 192, 193

Sandburg, Carl, 4
Santayana, George, 131
Sappho, 156
Shahn, Ben, 1
Sheeler, Charles, 1, 28, 38, 49
Silliman, Ron, 198, 199–200
Soupault, Philippe, 26, 33, 82, 136
Stein, Gertrude, 4, 26, 33, 34, 38, 136, 176,
    191, 196, 199–200
Stevens, Wallace, 1, 4, 28, 30–32, 38, 55, 67,
    73, 106, 169
Stieglitz, Alfred, 1, 28
Surrealism, 33, 82–83

Tate, Allen, 189, 194
Thirlwall, John, 6, 70, 145

Cambridge Companions to Literature

AUTHORS

Edward Albee edited by Stephen J. Bottoms

Margaret Atwood edited by Coral Ann Howells

W. H. Auden edited by Stan Smith

Jane Austen edited by Edward Copeland and Juliet McMaster (second edition)

James Baldwin edited by Michele Elam

Beckett edited by John Pilling

Bede edited by Scott DeGregorio

Aphra Behn edited by Derek Hughes and Janet Todd

Walter Benjamin edited by David S. Ferris

William Blake edited by Morris Eaves

Boccaccio edited by Guyda Armstrong, Rhiannon Daniels, and Stephen J. Milner

Jorge Luis Borges edited by Edwin Williamson

Brecht edited by Peter Thomson and Glendyr Sacks (second edition)

The Brontës edited by Heather Glen

Bunyan edited by Anne Dunan-Page

Frances Burney edited by Peter Sabor

Byron edited by Drummond Bone

Albert Camus edited by Edward J. Hughes

Willa Cather edited by Marilee Lindemann

Cervantes edited by Anthony J. Cascardi

Chaucer edited by Piero Boitani and Jill Mann (second edition)

Chekhov edited by Vera Gottlieb and Paul Allain

Kate Chopin edited by Janet Beer

Caryl Churchill edited by Elaine Aston and Elin Diamond

Cicero edited by Catherine Steel

Coleridge edited by Lucy Newlyn

Wilkie Collins edited by Jenny Bourne Taylor

Joseph Conrad edited by J. H. Stape

H. D. edited by Nephie J. Christodoulides and Polina Mackay

Dante edited by Rachel Jacoff (second edition)

Daniel Defoe edited by John Richetti

Don DeLillo edited by John N. Duvall

Charles Dickens edited by John O. Jordan

Emily Dickinson edited by Wendy Martin

John Donne edited by Achsah Guibbory

Dostoevskii edited by W. J. Leatherbarrow

Theodore Dreiser edited by Leonard Cassuto and Claire Virginia Eby

John Dryden edited by Steven N. Zwicker

W. E. B. Du Bois edited by Shamoon Zamir

George Eliot edited by George Levine

T. S. Eliot edited by A. David Moody

Ralph Ellison edited by Ross Posnock

Ralph Waldo Emerson edited by Joel Porte and Saundra Morris

William Faulkner edited by Philip M. Weinstein

Henry Fielding edited by Claude Rawson

F. Scott Fitzgerald edited by Ruth Prigozy

Flaubert edited by Timothy Unwin

E. M. Forster edited by David Bradshaw

Benjamin Franklin edited by Carla Mulford

Brian Friel edited by Anthony Roche

Robert Frost edited by Robert Faggen

Gabriel García Márquez edited by Philip Swanson

Elizabeth Gaskell edited by Jill L. Matus

Goethe edited by Lesley Sharpe

Günter Grass edited by Stuart Taberner

Thomas Hardy edited by Dale Kramer

David Hare edited by Richard Boon

Nathaniel Hawthorne edited by Richard Millington

Seamus Heaney edited by Bernard O'Donoghue

Ernest Hemingway edited by Scott Donaldson

Homer edited by Robert Fowler

Horace edited by Stephen Harrison

Ted Hughes edited by Terry Gifford

Ibsen edited by James McFarlane

Henry James edited by Jonathan Freedman

Samuel Johnson edited by Greg Clingham

Ben Jonson edited by Richard Harp and Stanley Stewart

James Joyce edited by Derek Attridge (second edition)

Kafka edited by Julian Preece

Keats edited by Susan J. Wolfson

Rudyard Kipling edited by Howard J. Booth

Lacan edited by Jean-Michel Rabaté

D. H. Lawrence edited by Anne Fernihough

Primo Levi edited by Robert Gordon

TOPICS